The National Underwr~~iter Company~~

WORKERS COMPENSATION GUIDE: COVERAGE AND FINANCING, THIRD EDITION

By Steven A. Coombs, CPCU, ARM, and David D. Thamann, J.D., ARM, CPCU

Workers Compensation Guide: Coverage and Financing, Third Edition is the single source that guides you through the entire spectrum of issues and considerations in the complex area of workers compensation.

From exclusions, to limits of liability, endorsements, and policy wording—this unique resource delivers valuable, expert insights every step of the way.

Written by **Steven A. Coombs,** CPCU, ARM, and **David D. Thamann,** J.D., ARM, CPCU, two of the foremost experts in the field, *Workers Compensation Guide: Coverage and Financing, Third Edition,* has been completely updated to incorporate vital new information on key areas.

This fully revised third edition includes:

- Additional case law to better explain key sections of the workers compensation policy

- Expanded analysis of the Longshore and Harbor Workers Compensation Act and the Jones Act

- Important updates to the workers compensation classification schedule, rating bureau information, and premium elements reference table

- Updated information covering which states use the NCCI plan for experience rating and which do not

- A new section on Alternate Employer Coverage

- Guidance on the three keys to conducting a successful workers compensation fraud investigation

- Expert analysis of several fraud-related cases from various jurisdictions

- Examination of the similarities and differences between the U.S. and Canadian workers compensation systems, including a chart presenting the maximum assessable/insurable earnings for all of the provinces; and a listing of workers compensation department contacts in each of the provinces

- Two new charts covering workers compensation requirements for employers, state-by-state; and Canadian workers compensation

- Appendices include a full version of the current workers compensation policy; the workers compensation experience rating chart; the Illinois workers compensation premium algorithm; analysis of the interplay among the FMLA, ADA, and workers compensation statutes; and more.

Workers compensation and employers liability affect different organizations in different ways. With *Workers Compensation Guide: Coverage and Financing, Third Edition* you will have everything you need to establish and monitor workers compensation and employers liability programs.

To place additional orders for *Workers Compensation Guide: Coverage and Financing, Third Edition* or any of our products, or for additional information, contact Customer Service at 1-800-543-0874.

Coverage Guides Also Available:

- Businessowners Policy

- Business Income

- Commercial Auto Program

- Commercial General Liability

- Commercial Property

- Condominium Insurance Coverage

- Construction Defects

- Critical Issues in CGL

- Directors and Officers Liability

- Employment Practices Liability

- Guide to Captives and Alternative Risk Financing

- Homeowners

- Insurance Claims: A Comprehensive Guide

- Mold Claims

- Personal Auto Policy

- Personal Umbrella

3rd Edition

Workers Compensation Guide
Coverage and Financing

Commercial Lines Series

Steven A. Coombs, CPCU, ARM
David D. Thamann, J.D., ARM, CPCU

The National Underwriter Company

This publication is designed to provide accurate and authoritative information in regard to the subject matter covered. It is sold with the understanding that the publisher is not engaged in rendering legal, accounting, or other professional service. If legal advice or other expert assistance is required, the services of a competent professional person should be sought.— from a Declaration of Principles jointly adopted by a Committee of the American Bar Association and a Committee of Publishers and Associations.

Copyright © 2016 by
THE NATIONAL UNDERWRITER COMPANY
4157 Olympic Blvd.
Suite 225
Erlanger, KY 41018

April 2016

International Standard Book Number: 978-1-941627-73-0

Library of Congress Control Number: 2016933397

Printed in the United States of America

About The National Underwriter Company

For over 110 years, The National Underwriter Company has been the first in line with the targeted tax, insurance, and financial planning information you need to make critical business decisions. Boasting nearly a century of expert experience, our reputable Editors are dedicated to putting accurate and relevant information right at your fingertips. With *Tax Facts*, *Tools & Techniques*, *National Underwriter Advanced Markets*, *Field Guide*, *FC&S*®, *FC&S Legal* and other resources available in print, eBook, CD, and online, you can be assured that as the industry evolves National Underwriter will be at the forefront with the thorough and easy-to-use resources you rely on for success.

The National Underwriter Company
Update Service Notification

This National Underwriter Company publication is regularly updated to include coverage of developments and changes that affect the content. If you did not purchase this publication directly from The National Underwriter Company and you want to receive these important updates sent on a 30-day review basis and billed separately, please contact us at (800) 543-0874. Or you can mail your request with your name, company, address, and the title of the book to:

The National Underwriter Company
4157 Olympic Boulevard
Suite 225
Erlanger, KY 41018

If you purchased this publication from The National Underwriter Company directly, you have already been registered for the update service.

National Underwriter Company
Contact Information

To order any National Underwriter Company title, please

- call 1-800-543-0874, 8-6 ET Monday – Thursday and 8 to 5 ET Friday

- online bookstore at www.nationalunderwriter.com, or

- mail to The National Underwriter Company, Orders Department, 4157 Olympic Blvd., Ste. 225, Erlanger, KY 41018

Acknowledgments

The authors wish to acknowledge and thank the legal research assistants Hannah Smith and Hillary Jamison, for their work in making this workers compensation book a presentable product. They put in long hours assembling the informative charts contained in this book and without these efforts, the workers compensation book would not be the useful and comprehensive product that it is.

Acknowledgements

About the Authors

Steven A. Coombs, CPCU, ARM, is a principal of Risk Resources, Inc., an independent risk management and insurance consulting firm. Prior to joining Risk Resources as president in 1992, he spent eight years with a national consulting firm, following several years as a national accounts underwriter for a large international insurance group. He serves as a consultant to many leading organizations, and provides litigation support services.

Mr. Coombs earned a Bachelor of Business Administration degree from Western Michigan University and a Master of Arts degree with a concentration in Risk Management and Insurance from DePaul University. He holds the Associate in Risk Management (ARM) certificate and the Chartered Property Casualty Underwriter (CPCU) designation. Mr. Coombs is active in various associations and is past President of the Society of Risk Management Consultants. He is a co-author of another book on construction insurance and also writes insurance related articles.

Mr. Coombs can be contacted via e-mail at scoombs@riskresources.net.

David D. Thamann, J.D., ARM, CPCU, is the managing editor of the *FC&S Bulletins*® and has been an *FC&S* editor since 1987. Before joining The National Underwriter Company, he was a claims supervisor and senior underwriter for American Druggists Insurance Company, a commercial property lead underwriter for Transamerica Insurance, and a commercial package underwriter for CNA and Safeco Insurance companies.

Mr. Thamann graduated from Salmon P. Chase College of Law and Xavier University.

The publications he wrote or contributed to include *Business Auto Coverage Guide, Personal Auto Coverage Guide, Workers Compensation Guide, Commercial Auto Program Coverage Guide* and *Commercial General Liability Coverage Guide*, all published by The National Underwriter Company. Mr. Thamann also writes articles for *Claims* magazine. He is a speaker or presenter at various insurance related seminars and meetings.

Publisher

Kelly B. Maheu, J.D., is Vice President in charge of the Practical Insights Division of ALM Media, which produces The National Underwriter's professional publications. Kelly has been with The National Underwriter

Company since 2006, and has served as the Managing Director of The National Underwriter's Professional Publishing Division as well as performing editorial, content acquisition, and product development roles.

Prior to joining The National Underwriter Company, Kelly worked in the legal and insurance fields for LexisNexis®, Progressive Insurance, and a Cincinnati insurance defense litigation firm.

Kelly has edited and contributed to numerous books and publications including the *Personal Auto Insurance Policy Coverage Guide*, *Cyberliability and Insurance*, *The National Underwriter Sales Essentials Series*, and *The Tools and Techniques of Risk Management for Financial Planners*.

Kelly earned her law degree from The University of Cincinnati College of Law and holds a BA from Miami University, Ohio, with a double major in English/Journalism and Psychology.

Legal Research Assistants

Hannah E. Smith is a graduate from the Salmon P. Chase College of Law.

Hillary A. Jamison is a third year law student at the Salmon P. Chase College of Law.

Editorial Services

Connie L. Jump, Manager, Editorial Operations.

Emily Brunner, Editorial Assistant.

Table of Contents

xi

Introduction

The Workers Compensation System

A Great Social Compromise

The workers compensation system was one of the triumphs of the industrial age. The system is the cumulative result of years of strife and compromise between employer/owners and employee/labor. The struggle toward this useful social compromise began in the 1870s with the organized labor movement and came to fruition in 1911 with the passage of the first state workers compensation law in Wisconsin.

As noted by the United States District Court, W.D. Arkansas, in *Cornell v. Liberty Mutual Group,* 2012 WL 912788, "the purpose of workers compensation statutes was to change the common law by shifting the burden of all work-related injuries from individual employers and employees to the consuming public. Employers were compelled to give up the common law defenses of contributory negligence, fellow servant, and assumption of risk; employees were required to give up the chance of recovering unlimited damages in fault-related cases in return for a certain recovery in all work-related cases."

In the workers compensation system, injured employees relinquish the right to sue their employers for employment-related injuries in return for a statutorily imposed mechanism that provides specific scheduled benefits. These benefits are funded, for the most part, through insurance policies that employers purchase from insurance companies. Indeed, in most states, employers must insure their workers compensation exposure or become qualified self-insurers. (Note that as of this writing, Texas allows employers to opt out of the workers compensation system.) Employers should not simply decide to operate without insurance. If they do, they risk being fined—and still have to pay the benefits that are set by law when an employee is injured on the job.

This work is a guide to the workers compensation system: how to calculate premium; how experience rating and modifiers work; and various financial plans and considerations. It also provides a detailed analysis of workers compensation and employers liability insurance by way of an examination of the standard workers compensation insurance policy. This policy is published by the National Council on Compensation Insurance

(NCCI), and is available for use in thirty-some states, plus the District of Columbia. The remaining states use similar forms that are approved and published by their respective workers compensation rating bureaus. The monopolistic state funds, federal workers compensation plans, coverage issues, and various other items of information are also covered. Moreover, information about the Canadian workers compensation system is offered, as well as workers comp fraud data.

There is perhaps no other type of insurance that uniformly affects the American population as much as workers compensation. Therefore, different types of readers may find different sections of this book of particular value. For example, human resource professionals, who often are charged with managing a program that a financial officer negotiated, may find the chapters on premium, experience rating, financial plans, and cost management especially useful. These chapters emphasize the correlation between program management and ultimate cost. Financial services professionals may gain insight into how to explain the system to current or prospective clients. Workers compensation adjusters should find interest in the chapters that deal with federal worker programs and general coverage issues.

The first chapters of this book (Chapters 1 to 6) examine the provisions of the NCCI workers compensation and employers liability policy, including its endorsements, on a clause-by-clause basis. How does the clause read; what does it mean? How have federal and state courts and administrative agencies interpreted it?

Many employers are located in a monopolistic state in which the employer is required to purchase insurance from the state fund. Chapter 7 details nonprivate workers compensation insurance—the monopolistic state funds of North Dakota, Ohio, Washington, and Wyoming. The workings of the residual markets maintained in some states are also mentioned.

Recognizing that state workers compensation systems were not adequate to protect all workers; for example, laborers working on waterways and on federal lands, the federal government enacted legislation such as the Longshore and Harbor Workers Compensation Act, the Jones Act, and other legislation protecting federal workers or workers on federal lands. Chapter 8 introduces and reviews federal workers compensation coverage—Longshore and Harbor Workers Compensation Act, Jones Act and other federal endorsements to the workers compensation policy.

Workers compensation is much more than an insurance policy. It is a system in the truest sense of the word; its cost is a basic cost of doing business. Because of this, the financial aspect of a company's workers compensation program often takes on a life of its own, outside the issues of coverage. Chapter 9 starts the book's section on financial considerations involved in workers compensation coverage. Chapter 9 discusses premium and how it is planned for, calculated, and arrived at. Chapter 10 introduces experience rating and the mod. Chapter 11 reviews various financial plans; Chapter 12 analyzes cost management issues; and Chapter 13 discusses a number of workers compensation coverage and legal issues: exclusive remedy; dual capacity; intentional tort; third-party-over; etc.

Chapter 14 deals with WC fraud data. Chapter 15 offers information about the Canadian workers compensation system.

This guide joins a number of guides published by the National Underwriter Company that review and analyze individual insurance forms. Among these are *Commercial General Liability* (eleventh edition), *Commercial Property*, *Businessowners*, *Business Auto*, *Commercial Auto Program*, *Homeowners*, *Personal Umbrella*, *Personal Auto*, *Employment Practices Liability*, and *Directors & Officers*.

Chapter 1

Policy Organization, General Section

Policy Organization

The workers compensation and employers liability insurance policy contains three separate and distinct parts of coverage. What coverages are applicable are indicated in the policy's information page, which is the workers compensation policy's equivalent of the declarations page in other property and casualty insurance formats. (The information page also lists the policy period, any applicable endorsements, and the premium for the policy.)

Part one is the workers compensation section, under which the insurer agrees to pay the benefits imposed upon the insured by the workers compensation law of the state or states listed on the information page in item 3.A.

Part two is the employers liability section, which protects the insured against liability imposed by law for bodily injury to employees in the course of employment that is not compensable under the workers compensation section. (Chapter 3 in this coverage guide contains a discussion of why employers liability coverage is necessary as part of a workers compensation coverage program.)

Part three applies to other states insurance. The insurer promises to reimburse the named insured for the benefits required by the workers compensation law of the state (or states) listed in item 3.C. of the information page if the insurer is not permitted to pay benefits required by the applicable workers compensation law directly to persons entitled to them. This coverage applies only to those states listed in item 3.C. of the information page, and if the insured begins work in any one of those states after the effective date of the policy, and if the insured is not insured for such work or is not self-insured for such work, all provisions of the policy will apply as though that state were listed in item 3.A. of the information page.

General Section

The workers compensation policy opens with a general section, something akin to an informative introduction to the policy. The general section contains five clauses.

The first clause identifies the policy as a contract of insurance between the employer (named on the information page) and the insurer. The benefits paid under a workers compensation claim may go to an employee, but the insured is the employer. In this way, the policy is a liability policy covering legal obligations imposed (in this case, statutorily) upon the insured. And, since the policy is a contract, this clause notes that the only agreements related to the coverage provided by the policy are those that are stated in the policy—no outside contracts or side agreements are to have an effect on the coverage. Of course, the terms of the policy can be changed or waived as any other contract can, but such modifications have to be accomplished by endorsements to the policy, endorsements which are issued by the insurer.

The first clause also specifies that the information page is part of (incorporated into as if it were an actual part of) the overall policy. The following data is listed on the information page: the effective dates of the policy; applicable endorsements; the insured and the insurer; the estimated premium; and the various states in which the coverage parts of the workers compensation policy apply.

The second clause confirms that an employer named in the information page is the named insured under the policy. The insured can be an individual, a partnership, a corporation, or some other entity. If the employer is a partnership, this clause specifies that an individual partner is an insured, but only in the capacity as an employer of the partnership's employees. The phrase recognizes the legal status of a partner; that is, it makes an individual partner an insured so that the partner's private holdings won't become subject to a claim by an injured worker.

The third clause notes that the coverage and benefits paid to the injured workers are based on the workers compensation law of each state or territory named in Item 3.A. of the information page. Item 3.A. is where the insured should list all states in which it conducts operations. The insured might have operations in more than one state, such as plants, retail stores, or traveling representatives; in some cases, major corporations have operations in every state. The insured might have one business domicile (the major place of business operations, or the official place of incorporation), but do business in multiple states; a business as noncomplex as a small plumbing contractor near a state border may have an exposure in two or three states. Or, the insured might not have multi-state operations nor employees that daily cross state lines, but may regularly send employees to lengthy seminars or meetings that are traditionally held out-of-state. In all these instances, the insured faces multi-state workers compensation exposures, and since the insured is charged with the responsibility of listing the appropriate state(s) or territory so that the proper benefits can be paid to injured employees, understanding and complying with this clause is crucial for insured employers.

This third clause also emphasizes the point that workers compensation coverage is applicable under and in accordance with state law, not federal compensation law. Quoting the policy, "The workers compensation law does not include any federal workers or workmen's compensation law, any federal occupational disease law, or the provisions of any law that provide nonoccupational disability benefits". Also, the "nonoccupational disability benefits" phrase shows that coverage under the policy is meant for injuries arising out of and in the course of employment, not disabilities that have nothing to do with employment; an example of this would be an employee of the named insured falling and breaking his leg while at home.

An additional note on this third clause: it shows that treatment of occupational diseases is covered under the workers compensation policy. The workers compensation part of the policy takes over the liability of the employer under the compensation laws of any state indicated on the information page, so any mandated obligation for occupational diseases is covered. Since the insuring clause of the workers compensation part of the policy refers simply to the "workers compensation law", and this term is defined in the third clause as including any occupational disease law, special endorsements are not necessary in states having separate occupational legislation. Listing the state on the information page takes care of all such liability under the compensation law of that state.

The fourth clause in the general section defines "state" as any state of the United States of America, and the District of Columbia. This does not mean that the workers compensation policy is applicable only in the fifty states and the District of Columbia. Any state or territory named in Item 3.A. of the information page shows the territorial applicability of the policy, but "state" is defined here just to clarify other paragraphs and phrases found throughout the policy. For example, if an employee is traveling in a foreign country on business, benefits for injuries suffered will be based on the workers compensation law of the state or states listed in Item 3.A.

The last clause in the general section declares that the policy "covers all of your workplaces listed in Items 1 or 4 of the information page; and it covers all other workplaces in Item 3.A. states unless you have other insurance or are self-insured for such workplaces." This clause shows the omnibus nature of the workers compensation coverage. If the insured has one workplace or twenty workplaces, this policy can apply; there is coverage if the insured lists all the workplaces on the information page. Furthermore, there is coverage even if the workplaces are not specifically listed, as long as the state(s) where the workplaces are located is noted in Item 3.A. Of course, this coverage does not apply if the insured has other insurance or is self-insured for such workplaces; otherwise, the insured would have duplicate coverage and that is something that insurers attempt to prevent.

Chapter 2

Workers Compensation Insurance

To "Pay Promptly When Due the Benefits Required by Law"

This is the heart of the workers compensation system—the pledge to provide a statutorily mandated schedule of benefits to persons injured in the course of employment. Under part one of the workers comp policy, the insurer agrees to pay the benefits imposed by law on the insured employer arising from injuries sustained by an employee during and in the course of employment.

The workers compensation insurance section is part one of the policy and contains eight clauses.

How This Insurance Applies

Workers compensation insurance applies to bodily injury by accident or by disease. Bodily injury includes resulting death. This clause attaches stipulations to the declaration.

First, bodily injury by accident must occur during the policy period.

Second, bodily injury by disease must be caused or aggravated by conditions of employment, with the employee's last day of last exposure to the conditions causing or aggravating the bodily injury occurring during the policy period. For example, in order for workers compensation insurance to apply to a worker who is suffering from lung disease, the insured would need to show the following: the worker's disease was caused by or aggravated by the working conditions (such as, having to constantly inhale smoke or other indoor air pollutants) and, the insurance policy has to be in force at the time the employee was last exposed to the conditions.

There are several items to note concerning this clause. First, the insurance applies to "bodily injury." The workers compensation policy does not define that term, however, and that can lead to disputes over the question of coverage should an employee make a claim based on, for

5

example, mental stress. Is mental stress a bodily injury under the workers compensation policy? This issue is discussed more fully in Chapter 13, but suffice it to say that since the policy does not define "bodily injury," the question is left to individual state laws and court decisions to settle.

Another point to note is that the coverage is for bodily injury caused by accident or by disease. Just as a slip and fall injury at work is covered, so also is a disease-based injury, such as asbestosis or electromagnetic field health hazards—as long as such disease is caused or aggravated by the employment.

Finally, the clause certifies that coverage is provided if the bodily injury occurs during the policy period. This makes the workers compensation policy an occurrence-type policy, similar to the commercial general liability occurrence form.

We Will Pay

In this clause the policy specifies that the insurer will "pay promptly when due the benefits required…by the workers compensation law"—a very simple and straightforward insuring agreement. Whatever the particular state workers compensation law declares the benefit to be—say for a broken arm—that is what the insurer will pay. A complication can arise, though, over the fact that an employee who is injured while working in a certain state can claim the compensation benefits of that state regardless of the fact that the employer is based in another state. In other words, an injured employee can choose among several possible states (depending on the laws of the states and the circumstances of the injuries) for his or her benefits. For example, just because company A is located in Maryland does not mean that an injured employee always has to file for workers compensation benefits in Maryland; if that employee is injured while on business in Pennsylvania, he or she could seek the compensation benefits of Pennsylvania.

This can seem to be unacceptable "forum shopping"—picking and choosing where to file a claim to get higher benefits—but in reality, such a practice is limited by the various state laws and by some judicial decisions, such as *Bradshaw v. Old Republic Insurance Company*, 922 S.W.2d 503 (Tenn. 1996). In this case, Bradshaw worked for a Tennessee company but was injured while on business in Maryland. He filed for benefits in Maryland but was turned down; he then filed in Tennessee and was turned down again. A Tennessee court declared that the election of remedies rule barred the Tennessee claim since the employee had "affirmatively acted" to get benefits in another state. Just because that other state denied his claim, the employee could not then seek the benefits in Tennessee. He had made his choice (Maryland) and to allow a second choice (or a third or fourth) would be unfair to the workers compensation system and a burden to the legal system.

In another Tennessee case, *Eadie v. Complete Company*, 142 S.W.3d 288 (2004), the Supreme Court of Tennessee declared that "an employee who suffers a compensable injury in another state may be barred from recovering benefits under Tennessee law through the election of remedies doctrine." In another example under Tennessee law, the Supreme Court of Tennessee in *Madden v. The Holland Group of Tennessee*, 277 S.W.3d 896 (2009), reiterated the point that the election of remedies doctrine may preclude an injured employee who has pursued a workers comp claim in another jurisdiction from filing the same claim in Tennessee.

These cases represent examples of the "election of remedies" doctrine that states use to limit forum shopping. This doctrine is designed to prevent forum shopping, vexatious litigation, and double recovery for the same injury." (Note that Tennessee is not the only state to honor this doctrine.)

There is another point to consider: the insurer has agreed to pay the benefits required by the *workers compensation law*, a phrase defined on the policy as the "workers compensation law… of each state or territory named in Item 3.A. of the information page." This makes it important for the insured employer to specifically list those states in which the employer has a workers compensation exposure. If, in the example noted in the first paragraph, the employer did not list Pennsylvania in Item 3.A. of the information page, payment for any benefits won by the claimant employee could be denied by the insurer since Pennsylvania was not a listed state. Of course, Other States Insurance (discussed in Chapter 4) can alleviate this potential problem. But an insured who has workers compensation exposures in more than one state should make sure those states are listed either in Item 3.A. or Item 3.C. of the information page.

We Will Defend

With this clause, the insurer promises to defend, at its expense, any claim, proceeding, or suit against the insured for benefits payable by the workers compensation policy. It should be noted that the insurer reserves the right to settle claims or lawsuits, so the insured has no veto power over the matter. For example, if the insured does not want to pay benefits to an injured employee because the insured believes the employee is faking the injury, the insurer need not get the permission of the insured in order to pay the claim if it so decides. This is analogous to the duty to defend language in the commercial general liability policy.

In this clause, the insurer also states clearly that it has no duty to defend a claim or lawsuit that is not covered under the terms of the policy. This is for those courts that would say that if a clear denial of the duty to defend under certain circumstances is not placed in the policy language, then the insurer must defend any and all claims or lawsuits.

We Will Also Pay

The insurer will pay certain enumerated costs as part of any claim, proceeding, or lawsuit that is defended. The listed costs are: reasonable expenses incurred at the insurer's request (but not loss of earnings); premiums for bonds to release attachments and for appeal bonds; litigation costs taxed against the insured; interest on a judgment as required by law; and expenses incurred by the insurer.

These payments are similar to the supplementary payments that are offered under a CGL coverage form. The payments are in addition to the amounts payable as workers compensation payments, so any of these costs that are paid by the insurer will not diminish the amounts available for workers compensation benefits.

Other Insurance

With this clause, the insurer declares that it will not pay more than its share of benefits and costs covered by the workers compensation policy and other insurance, including self-insurance. The sharing is to be on an equal basis until the loss is paid. Since the benefits paid under workers compensation are set by state law and not subject to the vagaries of a jury, there is no specified limit of liability on the workers compensation policy; however, any amounts to be paid as benefits will be split equally among affected insurers and self-insureds.

Payments You Must Make

This clause of the workers compensation coverage details when the insured, instead of the insurer, has to make payments arising out of an injured worker's claim. Here the policy points out that the insured is responsible for any payments in excess of the benefits regularly provided by the workers compensation law.

This excess is usually the result of the insured's violating workers compensation laws, such as: serious and willful misconduct, knowingly employing someone in violation of law, failure to comply with a health or safety law, or discharging or discriminating against any employee in violation of law. As an example, if the insured knowingly hires a minor in violation of state workers compensation laws and the minor is injured on the job, the insured will be charged a penalty by the state. The insurer will pay the benefits due the injured worker, but the insured is responsible for the penalty levied by the state. This is an attempt by the insurer to make the insured pay for his or her own intentional conduct that violates a law or regulation, something akin to the expected or intended injury exclusion on the CGL form.

Note that if the insurer makes any of these excess payments on behalf of the insured, the insured must reimburse the insurer promptly. There is no explanation on the policy as to just what "promptly" means, but it is unlikely that an insurer would allow payments due to languish over any length of time.

Recovery from Others

This is basically a subrogation clause. It entitles the insurer to recover its workers compensation payments from a party that can be shown to be actually liable for an employee's injuries. The insured has the duty to do everything necessary to protect the rights of the insurer and to help enforce those rights. So, for example, if a customer of the insured is somehow responsible for injuries suffered by the insured's employee, the insured is not supposed to waive the right of recovery in an attempt to keep the customer happy. Such a course of action would violate the insurer's rights and lead to a possible dispute over coverage between the insured and the insurer.

This clause does not speak to pre-injury waivers. Therefore, it must be concluded that if the insured has agreements with his or her customers that hold the customers harmless for injuries that may be suffered by the insured's employees arising out of the customers' negligence, such agreements do not violate the provisions of this clause.

Statutory Provisions

Where required by law, workers compensation insurance is subject to several statutory provisions. These clauses provide that: notice to the insured of an injury constitutes notice to the insurer; default, bankruptcy, or insolvency of the insured does not relieve the insurer of obligations under the policy (indeed, the insurer states that it is directly and primarily liable to any person entitled to payable benefits); jurisdiction over the insured is jurisdiction over the insurer for purposes of the workers compensation law—that is, the state law that decides if and what compensation is to be paid to the injured employee is the guide for both the insured and the insurer.

The statutory provisions also note that terms of the insurance coverage that conflict with the workers compensation law are changed to conform to the law. In other words, state law takes precedence over the wording of the insurance policy. Workers compensation coverage is guided by state law, not by an insurance policy and not by federal law.

Chapter 3

Employers Liability Insurance

Employers liability insurance is the second part of coverage contained in the standard workers compensation policy. It protects the insured against liability imposed by law for injury to employees in the course of employment that is not compensable as an obligation imposed by workers compensation, occupational disease, or any similar laws. The coverage under this part of the workers compensation policy corresponds to liability coverage found on other forms.

Despite the fact that workers compensation is usually considered to be the exclusive remedy for covered employees for work-related injuries, there are several reasons why employers liability coverage is desirable.

Some states do not make workers compensation insurance compulsory or do not require the statutory coverage unless an employer has three or more employees. In either of these circumstances, workers compensation insurance is elective. There may also be instances when an on-the-job injury or disease is not considered to be work-related and therefore not compensable under the statutory coverage. Nevertheless, the employee may still have reason to believe that the employer should be held accountable, and proceed with legal action. Moreover, the monopolistic states do not permit private insurers to write workers compensation coverage, so if a bodily injury claim made by an employee is considered outside the workers comp system, employers liability coverage will offer the employer some insurance protection. Additionally, the workers compensation laws of some states have been interpreted as permitting lawsuits and recovery against employers by spouses and dependents of injured workers, even though the workers are compensated for their injuries. The basis of such lawsuits is loss of consortium—loss of companionship, comfort, and affection.

Finally, employers are increasingly being confronted with claims and lawsuits in so-called third-party-over actions; these arise when an injured employee sues a negligent third party who, in turn, sues the employer for contributory negligence. For example, a third-party-over action might arise in the following circumstance: a store clerk's eye is injured by an exploding soda bottle cap. The employee sues the soda bottling company (because the judgment would probably exceed workers compensation benefits). The bottler joins the employer in the suit, claiming negligent storage of the bottles. This is a *third-party-over* action.

Under such circumstances as these, the employer can look to employers liability insurance for coverage.

The employers liability insurance part of the policy contains nine clauses.

How This Insurance Applies

Employers liability insurance applies to bodily injury by accident or by disease. The bodily injury must arise out of and in the course of employment, and the employment must be necessary or incidental to the named insured's work in a state or territory listed in Item 3.A. of the information page. (The same issues regarding the naming of states in 3.A. that apply to workers compensation insurance apply here; see Chapter 1 for comment.) The bodily injury by accident must occur during the policy period, and the bodily injury by disease must be caused or aggravated by the conditions of the employment. Finally, if the named insured is sued, the original lawsuit must be brought in the United States, its territories or possessions, or Canada (the coverage territory).

Arise Out of and in the Course of Employment

One of the crucial elements of this insurance coverage is the phrase "arise out of and in the course of employment." The various states' workers compensation laws do not offer a definition of the phrase and neither does the insurance policy. So, it has fallen to the courts to define the phrase; the following information serves as examples.

In *Appeal of Griffin*, 671 A.2d 541 (N.H. 1996), the New Hampshire Supreme Court, in deciding that an injury due to a fight with co-workers was employment related, explained the "arising out of and in the course of employment" requirement. The court said that to meet the scope-of-employment test, the claimant must prove: that the injury arose out of employment by demonstrating that it resulted from a risk created by the employment; and, that the injury arose in the course of employment by demonstrating that it occurred within the boundaries of time and space created by the terms of employment, and that it occurred in the performance of an activity related to employment.

In *Carnahan v. Morton Buildings*, 2014 WL 4678301, the Court of Appeals of Ohio, Third District, ruled that a claimant's injuries resulting from an all-terrain vehicle (ATV) accident on property at which the claimant was constructing a pole barn for his employer did not arise out of his employment. The claimant was injured touring the property after finishing the pole barn project. The court ruled the injuries did not arise out of employment because the scene of the accident was not in proximity to the pole barn jobsite, the employer did not have control over the scene of the accident, and the claimant's participation in the ATV ride and his presence at the scene of the accident provided no benefit to the employer.

The words "arise out of" refer to the causal relationship between the employment and the injury; see *Maher v. Workers Court of Appeals Board*, 661 P.2d 1058 (1983). Also see *City of Tulsa v. O'Keefe*, 329 P.3d 761 (2014) where in the Court of Civil Appeals of Oklahoma, Division No. 3 stated that "to prove that a workers compensation claimant's injury arose out of the claimant's employment, there must be a causal relationship between the injury suffered and the risks incident to the claimant's mission for the employer."

An accident arises out of employment when it occurs while the employee is engaged in some activity or duty that he or she is authorized to undertake and that is calculated to further, indirectly or directly, the employer's business; see *Scullin Steel Company v. Whiteside*, 682 S.W.2d 1 (1984).

Professor Larson opines that the "arising out of" formula refers to the time and space limitations of the claimant's employment, and a causality nexus between the injury and the claimant's employment responsibilities and duties; see 1 Larson *The Law of Workmen's Compensation*, §6.000 *et seq.* (1989). And, in *Trezza v. USA Truck*, 2014 Ark.App. 555, the Court of Appeals of Arkansas stated that the test to determine whether workers compensation claimants are performing employment services is "whether the injury occurred within the time and space boundaries of the employment, when the claimant was carrying out the employer's purpose or advancing the employer's interest directly or indirectly."

The term "in the course of employment" is not necessarily synonymous with "arising out of" as noted by the Court of Appeals of Virginia in *Bernard v. Carlson Companies* 60 Va.App. 400 (2012), and both conditions must be proved before compensation will be awarded. "In the course of employment" refers to the time, place, and circumstances under which the accident or injury occurred; see *Hoover v. Ehrsam Company*, 544 P.2d 1366 (1976). And, an employee is in the course of employment where he or she is engaged in the furtherance of the employer's business, or doing a duty he or she was employed to do; see *Malacarne v. Yonkers Parking Authority*, 359 N.E.2d 992 (1976). Couch states that in order to establish that an accident arose "in the course of employment", a temporal and spatial nexus to the employment must be established. Moreover, as a general rule, for an injury or death to occur in the course of employment, it must occur within the period of employment, at a place or area where the employee may reasonably be expected to be, and while the employee is performing his or her work duties or engaged in an activity at least incidental to his or her employment; see 9A *Couch on Insurance*, §135:5. Finally, in 8 *Couch on Insurance*, §115:70, it is stated that the words "in the course of employment" refer to the time and place of an accident and the circumstances under which it occurs. Whether a given injury is in the course of employment is determined by the facts and circumstances of the particular case, and in making the determination, the entire sphere and period of employment may be considered and whether the employee placed himself or herself outside his or her employment.

In the *Trezza* case noted previously, the Court of Appeals of Arkansas affirmed a ruling that the injured employee failed to prove that his ankle injury occurred in the course of employment. The employee injured his ankle when he got out of his truck to go to the bathroom and stumbled or stepped incorrectly. The court found that the claimant's work day had ended when he was injured because he had logged off duty and did not intend to perform any further job functions for thirty-four hours; he was not taking a necessary bathroom break so that he could return to his work duties and instead, was off work and not required to do anything; and, his injury did not occur in his truck and was not related to sleeping in his truck.

We Will Pay

Under employers liability insurance, the insurer promises to pay all sums that the insured legally must pay as damages because of bodily injury to employees. The covered damages, where recovery is permitted by law, include: (1) the insured's liability for damages claimed against a third party by one of the insured's employees (third-party-over actions); (2) damages assessed for care and loss of services; and (3) consequential bodily injury to a spouse, child, parent, or sibling of the injured employee. In addition, the employers liability insurance applies to damages assessed against the insured in a capacity other than as an employer (a dual capacity action).

Note that the language of the employers liability coverage complements the language of the employers liability exclusions that are on the standard commercial general liability (CGL) form; the covered damages under employers liability correspond well with the damages excluded under the CGL form. As examples: the CGL form excludes coverage for bodily injury to an employee of the insured (or to an employee's spouse, child, parent, brother, or sister for consequential bodily injury) that arises out of and in the course of employment by the insured; the CGL form's exclusions apply whether the insured may be liable either as an employer or in any other capacity (dual capacity); and the exclusions apply if the insured has an obligation to share damages with or repay someone else who must pay damages (third-party-over actions). This is in keeping with the idea that employee injuries should be covered by workers compensation policies and not general liability policies.

Employers Liability Exclusions

Employers liability coverage is subject to twelve exclusions that highlight the nature of this coverage.

For example, there are exclusions making the point that this policy is meant to apply under state laws and not federal laws. The insurance does not cover bodily injury to any person subject to the Longshore and Harbor Workers Compensation Act, the Defense Base Act, the Federal Coal Mine Health and Safety Act, or any other federal workers compensation law. Bodily injury to any person in work that is subject to the Federal Employers' Liability Act or any other federal laws obligating an employer to pay damages to an employee due to bodily injury arising out of or in the course of employment is also excluded. And, damages payable under the Migrant and Seasonal Agricultural Worker Protection Act and under any other federal law awarding damages for violation of those laws or regulations are excluded.

The employers liability insurance does not cover any obligation imposed by a workers compensation, occupational disease, unemployment compensation, or disability benefits law or any similar law. This exclusion is meant to emphasize the difference between the workers compensation insurance part of the WC policy and the employers liability insurance part.

Other exclusions apply to intentional acts and violations of laws, showing that this coverage is meant for accidental incidents. Employers liability insurance does not cover liability assumed under a contract (note that liability assumed by the insured under an insured contract is covered by the CGL form—another example of one coverage form complementing the other). Employers liability insurance does not cover fines or penalties imposed for violation of federal or state law. It does not cover punitive or exemplary damages because of bodily injury to an employee who is employed in violation of law. And, the insurance does not cover bodily injury to an employee while employed in violation of law with the actual knowledge of the named insured or any executive officers. This can act as a dual sword of punishment to an insured. For example, if the insured knowingly violates state law and hires a minor for hazardous work and the minor is injured on the job, the insured will no doubt be hit with fines and be sued by the injured minor for compensatory and punitive damages. When that happens, the employers liability insurance will not be applicable for the insured and the insured will carry the monetary burden.

There is an exclusion that applies to damages arising out of coercion, criticism, demotion, evaluation, reassignment, discipline, defamation, harassment, humiliation, discrimination against or termination of any employee, or any personnel practices, policies, acts, or omissions. This multi-worded exclusion emphasizes the point that employers liability insurance is meant for bodily injury suffered by an employee by accident or by disease, and not for mental stress or embarrassment or for something other than bodily injury arising out of a personnel practice or company policy. Even if a court were to equate the mental stress or anxiety of a demotion or harassment with bodily injury, this exclusion is so worded that the policy will not provide employers liability coverage—any "damages" arising out of the listed actions are not covered.

Finally, the policy has an exclusion for bodily injury occurring outside the United States, its territories or possessions, and Canada. This exclusion could pose a huge problem in today's business world since many companies do business on an international scale. However, the exclusion has an exception for bodily injury to a citizen or resident of the U.S. or Canada who is temporarily outside these countries. So, if an employee of the named insured company is in Japan on a business trip and is injured while on the job, employers liability insurance is available to the insured if needed.

We Will Defend

The policy gives the insurer the right and duty to defend the insured against any claim, proceeding, or lawsuit for damages payable by the employers liability insurance. The insurer reserves the right to settle the claims and lawsuits, so the insured has no veto power over the matter. The defense of the insured is at the expense of the insurer, so the costs of defense do not impact the declared limits of insurance.

This defense clause adds the stipulations that the insurer has no duty to defend a claim or lawsuit that is not covered by the insurance, and no duty to defend or continue defending after the applicable limit of liability is paid. The purpose of the first caveat is to counter the idea put forth by some courts that unless the insurer specifically declares that it has no duty to defend under certain circumstances, the insurer has to defend the insured under all circumstances, even if there is no coverage under the terms of the policy. The purpose of the second caveat is to keep insurers from continuing to spend money on the defense of the insured after the limits of liability are paid. Now, whether this means that the insurer can simply put the limits of liability into a fund before trial and then walk away from the defense of the insured, is not clear; however, the thinking of most courts today is that such a practice is not acceptable, legally or morally.

We Will Also Pay

This provision is the same as that found under part one of the workers compensation policy, discussed in Chapter 2. The payments promised here by the insurer are similar to the supplementary payments that are offered under the standard CGL coverage form, and do not diminish the limits of liability as shown on the information page.

Other Insurance

This provision is similar to the other insurance clause found under part one of the policy. A discussion of the clause is in Chapter 2.

Limits of Liability

The insurer's liability to pay for damages under employers liability insurance is limited. The limits of liability are shown on the information page in item 3.B., and are listed as follows: an amount per each accident is listed for bodily injury by accident; a policy limit is listed for bodily injury by disease; and an amount per each employee is listed for bodily injury by disease. This listing of specific limits of liability is, of course, a different approach than the payment schedule under part one of the policy; payments under part one of the policy are guided by the state workers compensation law and not the policy itself. Employers liability is more like a commercial general liability policy, in this regard.

The "by accident" limit is based on each accident so that the insurer will pay no more than the listed amount in any one accident regardless of how many employees are injured. For example, if three employees are injured in the same accident and the bodily injury by accident limit is $100,000, then that is the total amount payable by the insurer. This is not to say that all three employees will receive equal amounts—that is to be decided by the facts of the case—but, they will receive a total of $100,000.

The "by disease" limit has an aggregate limit and an each employee limit. The aggregate limit shown on the information page is the total amount payable by the insurer for all bodily injuries arising out of a disease, regardless of the number of employees who suffer injury from the disease. So, for example, if thirty employees suffer injury from a disease for which the employer is legally liable, the total amount available for all the injured employees is the amount listed as the policy limit for bodily injury by disease. The disease limit is also subject to an each employee limit in that, regardless of the aggregate limit, each employee injured by disease can collect only up to the amount listed on the information page.

As an example, the insured has a $250,000 policy limit for injury by disease and a $25,000 limit for each employee for injury by disease. If the thirty employees noted in the previous paragraph are injured by disease, they have a $250,000 pool to be divided among them, but each employee can only be paid under this policy a total of $25,000. These scheduled limits of liability may not be enough to completely pay the amounts for which the insured is found liable, but scheduled limits of liability are legal and not very likely to be disregarded by courts. Moreover, the policy explicitly states that the insurer will not pay any claims for damages after it has paid the applicable limit of its liability under this insurance.

Recovery from Others

This is the subrogation clause for employers liability insurance. It is similar to the clause in the workers compensation insurance part of the policy which is discussed in Chapter 2.

Actions against Us

This provision spells out a bit of the contractual relationship between the insured and the insurer. The insured has agreed not to exercise a right of action—that is, file a lawsuit—against the insurer unless certain things have occurred. Basically, the insured agrees not to sue the insurer unless a claim has been filed against the insured, all the provisions of the policy have been followed by the insured, a definite amount of liability has been assessed against the insured, and then, the insurer has, for whatever reason, refused to pay the amount due.

This clause also makes the point that the workers compensation policy is a contractual agreement between the insured and the insurer and so, no outside party—one not a party to the contract—has the right under this policy to sue the insurer to enforce the provisions of the policy.

The insurer agrees through this provision not to abandon its contractual commitments under the policy to the insured even if the insured goes bankrupt or becomes insolvent. Existing claims will still be paid even if the insured is no longer in business.

Chapter 4

Other States Insurance

This part of the workers compensation and employers liability insurance policy provides *other states insurance*. This coverage functions as a complement to part one of the policy, in that part one (workers compensation insurance) applies to obligations imposed on the insured by the compensation laws of states listed in Item 3.A. of the information page, while other states insurance applies only if a state(s) is shown in Item 3.C. of the information page. This means that if an insured is confronted with a claim under a workers compensation law of a state to which the insured had not fully expected to be subject—a state not listed in Item 3.A. of the declarations—there is no coverage under part one of the policy; but the insured could find coverage for such a claim by utilizing the other states insurance part of the workers compensation policy.

Other states insurance applies if one or more states where the insured could possibly end up working in are shown in Item 3.C. of the information page. The insured has no actual known exposure in those states listed in Item 3.C. when the policy becomes effective, but the insured thinks an exposure may arise (e.g., an employee might travel to one of those states on business or be unexpectedly assigned to an out-of-state construction project). If the insured begins work in one of the listed states after the effective date of the policy, the policy applies as if that state were listed in Item 3.A. for workers compensation and employers liability purposes.

To avoid an uninsured loss due to oversight, it has been suggested that the statement, "All states except North Dakota, Ohio, Washington, and Wyoming (monopolistic states) and states designated in Item 3.A. of the information page," be inserted in Item 3.C. However, an insurer licensed to operate in only a limited number of states should not include this broad statement in the workers compensation policy because it might convey to some the impression that the insurer has the ability to write insurance in all states. This is not the case, of course, since other states insurance does not give any insurer the approval to write workers compensation coverage in a particular state if that insurer is not licensed to do so.

A fairly common situation under which the other states insurance is useful is that of an insured firm that can have employees traveling in states other than the state where the firm is located. For example, if the insured has its office in Illinois and all its employees work there, the insured would list Illinois in Item 3.A. of the information page of the policy. Due to new business opportunities, the insured believes that it will have some employees travel into Iowa, Missouri, Indiana, and Wisconsin on business. To properly cover this possible exposure, the insured would list the four states in Item 3.C. of the information page (of course, if the insured thinks its employees would be going to more than the four states named, the insured can use the "all states ..." language noted in the previous paragraph). If the insured does begin any work in those states listed in Item 3.C. after the effective date of the workers compensation policy, the insured would have workers compensation insurance if needed. The insurer agrees to pay the benefits required by the workers compensation law of the listed states, or, if not permitted to pay the benefits directly to the injured employee, the insurer agrees to reimburse the insured for the benefits that it paid the employee.

Notice Clauses

A key point in this part of the workers compensation policy is the importance of giving notice to the insurer. The policy emphasizes that if the insured already has ongoing work on the effective date of the policy in any state not listed in Item 3.A. of the information page, "coverage will not be afforded for that state unless we (the insurer) are notified within thirty days." For example, if the insured has employees working in Delaware at the time his workers compensation policy renews, and Delaware is not listed under Item 3.A. of the information page, the insured must notify the insurer of the Delaware exposure within thirty days or there is no coverage for workers compensation claims that may arise after that time period expires.

Note that this thirty day time period is, presumably, thirty days after policy inception, but the policy's wording is not clear on that point. In order for the insured to be safe, the insurer should be notified of work begun in states other than those listed in Item 3.A. as soon as such work begins, and not wait for any thirty day time period to go by. In fact, in support of this immediate notice idea, the policy has another paragraph that reminds the insured to, "Tell us (the insurer) at once if you begin work in any state listed in Item 3.C. of the information page." Through these measures, the insurer is simply trying to exercise a degree of control over the loss potential.

Chapter 5

Duties after Injury Occurs/Conditions

This chapter deals with parts four and six of the workers compensation and employers liability insurance policy. (Part five of the workers comp policy, premium, is discussed in chapter nine.) Part four of the policy sets out the duties that the named insured must perform if an injury occurs lest the insured breach contractual obligations, thereby making the insurance contract voidable. Part six discusses certain conditions that affect the policy and some of the actions of the insured and the insurer in their dealings with one another.

The Duties of the Insured

The policy lists seven duties that the insured is to undertake in the event of an injury occurring to an employee.

First and foremost is the duty to notify the insurer if an injury that may be covered by the policy occurs. The obvious reason for this is so that the insurer can process an injury claim promptly. Such promptness can aid the insured, the insurer, and the injured employee. With prompt notice, the insured gets the ball rolling so that the insurance coverage he has already paid for can be applied to the claim. The injured worker gets quick appropriate medical attention and care, knowing that such care is going to be paid for by the insurer. The insurer can set up its claim file and fulfill its contractual obligations to "pay promptly when due" the workers compensation benefits required by law; and, if a lawsuit results from the injury, prompt notice allows the insurer to have the facts and figures of the accident so that a defense can be planned or a subrogation lawsuit can be successfully made. It is true that some insureds may want to hide a worker's injury in order to protect its experience rating factor, but that would not only violate the insured's duties under the policy contract, but also set the stage for possible future problems in the insurer-insured-employee relationship.

The next listed duty of the insured is to provide for immediate medical and other services required by the workers compensation law. This may conflict with the duty noted in the last paragraph of this part of the policy. That last paragraph warns the insured not to voluntarily make payments, assume obligations, or incur expenses, except at the insured's own cost. If, in the process of providing immediate medical services, the insured incurs expenses, are such expenses reimbursable by the insurer? The policy is not clear on this point; however, in all probability, the insured will be reimbursed. Note that the insurer has already promised to pay reasonable expenses incurred by the insured at its request, and since the insurer has "requested" the insured to provide immediate medical services if an injury occurs, it can be said that the insurer has already agreed to the reimbursement. Besides, the duty of the insured is to not voluntarily make payments or incur expenses; but, if the immediate medical services are required by law, that is not exactly voluntary on the part of the insured.

If an injury occurs, the insured must give the insurer or the agent the names and addresses of the injured persons and of witnesses, and other information needed by the insurer. And, the insured is required to promptly give the insurer all notices, demands, and legal papers related to the injury, claim, or lawsuit. This helps the insurer process the claim as soon as possible, and to plan for any future legal action on behalf of or against the insured.

The insured has the duty to cooperate with the insurer and to assist in the investigation, settlement, or defense of any claim, proceeding, or lawsuit. This is not to say that the insured has the final say in any settlement; the insurer has already reserved to itself that task. But, the insured has an affirmative duty to cooperate with the insurer in the claims process, and most courts would require the insured to fulfill this duty or be held in breach of contract.

The final listed duty of the insured deals with the insurer's right of subrogation. The insured must do nothing after an injury occurs that would interfere with the insurer's right to recover from others. The duty says nothing about an insured signing a waiver or some other type of hold harmless agreement prior to an injury that would restrict or even deny a right to recover from others, so such agreements would apply to the insurer as well as to the insured. Insureds should make such agreements known to the insurer before the policy takes effect.

Note again, if the insured violates these duties, there is the chance that the insurer will claim breach of contract, thus making the policy voidable. The insurer would have to prove such a breach, but if it can do so, the insured could end up with no insurance coverage for a workers compensation claim.

Conditions

There are five conditions listed on the workers compensation policy, dealing with inspections, long term policies, the transfer of the named insured's rights, cancellation of the policy, and just who acts as the sole representative on behalf of all the insureds.

The inspections clause gives the insurer the right (but not the obligation) to make an inspection of the workplace "at any time." This condition has given rise to a theory that would allow the injured employee to maintain an action for negligence against the workers compensation insurance carrier itself. The reasoning behind this is that some insurance carriers take it upon themselves to inspect the workplace for safety engineering purposes, and if an accident then occurs, the injured worker can charge negligence on the part of the insurer for failure to perform its assumed duty to uncover and correct unsafe working conditions.

When injured employees have filed lawsuits against workers comp insurers based on allegations of a negligent safety inspection, most judicial decisions have come down on the side of the insurer.

A federal district court in Michigan stated in *Kotarski v. Aetna Casualty & Surety Company*, 244 F.Supp. 547 (E.D. Mich. 1965) that nothing in Michigan's workers compensation act reveals the intention to allow the insurer that is performing safety inspections as an integral part of its business function to be sued as a negligent third party on the theory that its liability arises from negligent performance of a voluntary undertaking. (Note that *Kotarski* was later disavowed as a correct statement of Michigan law in a 1968 case; however, this 1968 ruling was itself overturned by statutory amendment, and the opinion in the *Kotarski* case was adopted by the Michigan legislature and incorporated into the Michigan Workers Compensation Act.)

In *Hamel v. Factory Mutual Engineering Association*, 564 N.E.2d 395 (1990), the Supreme Judicial Court of Massachusetts, Middlesex, stated "insurance companies that engage in accident prevention work, the social desirability of which cannot be questioned, should be able to do so without incurring unlimited liability for failing to discover a hazard that some jury might think ought to have been discovered. If an insurance company can escape tort liability altogether by not making any inspections on the premises of the insured, but may incur unlimited tort liability by making some inspections, it more than likely will decline to make any, unless required to do so by statute. The ultimate losers will be workmen and their families".

In *Barrette v. Travelers Insurance Company*, 246 A.2d 102 (Conn. Super. Ct. 1968), the Connecticut Supreme Court decided that an employer's compensation carrier is not subject to suit by an injured employee for alleged negligence in the failure to inspect machinery, failure to warn the employee of the danger, or neglecting to provide devices to negate the danger.

In *Reid v. Employers Mutual Liability Insurance Company*, 319 N.E.2d 769 (Ill. 1974), the Illinois Supreme Court held that the workers compensation insurer engaged in making safety inspections incident to its compensation coverage was not amenable to a lawsuit by an employee for injuries caused by the carrier's negligence in performing safety inspections. And, in a decision issued by the United States District Court in Colorado that favorably cited the *Reid* case, the district court stated that "there appears to be a definite trend toward the recognition of immunity for compensation carriers in the performance of safety inspections of an employer's premises"; this case is *McHargue v. Stokes Division of Pennwalt Corporation*, 649 F. Supp. 1388 (1986).

There are, of course, some cases on the other side of the issue. In a New Hampshire case, *Corson v. Liberty Mutual Insurance Company*, 265 A.2d 315 (N.H. 1970), a workers compensation insurer that undertook the task of assisting accident prevention by inspections and advice rendered to the insured employer was held to be liable to an injured employee for a negligent inspection. In *Rothfuss v. Bakers Mutual Insurance Company*, 257 A.2d 733 (N.J. Super. Ct. App. Div. 1969), the New Jersey Supreme Court declared that a workers compensation carrier is a third person liable to an employee in a common law action if its acts negligently cause harm to the employee. And, in *Cline v. Avery Abrasives, Inc.*, 409 N.Y.S.2d 91 (1978), the Supreme Court, Monroe County, New York held that an insurer, by performing safety inspections, is doing something clearly distinct from its contractual obligations to make payments of benefits under the insurance contract. Accordingly, the court ruled that a workers compensation insurance carrier is not immune from suit for claimed negligent safety inspection of the employer's premises.

However, as noted previously, the majority ruling is on the side of insurers. This is best summed up in a ruling from the Eighth Circuit. In *Kifer v. Liberty Mutual Insurance Company*, 777 F.2d 1325 (1985), the United States Court of Appeals, Eighth Circuit, noted that "the rule of law adopted in most of the decisions permitting this type of action against the workers compensation carrier has been overturned by statutory amendment". Moreover, the court went on, "in a number of states, the carrier is also expressly granted immunity from suit or is equated with the employer for most purposes under the statute, including immunity.

There is a discernible legislative trend toward granting immunity from suit to workers compensation carriers for their alleged negligence in the making of safety inspections ... and we may properly take cognizance of this emerging trend". Indeed, this trend is acknowledged in *Cornell v. Liberty Mutual Group*, 2012 WL 912788, wherein the United States District Court for the Western District of Arkansas noted that the Arkansas workers comp act provides that "an insurance company that performs a safety consultation under this provision shall have no liability with respect to any accident based on the allegation that the accident was caused or could have been prevented by a program, inspection, or other activity or service undertaken by the insurance company for the prevention of accidents in connection with the operations of the employer."

Regardless of which side of the argument prevails in any given state, it should be pointed out that the current workers compensation and employers liability insurance policy contains a rather specific disclaimer about the inspection of the workplace and the duty such an inspection places on the insurer. In the inspection condition of the policy, the insurance company declares that inspections it may carry out are not safety inspections; they relate only to the insurability of the workplaces and the premiums to be charged. Furthermore, the insurer states that it does not undertake to perform the duty of any person to provide for the health or safety of the employees, and does not warrant that the workplaces are safe or healthful, or that they comply with laws, codes, or standards. Thus, the insurer strives to intentionally limit its obligation to pay under the workers compensation policy.

The long term policy clause notes that, if a policy is written for longer than one year and sixteen days—say, for example, two or three years—then all the provisions in the existing policy apply as if under a brand new policy. In other words, the annual renewal is treated as an automatic rewrite of the existing policy, though both the insured and the insurer should examine current exposures in order to get proper premium for proper coverage.

The transfer of rights clause acts to prevent the insured from transferring his or her rights or duties to another party without the written consent of the insurer. This is meant to protect the insurer from getting an insured that it neither contracted for nor would want to insure in any instance. An exception is made, of course, for the legal representative of the insured in case the insured dies; notice must be given to the insurer within thirty days after the insured's death in order for the legal representative to be viewed as the insured.

The cancellation clause details how the insured or the insurer can cancel the policy. The clause allows the insured to cancel the policy at any time, even with only one day notice, as long as written notice is mailed to the insurance company in advance of the cancellation date. It should be noted that the clause states that notice need only be mailed in advance and not received by the company in advance. If the insurer cancels the policy, it must mail or deliver to the insured not less than ten days advance written notice stating when the cancellation is to take effect. For the insurer also, mailing the notice will prove sufficient to prove notice. Presumably, should any dispute arise over the cancellation date, a court will decide if the terms of the clause were heeded, but regardless of which party is mailing the cancellation notice, it would be prudent to mail it by certified mail, return receipt requested. This clause also states the obvious—if the cancellation provisions conflict with state law, the state law prevails and this policy and the insurer recognize that fact.

The final condition on the policy makes the first named insured the sole representative to the insurer, so that important items such as changing the policy provisions or cancelling the policy can be dealt with without having the insurer sort through possibly conflicting statements or wishes from the various insureds. This is simply a good and sensible business practice.

Chapter 6

Endorsements

There are many endorsements authorized for use with the workers compensation and employers liability insurance policy. This chapter lists some of them and analyzes their content. It should be noted that there are state-specific endorsements that are applicable only in that particular state named in the endorsement that bring the policy into conformity with state law or regulation; but, those are too numerous to discuss in this guide. And, there are endorsements that pertain to federal laws on the subject of workers compensation, such as the maritime coverage endorsement and the federal employers liability coverage endorsement. These are discussed in a later chapter.

The endorsements in this chapter are presented in numerical order.

Alternate Employer Endorsement WC 00 03 01 A

This endorsement applies only with respect to bodily injury to the named insured's employees who are in the course of special or temporary employment by the alternate employer listed on the endorsement. An example of when this endorsement can be used is the following: a supplier of temporary office help (the insured) is required by its customer (the user of the temporary office help, that is, the alternate employer) to provide this insurance to protect the customer from claims brought by the insured's employees against the alternate employer. If the named insured has an employee who is injured while working for the alternate employer listed on the endorsement, WC 00 03 01 A will provide coverage for claims made by the employee against that alternate employer. Of course, the insurance afforded by the endorsement is not intended to satisfy the alternate employer's duty to secure its own obligations under the workers compensation law of the state.

Employers Liability Coverage Endorsement WC 00 03 03 B

This endorsement is usually used in monopolistic states where the workers compensation system is not open to coverage by private insurance companies. WC 00 03 03 B states up front that part one of the workers compensation policy (workers compensation insurance) does not apply to work in a state shown in the schedule. On the other hand, part two (employers liability insurance) applies to work in the listed states as though the states were shown in Item 3.A. of the information page. Basically, WC 00 03 03 B provides stop gap coverage for employers in those states where the state runs the workers compensation program but does not offer employers liability coverage. (Note that in Ohio, endorsement WC 34 03 01 B is used in place of WC 00 03 03 B.)

Joint Venture as Insured
Endorsement WC 00 03 05

WC 00 03 05 is fairly straightforward. It states, "If the employer named in Item 1 of the information page is a joint venture, and if you are one of its members, you are insured, but only in your capacity as an employer of the joint venture's employees." The workers compensation policy makes no mention of business arrangements such as joint ventures, but, joint ventures can, of course, be employers. This endorsement makes the point that the insurance afforded by the workers compensation policy is limited to being an employer of those employees that are working for the joint venture. If an employer is involved in a joint venture but also has other business interests and operations, he will need a separate workers compensation policy to apply to injuries suffered by those employees working in the other businesses and operations; WC 00 03 05 will not respond to such claims.

Medical Benefits Exclusion
Endorsement WC 00 03 06

Some states permit insureds to pay medical benefits directly, instead of channeling them through the workers compensation policy. Endorsement WC 00 03 06 is attached in such situations. It states that workers compensation medical benefits of a state listed on the endorsement are not covered. The endorsement directs that the insured pay medical benefits as required by law and to the satisfaction of the insurer.

Medical Benefits Reimbursement
Endorsement WC 00 03 07

This endorsement is similar to WC 00 03 06, discussed previously. It states that the insured will provide medical benefits as required by law in the states listed. The insurer also must be satisfied with the way in which benefits are being paid. In addition, the insured is obligated to reimburse the insurer for any medical benefits that it may legally be required to pay.

Partners, Officers and Others
Exclusion Endorsement WC 00 03 08

Some states allow partners and executive officers to choose to be subject to the workers compensation laws. If these people so choose, the premium basis of the workers compensation policy includes their remuneration. However, where the individual partners or executive officers choose not to be covered by the workers compensation laws, WC 00 03 08 should be attached to the policy. The endorsement states that the policy does not cover bodily injury to any person described in the schedule and that the premium basis for the policy does not include their remuneration. Note that individuals can be named on this endorsement only when the state workers compensation law allows it.

Sole Proprietors, Partners, Officers and
Others Coverage Endorsement WC 00 03 10

In contrast to WC 00 03 08, endorsement WC 00 03 10 is used when partners and executive officers choose to be subject to the workers compensation laws. The endorsement notes that the persons described on the schedule have chosen to be subject to the law and that the premium basis for the policy includes their remuneration. As with the previous endorsement, individuals can be named in this endorsement only when it is allowed by the state workers compensation law.

Voluntary Compensation and Employers
Liability Coverage Endorsement WC 00 03 11

WC 00 03 11 can be used to cover all employees, like domestic or farm workers, who are not subject to the workers compensation laws, and it can be attached to an existing workers compensation policy that is in place for those employees that are required by state law to be covered by the workers compensation system.

Coverage provided under this endorsement is identical to that for employers and employees required to be insured under the law. WC 00 03 11 states that the insurer "will pay an amount equal to the benefits that would be required of you if you and your employees described in the schedule were subject to the workers compensation law shown in the schedule. We will pay those amounts to the persons who would be entitled to them under the law." In other words, benefits are provided for injuries that would have been compensable in the same manner as they would have been provided had the employment been subject to any applicable state workers compensation laws.

The insurance provided by WC 00 03 11 applies to bodily injury sustained by an employee in the group of employees described in the endorsement's schedule. The bodily injury must occur in the course of employment necessary or incidental to work in a state listed in the schedule and must occur during the policy period. The insurance does not cover any obligation imposed by a workers compensation law or bodily injury intentionally caused or aggravated by the named insured.

Note that before any payments are made to those entitled to them, the beneficiaries must release the insured and the insurer, in writing, of all responsibility for the injury. Any right to recover from others who may be responsible for the injury must be transferred to the insurer, and the injured party must cooperate fully with the insurer in enforcing the right of recovery. If the persons entitled to the benefits of the insurance fail to do these things, or if they claim damages from the insured or the insurer, the duty to pay under this endorsement ends at once.

Voluntary Compensation and Employers Liability Coverage for Residence Employees Endorsement WC 00 03 12 A

WC 00 03 12 is something of a companion endorsement to WC 00 03 11. Both offer voluntary compensation coverage, but as WC 00 03 11 should be used by corporations and business entities, WC 00 03 12 can be used by homeowners. If a homeowner wants workers compensation coverage for a domestic worker, such as a housekeeper or a gardener, WC 00 03 12 is the fitting manner for coverage.

WC 00 03 12 adds voluntary compensation and employers liability coverage for residence employees to a homeowners policy, a personal liability policy, or some other policy that provides similar personal liability coverage. The insurance applies to bodily injury by accident or disease sustained by the named insured's residence employees and must arise out of and in the course of employment by the named insured. So, an advantage of this coverage is that if a domestic worker who cannot be brought within the workers compensation system due to state law is injured and sues the named insured employer, WC 00 03 12 will provide protection to the named insured.

The insuring agreement, exclusions, and other provisions of WC 00 03 12 are similar to those of WC 00 03 11, but there is an important point to mention. In keeping with the "personal"—as opposed to the "business"—nature of WC 00 03 12, the endorsement has an exclusion that states that coverage does not apply to bodily injury arising out of any of the named insured's business pursuits.

Waiver of Our Right to Recover from Others Endorsement WC 00 03 13

The insurer, through this endorsement, waives its right of subrogation against third parties who may be responsible for an injury if those third parties are named in the endorsement's schedule.

Workers Compensation and Employers Liability Coverage for Residence Employees Endorsement WC 00 03 14 A

In jurisdictions where domestic, agricultural, and casual workers are subject to the state's workers compensation laws, the employer is required to provide coverage. One way to arrange for this coverage is through the use of WC 00 03 14. This endorsement contains basically the same provisions as the standard workers compensation and employers liability policy and is to be attached to a personal liability policy, a homeowners policy, or any policy affording similar personal liability coverage with respect to the residence premises of the insured. The effect is the same as if the employee were covered by a standard workers compensation policy since the insurer agrees to pay benefits required by the state's workers compensation laws.

Domestic and Agricultural Workers Exclusion Endorsement WC 00 03 15

Domestic, agricultural, and casual employees are not treated in a uniform manner under the workers compensation systems of the various states. Some states have written their workers compensation laws to include domestic and agricultural employees either on a compulsory basis, or to allow employees to provide coverage voluntarily. WC 00 03 15 can be used by insureds to deny workers compensation benefits coverage to any agricultural, domestic, or household worker as long as the state law allows this course of action. Those workers denied coverage have to be listed in the endorsement's schedule.

Employee Leasing Client Endorsement WC 00 03 19

This endorsement is attached to policies issued to labor contracting businesses. It specifies that coverage for leased workers will be provided by the business that is leasing the employees under contract (the client), not the labor contractor. The endorsement requires that the labor contractor provide its insurer with the following information within thirty days of entering a labor contract: contract effective date and term; client's name; client's federal employer identification number; client's mailing address; and number of workers leased, description of duties of each, and work location for each. Clients of the labor contract must maintain workers compensation coverage for their direct and leased workers, and proof of that coverage must be submitted to the labor contractor's insurer. If proof is not submitted, the labor contractor must pay premium for the leased employees and the insurer may cancel the labor contractor's policy.

Labor Contractor Exclusion
Endorsement WC 00 03 21

This endorsement defines employee leasing as an arrangement in which a business engages a third party to provide it with workers for a fee or other compensation. The third party is referred to as the labor contractor. The entity leasing the employees is called the client. The endorsement excludes coverage for workers that the labor contractor leases to clients listed on the endorsement. Coverage must be provided by the client. The endorsement is attached to a labor contractor's policy. Temporary workers are not considered leased workers.

Employee Leasing Client Exclusion
Endorsement WC 00 03 22

This endorsement limits coverage under the policy to employees of the insured who are not leased from third parties; it excludes coverage under the policy for workers that the insured leases from labor contractors. It defines labor contractor and client in the same way as does WC 00 03 21.

Anniversary Rating Date
Endorsement WC 00 04 02

As discussed in Chapter 10, most companies are subject to experience rating. The experience modification is subject to change on the anniversary rating date of the company, which usually corresponds with the inception date of the policy. However, there are times when the anniversary rating date differs from the policy inception date. When this happens, WC 00 04 02 is attached. The endorsement states that the premium, rates, and experience modification used on the policy may be changed at the anniversary rating date that is shown in the endorsement.

Experience Rating Modification Factor
Endorsement WC 00 04 03

This endorsement is attached when the experience modification that applies to the policy is not available when it is issued. WC 00 04 03 states that the factor will be endorsed onto the policy when it becomes available. The premium is subject to change if the modification differs from the one used to issue the policy.

Premium Discount Endorsement WC 00 04 06 or WC 00 04 06 A

Chapter 9 includes a discussion of the premium discount. Endorsements WC 00 04 06 and WC 00 04 06 A may be used to outline the premium discount percentages that apply to the ascending premium amount.

Retrospective Premium Endorsement One Year Plan WC 00 05 03 C

This endorsement acknowledges that a one-year retrospective rating plan is in effect. The endorsement outlines the retrospective premium formula and program elements, including the policies subject to retro rating; loss limitation, if any; loss conversion factor; minimum and maximum premium factors; basic premium factors; and the tax multipliers, excess loss premium factors, and retrospective development factors as they apply in the states where retrospective rating is applicable. Additional information on how retrospective rating works is provided in Chapter 11.

Retrospective Premium Endorsement Three Year Plan WC 00 05 04 C

This is similar to endorsement WC 00 05 03 C, but it pertains to a three-year retro program.

Retrospective Premium Endorsement One Year Plan—Multiple Lines WC 00 05 12 C

This endorsement is used when a one-year retrospective rating plan applies to multiple lines of insurance, such as workers compensation and employers liability, general liability, and auto liability. It lists the same items that are included in WC 00 05 03 C for all policies that are included in the retrospective rating program.

Retrospective Premium Endorsement Three Year Plan—Multiple Lines WC 00 05 13 C

This is similar to endorsement WC 00 05 12 C, but it pertains to a three-year retro program that covers more than one line of insurance.

Benefits Deductible Endorsement WC 00 06 03

Some states permit a deductible to be applied to medical, indemnity (wage loss), or medical and indemnity benefits. Endorsement WC 00 06 03 is used to list the deductibles for each type of benefit, as well as the states in which they apply. The deductible amounts apply separately to each claim for bodily injury by accident or disease, unless state law requires payment on a per accident or per disease basis. If the second case applies, the deductibles are applied separately to each accident or disease, regardless of how many employees are injured in the respective accident or by the disease.

The endorsement also specifies that the insurance company will pay the deductible amount for the insured. The policy may be canceled if the insured does not reimburse the carrier for deductible amounts paid within thirty days of a billing notice. In jurisdictions where the insured is permitted to directly pay the deductible, the insurance company becomes the guarantor for the payments.

Chapter 7

Nonprivate Insurance

Monopolistic State Funds

One area of workers compensation insurance that can be a source of confusion concerns the procedures employers with interstate operations must follow when coverage is necessary in states that have monopolistic state funds. There are four such states in this category: North Dakota, Ohio, Washington, and Wyoming.

The discussion that follows concerns these four states. It outlines, in summary form and on a state-by-state basis, some of the procedures that must be followed in determining whether workers compensation needs to be purchased and, if such insurance is required, how to go about purchasing it.

North Dakota

The Workforce Safety & Insurance Fund administers the insurance under the act in North Dakota. The address of the bureau is: Workforce Safety & Insurance, 1600 E. Century Avenue, Suite 1, Bismarck, ND 58503; Toll free: 1-800-777-5033; ndwsi@nd.gov.

All public employees and most employees (one or more) within the categories of private or hazardous employments are classified as compulsory under the workers compensation act of this state.

Employers exempt from the act are those who employ farm labor, domestic servants, and casual workers. Nonhazardous employments and employers, including officers of a business corporation, excepted from the compulsory provisions of the act are eligible however, for coverage on a voluntary basis. If an employer in this situation does not wish to purchase insurance, it still retains its common law defenses, but is vulnerable to judgments that might exceed the state's specified workers compensation benefits.

North Dakota has reciprocal agreements with a number of states which have the effect of exempting nonresident employees who are covered by workers compensation insurance in their home state from the provisions of the North Dakota act while temporarily within this state. This extraterritorial provision, however, does not apply to resident employees of North Dakota.

Those states that have reciprocal agreements with North Dakota are: Colorado, Idaho, Montana, Nevada, Oregon, South Dakota, Utah, Washington, and Wyoming. Employees from all other states must be covered by workers compensation insurance from the North Dakota fund.

When a firm desires workers compensation insurance in the state of North Dakota for out-of-state employees, it can either write or call the bureau giving an estimate of its expected payroll in that state and describing the type of work to be performed. The bureau will then inform the employer about the cost of insurance per classification and about the total advance premium necessary to deposit prior to the commencement of work in North Dakota.

When such a request involves a subcontractor, a certificate of insurance is issued for the prime contractor. The bureau also submits a copy of this certificate to the secretary of state indicating that the subcontractor is in good standing with the workers compensation bureau. The subcontractor is then in a position to request a contractor's license from the secretary of state thereby enabling him to commence work in North Dakota.

Ohio

In Ohio, the Bureau of Workers Compensation administers the state insurance fund. The agency is governed by chapters 4121 and 4123 of the Ohio Revised Code. The address for the bureau is: Ohio Bureau of Workers Compensation, 30 W. Spring Street, Columbus, Ohio 43215; 1-800-644-6292; Fax 1-877-520-6446. The bureau is the administrative branch of the Ohio system of workers compensation. Its responsibility is to process all claims, keep account records, conduct audits, and to collect premiums from employers, among other duties.

All employers of one or more full or part time employees must either purchase insurance from the fund or qualify as self-insurers. Also subject to the law, on a compulsory basis, are employers of domestic workers who earn $160 or more in cash from a single household in any calendar quarter.

The act is also compulsory for state, county, city, township, and incorporated village officials, as well as school districts.

If an employer is a partnership or a sole proprietor, the employer may elect to include, as employees, any members of such partnership or the owner of the sole proprietorship. It is important to note, however, that the employer must provide written notice naming the persons to be covered. No partner or proprietor is considered an employee until such notice is made and acknowledged.

Nonresident employees who are covered by workers compensation insurance in their own state are exempt from the provisions of the Ohio act for a maximum period of ninety days. After that period, the employer must purchase insurance for its employees from the Ohio fund. However, any nonresident employer who hires employees from within the state of Ohio for work in that state must purchase coverage from the Ohio fund.

When an employer desires workers compensation insurance in the state of Ohio, it must request an application (form U-3) from the underwriting section of the bureau or from any one of its sixteen district offices.

To insure proper handling of its account, an employer must be sure its application adequately describes the operation for proper classification. The employer must also report its payroll according to the correct classification. The coverage is effective on the business day that the employer's check *is received* by the bureau.

When coverage begins, the employer must make an estimate of payroll for eight months. The bureau will then apply the rate to the estimate and bill the employer for that amount. This advance deposit insures coverage during the six month period plus the two month grace period for reporting actual premiums. The state insurance fund manual, which contains a description of each classification, rates for each classification, and rules governing risks, is published annually by the bureau and is available to employers upon request.

The bureau operates on a fiscal year of July 1 to June 30 for premium purposes. In June and December of each year, the bureau sends out payroll reports to be completed by employers. Payroll reports are due on January 31 and July 31. Coverage lapses if premiums are not paid by March 1 and September 1.

Washington

The state agency that administers the workers compensation insurance program in Washington is the Department of Labor and Industries. The address for the agency is: Department of Labor and Industries, P.O. Box 4400, Olympia, Washington 98504-4000; (360) 902-5800; Fax: (360) 902-5798; 1-800-547-8367.

Almost all employees must be covered by workers compensation insurance. Those exempt from the act are: sole proprietors and partners; corporate officers; casual employees not connected with a trade, profession or business; domestic servants—unless two or more are regularly employed forty or more hours a week; and any person employed to do maintenance, repair, remodeling or similar work in or about the private home of the employer, provided the work does not exceed ten consecutive work days.

Also exempt are: persons performing services in return for aid or sustenance from any religious or charitable organization; an employee subject to either the Longshore and Harbor Workers Act or the Jones Act; law enforcement officers and fire fighters hired prior to October 1, 1977; minor children under eighteen years of age on a family farm; musicians and entertainers; and insurance brokers or salesmen.

Self-insurance is permitted if an employer can meet certain qualifications. Self-insuring employers must show their financial ability by providing a surety bond or a deposit equal to an amount that is calculated annually by the Department of Labor and Industries. Such employers must also establish their own safety organizations to provide service similar to that provided by the safety division of the department. Furthermore, these firms must have been in business for three years and have a net minimum worth of $5 million.

Employers that have employees who are not residents of Washington may be exempt from the workers compensation law of Washington if work is of a temporary nature and this state has a reciprocal agreement with the home state of such employee. In these cases, employers are required to submit a certificate to the Department of Labor and Industries stating to the effect that employees will be working in the state of Washington for a period of time and that they are covered under the workers compensation act of their home state.

Those states that have reciprocal agreements with Washington are: Idaho, Montana, Nevada, North Dakota, South Dakota, Oregon, and Wyoming. Employees of all other states must be covered under the workers compensation act of Washington, assuming the type of work being performed is not exempt from the law.

In order to apply for workers compensation insurance in the state of Washington, an employer must request an application from the department or any one of its fifteen district offices. This "master business application" will open accounts with five agencies in Washington, thus avoiding multiple applications. Classification is made according to the business that the firm is engaged in and not by individual employments.

Two premiums are charged for coverage and there is one assessment: (1) the industrial insurance premium; (2) the medical aid premium; and (3) the supplemental pension fund assessment.

The industrial insurance premium is paid entirely by the employer. This rate is assessed according to the number of workers hours and premiums are paid quarterly. The medical aid premium is shared equally by the employer and employee. Both premiums are experience rated after three years. Also shared equally is the assessment for the pension fund.

After coverage is written by the department, the employer must complete quarterly reports of payroll. These become due thirty days following the end of the quarter that is being reported.

Wyoming

In the state of Wyoming, workers compensation coverage is compulsory only for specifically required industries or occupations. The Workers' Safety and Compensation Division administers the state fund. The address is: Workforce Services, Workers Compensation, 1510 E. Pershing Boulevard, Cheyenne, Wyoming 82002-0700; (307) 777-7786; Fax: (307) 777-3646.

Employers who employ workers in required (or extra-hazardous) industries or occupations as described within the state's workers compensation act—such as mining, heavy construction, lumber products, chemical products—must provide coverage for their employees through the state fund. This coverage for such employees is compulsory and may not be provided through a private carrier. Coverage for all other industries and occupations is optional at the choice of the employer and is not compulsory, either through the state fund or through a private carrier. Effective July 1, 1992, specific industries are excluded from coverage through the state fund unless coverage is elected for all employees. The elective coverage is in effect for a minimum three year period. Coverage may be withdrawn by the employer after the three year period if the employer is current on all contributions and payments required by the act.

Employer premiums are set through an industry based rating system with experience modification assigned after an employer has been registered in the state fund for two fiscal years.

Any nonresident employee and his nonresident employer who are temporarily engaged in work within the state of Wyoming are exempt from the provisions of Wyoming's workers compensation act. Wyoming residents employed by a nonresident employer in a required industry or occupation must be provided coverage through the Wyoming workers compensation act.

Wyoming employers and employees covered under the state's workers compensation act but temporarily working out of state are still covered by the Wyoming law. Employers who hire workers in another state to perform work in the other state must provide coverage for those employees under the laws of the other state.

Nonresident employers who hire Wyoming resident employees in a required industry or occupation must complete and file an application for coverage with the Wyoming workers compensation division. A nonresident employer is defined as one who has not been domiciled in Wyoming for at least one year prior to commencing operations in the state.

The workers compensation act requires a minimum $10,000 surety bond for all nonresident employers required to register and provide coverage with the state fund. Employers performing work in Wyoming under contract are subject only to the $10,000 bond requirement if the contract amount does not exceed $100,000. For each additional $100,000 or fraction thereof of contract, an additional $1,000 is required, up to a maximum bond required of $50,000.

Residual Markets

Workers compensation coverage can be provided by private insurance companies in all but the four monopolistic states. Since workers compensation is a required coverage under most circumstances, it must be available to all businesses that are subject to the law. There are times, however, when businesses are unable to obtain insurance in the nonmonopolistic states from insurance companies because of their size, the type of work they do, or poor workers compensation loss experience.

In response to this need, jurisdictions have established residual market systems, which sometimes are called the markets of last resort. There are two basic methods of providing insurance for the residual market.

Some states have established competitive state workers compensation funds. These funds compete with private insurers for desirable business in addition to providing insurance for companies that cannot obtain it in the open market. The state funds usually provide coverage only for operations within their states. Some of them are operated as independent insurance companies; some maintain their governmental agency structure.

An assigned risk system handles the residual market in another way. States that use this system assign residual business to private insurance companies who operate in the state. The assignments usually are based on the amount of business the insurer writes voluntarily in the state. Some insurers participate in the assigned risk system as reinsurers; others participate by directly providing coverage to those businesses assigned to them. Surcharges or premium differentials may apply to insureds who participate in an assigned risk program.

(Note: see the appendices for states that use residual market systems.)

Chapter 8

Federal Workers Compensation Coverage

Introduction

The United States Longshore and Harbor Workers Compensation Act (L&HWCA), 33 USC 901-952, was enacted in 1927, sixteen years after the first state workers compensation law was passed. (A federal law was passed since the United States Constitution grants exclusive jurisdiction in all maritime matters to the federal government.) The federal act was designed to provide the benefit of workers compensation to employees (other than seamen) who work in maritime employment upon the navigable waters of the United States and who are usually considered outside the scope of state compensation laws. Even so, the purpose of this federal compensation law is no different than that of a state compensation law; namely, to compensate workers for injuries that affect their wage earning capabilities and that arise out of the workers' employment.

The Jones Act, 46 USC 688, is a federal statute, the Merchant Marine Act of 1920, and states that a seaman injured in the course of his employment by the negligence of the owner, master, or fellow crew member can recover damages for his injuries. The act states that any seaman who suffers injury in the course of his employment may maintain an action for damages directly against the owners of the ship, and in the case of death, the seaman's personal representative can maintain an action for wrongful death. Jurisdiction in such actions is under the court of the district in which the defendant employer resides or in which the principal office is located.

In addition to these federal laws, and as a way to comply with those laws while providing workers compensation insurance and employers liability insurance for affected workers, several endorsements are available for use.

This chapter offers a discussion of the L&HWCA, the Jones Act, and federal workers compensation endorsements. The endorsements are presented numerically.

The Longshore and Harbor Workers Compensation Act

Scope of Coverage

The coverage of the L&HWCA applies to compensation for disability or death of an employee if the disability or death results from injury occurring upon the navigable waters of the United States, including any adjoining pier, wharf, dry dock, terminal, marine railway, or other adjoining area customarily used in the loading, unloading, repairing, dismantling, or building of a vessel. Coverage under the L&HWCA, as stated by the United States Court of Appeals, Second Circuit in *Lockheed Martin Corporation v. Morganti*, 412 F.3d 407 (2005), requires both situs (physical presence on actual navigable waters) and status (person injured on actual navigable waters, providing that he is not excluded by any other provision of the L&HWCA.)

One of the original problems that arose with the L&HWCA was the status issue, in that anyone performing work however remotely connected to maritime employment attempted to obtain the benefits of the act. Therefore, in order to curb the jurisdictional scope of the act, not only does the coverage paragraph of the L&HWCA contain certain exclusions, but the definition of "employee" is limited to specific classes of workers.

The L&HWCA does not apply to an officer or employee of the U.S. government, any state or foreign government, or any city or county government; it also does not apply to an employee who is injured solely due to his own intoxication or due to his or a fellow employee's willful intention. The term "employee" means any person engaged in maritime employment, but this term does not include clerical, secretarial, security, or data processing work; it does not include individuals employed by a camp, restaurant, recreational operation, or retail outlet; nor does it include individuals employed by a marina, aquaculture workers, individuals employed to build any recreational vessel under sixty-five feet in length, or individuals employed to repair any recreational vessel, or to dismantle any part of a recreational vessel in connection with the repair of such vessel. (Note that this latter provision only applies to employees if state workers comp coverage is provided.) Masters or members of a crew of any vessel or any person engaged to load or unload or repair any small vessel under eighteen tons net are also not considered employees under the Longshore act.

Needless to say, disputes and legal challenges over the definition of "employee" continue. The current judicial mood seems to be to decide each case on its own circumstances. An example of this thinking is in *Bienvenu v. Texaco, Inc.*, 164 F.3d 901 (5th Cir. 1999).

In this case, the United States Court of Appeals for the Fifth Circuit put forth an informative discussion of the history of the L&HWCA and judicial interpretation of its scope, but ended up showing that the trigger of coverage is decided on a case-by-case basis. Here, the injured worker, Bienvenu, was responsible for maintaining and calibrating automated equipment located on fixed production platforms. Bienvenu was injured while on board a boat that transported him around the various platforms and he claimed benefits under the L&HWCA. Benefits were denied on the grounds that Bienvenu was not engaged in maritime employment and spent the vast majority of his working hours on fixed platforms; indeed, the fact was that Bienvenu spent only one hour out of twelve actually performing work on navigable waters. Nevertheless, the appeals court ruled that Bienvenu was entitled to L&HWCA benefits and that the percentage of work time spent on navigable waters was substantial enough to trigger L&HWCA coverage.

A later case used the *Bienvenu* case to expound on the definition of "employee". In *Early v. Wise Well Intervention Services, Inc.*, 2012 WL 826992, the United States District Court, W.D. Louisiana, said that, in order for an employee-claimant to receive L&HWCA benefits, the worker must satisfy both a situs and status test. The situs test concerns geographic areas covered by the L&HWCA, whereas the status test concerns an employee's type of work activities. The situs test includes injuries occurring upon the navigable waters of the United States. The status test, as noted in the *Bienvenu* decision, defines an employee as any person engaged in maritime employment, including any longshoreman or other person engaged in longshoring operations, and any harborworker including a ship repairman, shipbuilder, and ship-breaker. Furthermore, the court said in quoting from the *Bienvenu* opinion, a worker injured in the course of his employment on navigable waters is engaged in maritime employment and meets the status test only if his presence on the water at the time of injury was neither transient nor fortuitous. The presence, however, of a worker injured on the water and who performs a not insubstantial amount of his work in navigable waters is neither transient nor fortuitous.

Of course, there are opinions that do not match the *Bienvenu* and *Early* rulings.

In *Daul v. Petroleum Communications, Inc.*, 196 F.3d 611 (5th Cir. 1999), the court of appeals upheld the finding that a communications consultant (Daul) injured in a fall on a barge was barred from coverage under the L&HWCA. Daul was employed to provide cellular telephone service to users in the Gulf of Mexico, and his stated duties were: to maintain customer relations, call on customers, transport new equipment to customers, and to pick up broken or defective equipment. Daul was accompanying a technician from the communications company to install equipment on a barge docked in a canal. Daul was descending steps on the barge, carrying a desk phone, when he slipped and fell, allegedly because of slippery food material on the stairs. Daul filed a claim for benefits under the Longshore Act, but the claim was denied because Daul was found to be temporarily doing business on the premises, business that consisted of selling his employer's product. Daul was not entitled to coverage under the L&HWCA just because he suffered an injury while upon navigable waters.

In a case from the Ninth Circuit, a worker injured while working as a pile driver on a structure used for processing oil received from offshore wells was also denied coverage under the L&HWCA. The case is *McGray Construction Company v. Director, Office of Workers Compensation Programs and Harry Hurston*, 181 F.3d 1008 (9th Cir. 1999). Here, Hurston was working as a pile driver when a load fell from a crane and seriously injured him. His employer, McGray Construction, paid workers compensation benefits to Hurston, but he claimed that he was entitled to benefits under the L&HWCA. The original finding was that Hurston was entitled to the benefits; the employer appealed.

The appeals court noted that in order to be covered by the L&HWCA, a person must be an employee as defined in the act. The court said that there are two tests that a person must pass to fit the definition: a situs test and a status test, both of which are independent of each other. There was no question that Hurston met the situs requirement; the place where he was injured was found to be an adjoining pier, which is listed in the act as a covered premises. However, Hurston did not meet the status test because his job was not maritime employment. Hurston was hired for piledriving which was pier construction and not ship construction. The court emphasized that Hurston's work was in no way longshoreman's or shipbuilder's work or anything like those categories. The court upheld the idea that the crucial factor is the nature of the activity to which a worker may be assigned; Hurston's work in this instance was clearly nonmaritime in nature.

In these examples, the deciding element was upholding the purpose of the L&HWCA, that is, to compensate workers for injuries suffered in maritime employment related injuries. The question remains, though, as to just what maritime employment is, and these cases show that no one, iron clad, unanimous opinion exists.

But, if courts continue to decide the scope of coverage under the L&HWCA on a case-by-case basis, employers and employees should know that judicial interpretations of the law may very well favor an emphasis on upholding the purpose of the law (to compensate workers for work related injuries) in contrast to a strict reading of the words and phrases of the act. Examples of this happening are: *Levins v. Benefits Review Board*, 724 F.2d 4 (1st Cir. 1984); *Parrott v. Seattle Joint Port Labor Relations Committee of the Pacific Maritime Association and Insurance Company of North America*, 22 BRBS 434 (1989); and *Bundens v. J.E. Brenneman Company*, 46 F.3d 292 (3d Cir. 1995).

In the *Levins* case, a federal court stated that: "it is the employee's actual duties rather than a formal job classification that must be looked at in determining coverage." This was a case where a book clerk worked in the office, but also was required to work as a runner on the pier whenever ships under 300 tons were loaded or unloaded. The clerk was injured while working outside the office—he fell in a parking lot—and he sought benefits under the L&HWCA. The federal circuit court agreed with the clerk that he was a covered employee. In the *Parrott* case, an administrative law judge decided that a claimant's duties as a night dispatcher delivering slips to foremen aboard vessels constituted maritime employment within the coverage of the L&HWCA. And, in the *Bundens* case, it was decided that a construction worker building a dock was a harbor worker and covered by the Longshore Act.

Another problem that can arise when it comes to the L&HWCA is a dispute over whether the situs requirement is met, that is, whether the injured worker was on actual navigable waters when the injury occurred. The Second Circuit Court in the *Lockheed Martin* case previously mentioned said that waterways are navigable in fact when they are used, or are susceptible of being used, in their ordinary condition, as highways for commerce. In addition, the court stated that for purposes of a claim under the L&HWCA, a person on any object floating in actual navigable waters must be considered to be on actual navigable waters.

Employer's Liability

Section 904 of the Longshore Compensation Act states that every employer is liable for and shall secure the payment to his employees of the compensation payable under the requirements of the act. In the case of an employer who is a subcontractor, the contractor shall be liable for and shall secure the payment of such compensation to employees of the subcontractor unless the subcontractor has secured such payment.

This liability of the employer is exclusive and precludes all other liability of the employer to the employee, his legal representative, or his dependents; in other words, the exclusive remedy theory is applied to the employer. Of course, if the employer fails to secure payment of compensation, an injured employee can file suit at law or in admiralty for damages and the employer cannot use the defenses that were common prior to the enactment of workers compensation laws: negligence of a fellow servant; the assumption of risk by the employee; or contributory negligence on the part of the employee. Furthermore, if a responsible employer fails to secure the compensation required under the L&HWCA, he can be fined up to $10,000 or be sentenced to not more than one year imprisonment. This same punishment is meted out if the employer attempts to avoid the payment of compensation by transferring, selling, or concealing any property belonging to the employer.

So, any employer that does not fulfill his obligations under the L&HWCA faces not only the clear probability of a lawsuit filed by the injured employee, but also a statutory punishment.

Third Party Actions

Having a party other than the employer involved in the injury of an employee is not a unique occurrence. The L&HWCA takes that into account whether the injury is caused by a person or a vessel. In the event of injury to an employee covered under the L&HWCA caused by the negligence of a vessel, the employee can bring an action against that vessel (an in rem action alleging negligence against the vessel owner) as a third party. Should that happen, the employer is not liable to the vessel for such damages directly or indirectly and any agreements or warranties to the contrary shall be void. Therefore, hold harmless agreements and third-party-over actions are precluded by the L&HWCA.

It should be noted that the third party liability of vessels is the subject of section 905 (b) of the L&HWCA. Section 933 of the act applies to compensation for injuries in which third persons are liable. An injured employee can file suit or a claim against a third person who is liable for the injuries. However, should the employee accept compensation from the employer under an award in an order filed by an administrative law judge that operates as an assignment to the employer of all rights of the employee to recover damages against the third person. The employer then has ninety days after the assignment to bring an action against the third person; if he fails to do so, the right reverts to the employee.

Compensation

The L&HWCA lists levels of compensation for disability or death under various sections. For example, the maximum rate of compensation of weekly benefits cannot exceed an amount equal to 200 percent of the applicable national average weekly wage as determined by the Secretary of Labor. Also, compensation for loss of hearing in one ear is fifty-two weeks pay; for loss of hearing in both ears, 200 weeks. The "proper and equitable" compensation for serious disfigurement of the face, neck, or head cannot exceed $7,500. Reasonable funeral expenses are not to exceed $3,000. Of course, these amounts can be revised either by law or by increases caused by inflation.

The L&HWCA and the Workers Compensation Policy

Longshore and Harbor Workers Compensation Act insurance may be provided by attaching endorsement WC 00 01 06 A to the standard workers compensation and employers liability insurance policy. The endorsement applies to work done in the states scheduled (including those states with a monopolistic state fund) and extends the definition of workers compensation law to include the L&HWCA; this is necessary because the policy declares in the general section that the term "workers compensation law" does not include any federal workers compensation law. The statutory obligation of an employer to furnish benefits required by the L&HWCA is thus satisfied. The coverage, exclusions, and conditions of part one of the workers compensation policy are applied to those parties involved under the L&HWCA.

Under part two of the workers compensation policy—employers liability insurance—the insurance applies to bodily injury by accident or by disease arising out of and in the course of the injured employee's employment. However, exclusion 8 precludes employers liability insurance from bodily injury to any person in work subject to the L&HWCA; endorsement WC 00 01 06 A drops this exclusion as it relates to such work. For operations subject to the L&HWCA, the standard limits of liability under part two of the policy are: $100,000 per each accident for bodily injury by accident; $100,000 per each employee for bodily injury by disease; and a $500,000 policy limit for bodily injury by disease. Increased limits are, of course, available for an additional premium.

The coverage, most of the exclusions, and conditions of the employers liability insurance are applicable to those parties covered by the L&HWCA. Now, since such insurance pays for damages for which the insured may become liable to a third party based on a third-party-over action, a question may arise. The L&HWCA precludes third-party-over actions, but the workers comp insurance policy of the insured has an employers liability insuring agreement that states that any liability damages based on such actions will be paid. Is there a contradiction present? No, because the insuring agreement on the policy declares that the damages will be paid where recovery is permitted by law. Since the law (the L&HWCA) does not permit third-party-over actions against the employer (the insured), the issue is moot.

State vs. Federal Coverage

Based on the nature of the work involved, with accidents and injuries happening on land as well as on or over water, conflicts may arise over which coverage takes precedence: state or federal. For example, in Logan v. Louisiana Dock Company, 541 So.2d 182 (La. 1989), Logan, the employee, was injured while repairing a barge on the defendant's dry dock. He filed for workers compensation and sued to obtain benefits. Louisiana Dry Dock responded that Logan could have sought benefits under the L&HWCA and so, he was not eligible for state workers compensation. A Louisiana court of appeals decided that just because there is a federal remedy, it does not necessarily mean there is no state remedy. The court, in finding for Logan, held that the L&HWCA does not expressly say that it is the exclusive remedy for injured workers; the proper approach is for state workers compensation laws to complement the federal law.

Note, however, that this finding was superseded by a Louisiana statute. In *Dempster v. Avondale Shipyards, Inc.*, 643 So.2d 1316, the Court of Appeals of Louisiana, Fifth Circuit, said that the *Logan* ruling that an injured worker was allowed to seek benefits from federal and state compensation schemes was made prior to the enactment of La. R.S. 23:1035.2. This statute declared that no state compensation shall be payable in respect to the disability or death of any employee covered by the Federal Employer's Liability Act, the Longshore and Harbor Workers Compensation Act, or any of its extensions, or the Jones Act. For cases occurring after the enactment of this state law, the court said that if the employee meets the requirements of these acts, the employee must file his compensation claim under federal law.

But, barring any state law to the contrary, the opinion in the *Logan* case represents the current judicial attitude. Indeed, the U.S. Supreme Court has decreed that state workers compensation laws and the L&HWCA are not mutually exclusive remedies and has, in effect, sanctioned the filing of a claim by longshoremen under both the federal law and the state law. In *Sun Ship, Inc. v. Pennsylvania*, 447 U.S. 715 (1980), and in *Herb's Welding, Inc. v. Gray*, 470 U.S. 414 (1985), the Supreme Court held that the L&HWCA supplements rather than replaces the state workers compensation law and that concurrent jurisdiction exists for land based maritime injuries.

It should be noted that amendments to the L&HWCA do require that a worker or dependent who is excluded from the definition of "employee" must first claim compensation under the appropriate state workers compensation program and receive a final decision on the merits of that claim before any claim may be filed under the Longshore and Harbor Workers Compensation Act.

The Jones Act

Scope of Coverage

Seamen are subject to admiralty law and, if injured, have the right to file claims for damages in admiralty courts where the proceeding is in the nature of a liability suit against the employer based on negligence. Also, note that in *Smith v. BP America*, 522 Fed.Appx. 859 (2013), the United States Court of Appeals, Eleventh Circuit, stated that pursuant to the Jones Act, "a seaman injured in the course of employment may elect to bring a civil action at law against the employer." Moreover, the court added, "a seaman who is injured by an unworthy condition on a ship has a right to recovery against the owner of the vessel beyond maintenance and cure."

The Jones Act allows for the providing of insurance for such liability through the use of the standard workers compensation and employers liability policy and endorsements. There are two programs available to furnish such insurance.

Under program I, the workers compensation policy has endorsement WC 00 02 01 A, the maritime coverage endorsement, attached to it. This endorsement does not address the workers compensation insurance part of the workers compensation policy. Furthermore, the workers compensation law definition does not include any federal workers compensation law. So, endorsement WC 00 02 01 A is not relevant to the workers compensation insurance part of the workers compensation policy. WC 00 02 01 A does state that the insurance afforded by the employers liability insurance part of the workers compensation policy for bodily injury to a master or member of the crew of a vessel is changed by the provisions of the endorsement. The endorsement applies the insurance to bodily injury by accident or by disease arising out of and in the course of the injured employee's employment that is described in the schedule on WC 00 02 01 A. The bodily injury must occur in the territorial limits of, or in the operation of a vessel sailing directly between the ports of, the United States of America or Canada. And, note that the injured worker must sue for damages under the Jones Act. This is in keeping with the nature of employers liability insurance since that coverage is based on sums that the insured "legally must pay as damages."

The employers liability insurance part of the workers compensation policy has several exclusions, and, for the most part, these exclusions do apply to any claims made by seamen against the insured. The endorsement deletes exclusion 10 pertaining to bodily injury to a master or member of the crew of any vessel. And, endorsement WC 00 02 01 A adds two other exclusions. These two exclusions deal with items that are peculiar to maritime coverage insurance.

The first exclusion applies to bodily injury covered by a Protection and Indemnity (P&I) policy issued to the named insured. P&I coverage is an ocean marine form that provides legal liability coverage for marine exposures. For example, if a third party is injured in a collision with the insured's vessel, the P&I policy will respond to a claim. The exclusion on endorsement WC 00 02 01 A aims to prevent any injured party from an attempt to stack coverages since the endorsement does apply to bodily injury by accident.

The second exclusion states that the insurance does not cover the named insured's duty to provide transportation, wages, maintenance, and care. These items are considered historical rights given to sailors and one of the elements of the contract of hire. A sailor who falls sick in the service of the vessel has historically been entitled to wages, transportation back home, food and quarters to the end of the voyage, medical attention, and other similar services. The exclusion on WC 00 02 01 A makes the point that the insurer does not substitute itself for the insured in fulfilling an ancient common law of the sea. However, it needs to be noted that the insurer will drop this exclusion if the insured wants the coverage and will pay an additional premium.

Endorsement WC 00 02 01 A does limit the damages paid for bodily injury by accident and by disease; bodily injury by accident is on an each accident basis, and injury by disease is on an aggregate basis. Both items have the limits of liability scheduled on the endorsement and the insurer states clearly that it will not pay any claims after the applicable limits have been reached.

Under program II, the same coverage in program I is offered, along with the addition of voluntary compensation. The insurer agrees under this program to offer a settlement of a claim voluntarily in accordance with the statutory benefits called for by the workers compensation law of the state(s) specified on the voluntary compensation endorsement, WC 00 02 03. If the offer of a settlement is rejected, employers liability then will apply to such a claim or suit. Endorsement WC 00 02 03 applies insurance to bodily injury by accident or by disease sustained by an employee who is a master or member of the crew of a vessel described in the schedule. The bodily injury must occur in employment that is necessary or incidental to work scheduled on the endorsement.

The insurance provided by the endorsement does not cover any obligation imposed by a workers compensation law or bodily injury intentionally caused by the named insured. Furthermore, before any benefits are paid, the persons entitled to them must sign a release, transfer to the insurer all rights of recovery, and cooperate with the insurer in enforcing the right to recover from others. If the persons entitled to the benefits fail to do these things, then the duty of the insurer to pay ends at once.

Definition of "Seaman"

Since the Jones Act deals with the recovery for injury to or death of a *seaman*, that term needs to be examined. Lacking a concrete definition in the act itself, courts have established through judicial decisions certain factors that need to be met if a claimant is considered a seaman. Some of these factors are: the vessel on which the claimant is employed must be in navigable waters; the claimant must have a more or less permanent connection with the vessel, like performing a substantial part of his work on the vessel; and the claimant must be aboard to aid in the navigation of the vessel, as in the actual operation or maintenance of the vessel.

The U.S. Supreme Court attempted to clarify this somewhat in a 1995 case. In *Chandris, Inc. v. Latsis*, 515 U.S. 347 (1995), the Supreme Court said that a seaman must contribute to the function of the vessel or to the accomplishment of its mission, and that his or her connection to a vessel must be substantial in both duration and nature. And, the Court added that as a rule of thumb, a seaman should spend more than 30 percent of his or her time on the vessel. Since that time, lower courts have tried to use this direction from the Supreme Court to determine just what a seaman is, on a case-by-case basis.

In 1997, the Supreme Court took another shot at clarifying the issue. The case is *Harbor Tug & Barge Co. v. Papai*, 520 U.S. 548 (1997).

In that case, a worker was injured while on a one day assignment obtained through the union hiring hall to paint a tug at dockside. This worker fell from a ladder and hurt his leg. He sued for benefits under the Jones Act and, after the trial court decided he was not a seaman and could not receive Jones Act benefits, an appeals court declared that he was a seaman. The Supreme Court took the case and agreed with the trial court. The Court said that defining a seaman under the Jones Act is a mixed question of law and fact, but that coverage under the act should be confined to those who face a regular exposure to the perils of the sea; land based employment is inconsistent with the Jones Act.

The Court reaffirmed its ruling in the *Chandris* case and sought to further clarify that ruling. Essential requirements for a person to be a seaman are: there must be a substantial connection between the employee and the vessel in navigation, substantial in terms of both duration and nature; and, the employee's duties must contribute to the function of the vessel or to the accomplishment of the vessel's mission. The Court went on to declare that the fundamental purpose of the "substantial connection" requirement is to give full effect to the remedial scheme created by Congress, that is, to separate sea based maritime workers who are entitled to Jones Act protection from those land-based maritime workers who have only a transitory or sporadic connection to a vessel in navigation, and therefore, whose employment does not regularly expose them to the perils of the sea.

In line with this thinking are the following cases.

In *Hufnagel v. Omega Service Industries, Inc.* 182 F.3d 340 (5th Cir. 1999), an employee of an oil platform repair corporation brought a claim under the Jones Act for injuries he suffered while repairing a piling on a fixed oil drilling platform. Hufnagel had been hired to repair pilings located on an oil drilling platform off the cost of Louisiana. He ate and slept on a vessel (not owned or rented by Hufnagle's company) that was used by the repair workers as a temporary hotel while working on the oil platform. Hufnagel was struck in the face by a chain while working and, in his claim for compensation, said that he was a crew member of the vessel and was entitled to Jones Act compensation.

The federal district court concluded that Hufnagle was not a seaman. His work did not contribute to the function of the vessel or to the accomplishment of its mission, and he did not have a connection to a vessel in navigation that was substantial in terms of both its duration and its nature. The court said that whether a worker is a seaman and thus can bring a Jones Act action is determined by the worker's entire employment-related connection to a vessel, and not by the immediate circumstances or location of the worker's injury. Furthermore, the court went on, a fixed oil drilling platform was legally a man-made island and not a vessel. The undisputed evidence showed that as a matter of law, Hufnagel was primarily a land-based employee and not a Jones Act seaman.

In *St. Romain v. Industrial Fabrication and Repair Service, Inc.*, 203 F.3d 376 (5th Cir. 2000), a claimant who was injured while working as a plug and abandon helper sued for damages under the Jones Act. This injury occurred on an offshore platform that was permanently affixed to the outer continental shelf off the coast of Louisiana. St. Romain was employed as a plug and abandon helper which involved the decommissioning of oil wells under offshore platforms. St. Romain was assisting in the removal of casing when a spreader bar used to lift the pipe failed and a shackle and sling struck him; he claimed status as a seaman under the Jones Act.

The court said that the determination whether an injured worker is a seaman under the Jones Act is a mixed question of law and fact.

Applying the two part test the Supreme Court announced in the Papai case, the district court decided that St. Romain was not permanently assigned to any one vessel in navigation. He may have been exposed to the perils of the sea that are faced by traditional seamen, but this was not determinative of the issue of his status. As a matter of law, St. Romain's claim for seaman status failed.

The United States District Court, S.D. Texas, handled a case wherein a galleyhand who worked approximately eight months on board a vessel was injured and claimed coverage under the Jones Act. Using the guidelines set out by the Supreme Court, the District Court found that the claimant satisfied the substantial nature of being a seaman. The court noted the two-part test established by the Supreme Court (that is, the employee's activities must contribute to the function or mission of the vessel, and the employee must possess a connection to a single vessel or identifiable fleet of vessels that is substantial in both nature and duration) and then identified several other guiding principles.

The District Court said that seamen do not include land-based workers. And, Jones Act coverage depends not on the place where the injury is inflicted, but on the nature of the seaman's service, his status as a member of the vessel, and his relationship as such to the vessel and its operation in navigable waters. Finally, the court said that the duration of a worker's connection to a vessel and the nature of the worker's activities, taken together, determine whether a maritime employee is a seaman because the ultimate inquiry is whether the worker in question is a member of the vessel's crew or simply a land-based employee who happens to be working on a vessel at a given time. This case is *Joseph v. Marine Management Contractors, Inc.*, 2007 WL 1964527.

In *Brown v. Trinity Catering*, 2007 WL 4365384, the United States District Court, E.D. Louisiana, stated that "although determination of whether an injured worker is a seaman under the Jones Act is a mixed question of law and fact that is usually a question for a jury to decide, judgment as a matter of law is mandated where the facts and the law will reasonably support only one conclusion." The court noted that the United States Supreme Court in the *Chandris* case considered it important that a seaman's connection to a vessel in fact be substantial both in its duration and nature.

Jurisdiction of the Jones Act

The Jones Act provides that jurisdiction over actions for personal injuries is in a court of the district where the defendant employer resides or where the principal office is located. The maritime coverage endorsement

(WC 00 02 01 A) states that if the insured is sued, the original suit must be brought in the U.S. or Canada. Based on these phrases, a question may arise: should an injured seaman file a lawsuit based on the Jones Act in a state court or a federal court? The Jones Act is, after all, a federal law; at the same time, insurance coverage under the Jones Act can be provided by a policy used to comply with state workers compensation requirements.

Court decisions through the years have supported the proposition that federal and state courts have concurrent jurisdiction to enforce the right of action established by the Jones Act. However, since the act is a federal law, federal principles of law and rules of construction prevail if a conflict arises with a state law. For example, if an injured seaman files an action under the Jones Act in a state court, that court must use federal rules on the introduction and use of evidence regardless of the state regulations that exist. So a seaman has his choice of courts should he feel the need to file a lawsuit against his employer.

Concurrent jurisdiction is accepted, but what about dual recovery? Can an injured seaman accept recovery under both the Jones Act and a state workers compensation law? In perhaps a trend-setting case in Louisiana, a federal court decided that a workers compensation action is not precluded under the Jones Act under certain circumstances. The court, in *Dominick v. Houtech Inland Well Service, Inc.*, 718 F.Supp. 489 (E.D. La. 1989), indicated that since the state supreme court had ruled that insurance carried by the employer was considered insurance for state workers compensation purposes regardless of the fact that it may have been purchased by the employer as insurance for Jones Act claims, a workers compensation claim was maintainable. Thus, the injured seaman had two avenues for recovery for his claim open to him.

There are two points to remember, however, on this subject. First, the Jones Act as a federal law has precedence over conflicting state laws if indeed there is conflict. For example, if the Jones Act allowed compensation to injured seamen and a state law forbad such compensation, the Jones Act would supersede the state law. However, in areas where the state law does not conflict with the Jones Act, both laws can peacefully coexist. So, where a state allows a workers compensation action for pain and suffering incurred prior to death or allows action against tortfeasors other than employers, seamen that are injured in that state receive the benefit of the state laws. The state laws complement the federal law and an injured worker receives his just compensation.

The second point is that, historically, courts have allowed offsets for concurrent awards. So if a seaman receives compensation under the Jones Act for his injury, and then files a state workers compensation claim based on that same injury, a court may allow the workers compensation action as permitted by state law, but will offset any award by the amount already received. Thus, the possibility of double recovery being an unlimited source of compensation is remote.

Federal Workers Compensation Endorsements

There are some federal laws pertaining to workers compensation that affect workers employed in areas that are beyond the authority of an individual state. As a way to comply with these laws, several endorsements are available for use with the workers compensation policy.

Defense Base Act Coverage
Endorsement WC 00 01 01 A

This endorsement applies only to the work described in the schedule or described on the information page as subject to the Defense Base Act. Basically, WC 00 01 01 A modifies the workers compensation and employers liability insurance policy by replacing the definition of "workers compensation law" found on the policy with the following meaning: workers compensation law means the workers compensation law and occupational disease law of each state or territory named in Item 3.A. of the information page and the Defense Base Act (42 USC Sections 1651-1654). The definition goes on to state that it does not include any other federal workers compensation law or federal occupational disease law. As an example of putting WC 00 01 01 A to work, it can be used for contractors performing work at overseas military bases or under various public works contracts outside the continental United States of America.

This endorsement also declares that exclusion 8 under the employers liability insurance part of the workers compensation policy does not apply to work subject to the Defense Base Act. Exclusion 8 deals with bodily injury to any person in work subject to the Defense Base Act.

WC 00 01 01 A applies the workers compensation policy to the described work as though the location included in the description of the work were a state named on the workers compensation information page; therefore, the description of the work must include the location where the work is to be performed.

Federal Coal Mine Safety and Health Act
Coverage Endorsement WC 00 01 02 A

This endorsement is used when the workers compensation policy is to cover exposures subject to the Federal Coal Mine Health and Safety

Act. WC 00 01 02 states that the definition of workers compensation law includes the Coal Mine Act and applies only to work in a state shown in the schedule.

Workers compensation insurance applies under this endorsement to bodily injury by disease that is caused or aggravated by the conditions of the employment and the employee's last day of exposure to the conditions causing or aggravating such bodily injury by disease must occur during the policy period.

Federal Employers Liability Act
Coverage Endorsement WC 00 01 04

This endorsement applies only to work subject to the Federal Employers Liability Act (45 USC sections 51 - 60) and any amendment to that act in effect during the policy period. For example, the act makes an interstate railroad liable for bodily injuries sustained by an employee if the injured employee can show any negligence on the part of the railroad. Due to the interstate nature of the employment, such employees are not subject to state workers compensation laws and this endorsement covers the liability of the railroad.

The liability to pay for damages is limited and the limits are shown in the schedule. The limits of liability for bodily injury by accident are on an each accident basis; the limits for bodily injury by disease are on an aggregate basis.

Longshore and Harbor Workers Compensation Act
Coverage Endorsement WC 00 01 06 A

This endorsement applies only to work subject to the Longshore and Harbor Workers Compensation Act in a state shown in the schedule and provides compensation coverage to employees such as longshoremen, harbor workers, ship repairmen, and shipbuilders. The endorsement is attached to the workers compensation and employers liability insurance policy (WC 00 00 00) and expands the definition of workers compensation law to include the Longshore and Harbor Workers Compensation Act (33 USC sections 901 - 950) and any amendments to that act that are in effect during the policy period.

WC 00 01 06 A declares that exclusion 8 under the employers liability insurance part of the workers compensation policy does not apply to work subject to the Longshore and Harbor Workers Compensation Act. This is, of course, similar to the wording found on endorsement WC 00 01 01 A as noted above. It is also stated on the Longshore and Harbor Workers

Compensation Act coverage endorsement that the endorsement does not apply to the Defense Base Act, the Outer Continental Shelf Lands Act, or the Nonappropriated Fund Instrumentalities Act.

Nonappropriated Fund Instrumentalities Act Coverage Endorsement WC 00 01 08 A

This endorsement applies only to the work described in the schedule as subject to the Nonappropriated Fund Instrumentalities Act; the definition of "workers compensation law" is expanded by this endorsement to include the Nonappropriated Fund Instrumentalities Act. This act makes the Longshore and Harbor Workers Compensation Act apply to civilian employees of certain entities, such as, the army exchange service or the military motion picture service. Thus, workers compensation insurance and employers liability insurance is provided for those civilian companies and employees that administer the stores or dining areas that exist on military bases.

WC 00 01 08 A also notes that exclusion 8 of the employers liability insurance part of the workers compensation policy does not apply to work subject to the Instrumentalities Act.

Outer Continental Shelf Lands Act Coverage Endorsement WC 00 01 09 B

This endorsement applies only to the work described in the schedule as subject to the Outer Continental Shelf Lands Act (OCSLA). The coverage will apply to that work as though the location shown in the schedule were a state named on the workers compensation policy. Therefore, the description of the work must show the state whose boundaries, if extended to the outer continental shelf, would include the location of the work. However, note that the Supreme Court of the United States in *Pacific Operators Offshore v. Valladolid*, 132 S.Ct. 680 (2012) declared that the OCSLA provision extending L&HWCA does not require that the injury occur on the outer continental shelf.

The Outer Continental Shelf Lands Act makes the Longshore and Harbor Workers Compensation Act apply to work involving the development of the natural resources of the outer continental shelf. Workers who are employed in this type of activity receive workers compensation insurance, and employers of such workers receive employers liability insurance through this particular endorsement.

WC 00 01 09 B, like some of the previous endorsements noted above, expands the meaning of "workers compensation law" to include the particular law for which this endorsement is named and deletes exclusion 8 from the employers liability insurance part of the workers compensation policy.

Maritime Coverage Endorsement WC 00 02 01 A

Masters and members of the crews of vessels are not covered under state workers compensation laws or under the Longshore and Harbor Workers Compensation Act. They are subject to admiralty law and, if injured, have the right to sue their employers for damages. This endorsement affords coverage where the employer has such exposure and needs employers liability insurance.

This endorsement applies to and schedules limits of liability for bodily injury by accident or by disease. Such bodily injury must arise out of and in the course of employment as described in the schedule. The coverage does not apply to bodily injury that is covered by a protection and indemnity policy issued to the insured (a protection and indemnity policy is ocean marine insurance that applies to personal injury liability including bodily injury to employees). Insurance under this endorsement also does not apply to the duty of the insured to provide transportation, wages, maintenance, and cure for the employees unless the insured pays an extra premium for such coverage and this is noted in the schedule.

WC 00 02 01 A goes on to state that exclusion 10 under the employers liability insurance part of the workers compensation policy is removed; exclusion 10 deals with bodily injury to a master or member of the crew of any vessel.

In the early history of ocean marine insurance, an injured seaman could file an action in rem to seek compensation for his injury. In such an action, the seaman filed a suit directly against the ship and not the owner, thereby seeking compensation by claiming a property interest in the ship and bypassing the problem of whether or not the ship owner carried liability insurance. An endorsement did exist that provided coverage for such in rem lawsuits, but that endorsement is now obsolete since WC 00 02 01 A includes a statement that a suit or action in rem against a vessel owned by the insured is treated by the insurer as a suit against the insured himself requiring a defense by the insurance company.

Chapter 9

Premium

Part Five of the workers compensation and employers liability policy[1] governs how premiums are calculated, paid for and ultimately adjusted. Part Five includes seven individual components:

- Manuals

- Classifications

- Remuneration

- Premium Payments

- Final Premium

- Records

- Audit

This chapter first offers a brief history of the Premium section in standard workers compensation policies. This is followed by a review of each of the components listed above. This consists of restating the actual verbiage contained in Part Five and providing commentary regarding each component. It should be kept in mind that any references to "we" or "us" refers to the insurer; references to "you" and "your" refers to the named insured (employer).

This portion of the chapter is followed by an analysis of other factors which impact the development of workers compensation insurance premiums.

History

Prior to 1954, workers compensation policies contained an assortment of endorsements which set forth the various rules and procedures for calculating and handling premiums and adjustments. There was no reference in the basic policy to following the manuals utilized by insurers. So the premium-related procedures had to be endorsed onto the policy.

After a multi-year study conducted by NCCI focused on changes needed in the standard workers compensation policy, a new policy form was adopted in 1954. One of the major improvements of the new policy was a revised Premium condition, which referenced the manuals in use by the company (the insurer). The first paragraph of the Premium condition of the 1954 policy is as follows:

1. **Premium.** *The premium bases and rates for the classifications of operations described in the declarations are as stated therein and for classifications not so described are those applicable in accordance with the manuals by the company. This policy is issued by the company and accepted by the insured with the agreement that if any change in classifications, rates or rating plans is or becomes applicable to this policy under any law regulating this insurance or because of any amendments affecting the benefits provided by the workmen's compensation law, such change with the effective date thereof shall be stated in an endorsement issued to form a part of this policy.*

This change modernized how workers compensation policies were structured and automatically tied premium rating issues to the manuals of the insurer. This was a major simplification over the tedious process of issuing rating and premium and related endorsements.

But because the policy no longer contained all the information needed for an insured to determine how premiums were calculated and adjusted, the change imposed a greater responsibility on the insurer, agent, and broker to make certain the insured was reasonably informed in such matters. That continues today.

Our Manuals

The first clause in the Premium section of the workers compensation policy is called "Our Manuals" and deals with the use of manuals by the insurer:

> *All premium for this policy will be determined by our manuals of rules, rates, rating plans and classifications. We may change our manuals and apply the changes to this policy if authorized by law or a governmental agency regulating this insurance.*

> Source: Workers Compensation and Employers Liability Insurance Policy, WC 00 00 00C, National Council on Compensation Insurance, Effective January 1, 2015 (refer to Appendix A).

The first sentence makes it clear to the insured that the premium is based on the manuals used by the insurer. The term "manuals" may include books, booklets, handbooks, loose leaf binders, and so forth. The only limitation is that such manuals deal specifically with rules, rates, rating plans and classifications. These manuals may include (1) those prepared and maintained by rating bureaus, such as the National Council on Compensation Insurance (NCCI), and/or (2) proprietary materials prepared by an insurer, such as an underwriting manual.

Workers compensation rules, rates, rating plans and classifications are addressed by four different manuals authored and maintained by NCCI. These manuals are available to subscribers in both written and electronic forms. Manuals are also prepared by other rating bureaus, but given the limited space here, our focus is on NCCI materials.

Basic Manual for Workers Compensation and Employers Liability Insurance

This is the most relied on workers comp manual in the United States. It is used mostly by insurers, brokers and agents. This manual is hundreds of pages in length and covers the rules governing workers compensation rating (Part One) and classifications (Part Two).

Part One includes rules applicable to the following:

- Classification assignment

- Premium basis and payroll allocation

- Rating definitions and application of premium elements

- Insurance plan rules

Each of these broad areas contains a myriad of rules and examples which are intended to provide guidance to the manual user. For instance, Rule 1-Classification Assignment explains basic rating classifications and standard exception classifications. It addresses classification wordings, classification procedures, miscellaneous employees and changes/corrections in classifications. Each of these different areas is further broken down into groups of rules and explanations. Part One also contains extensive appendices containing charts and tables which address premium discounts, cancellation, increased limits, schedule rating plans, classifications by hazard group, and payroll determination formulas.

Part Two covers rating classifications. This section identifies the name of each classification, the class code assigned and brief explanations and commentary. This also includes state specific classifications, pending changes and individual rates for each classification. For example, one classification is Paper Manufacturing. The four digit classification code is 4239. There are notes applicable to this classification: "Includes card, bristol, paper, straw, fiber or leather board." There is a further reference to two other four digit classification codes to consider if there are any pulp manufacturing operations (these codes are 4206 and 4207).

Each state approves rates that apply to new and renewal policies. These are adjusted by most states annually. States approve different kinds of rates, which can sometimes be confusing. These different types of rates include:

Loss Costs. This is the loss component used in establishing rates. These are commonly referred to as rates, but they are more accurately referred to as loss costs. Loss costs are the expected losses for each $100 of workers compensation payroll. It is up to insurers to calculate the expenses it requires (the expense portion of the rate). It then seeks and obtains approval of combined rates (loss costs plus expenses) for each classification. Once approved by the appropriate rating authority, these combined rates are referred to as "manual" rates.

Voluntary Advisory Rates. These manual rates include the loss and expense components. Insurers can adopt these rates or file different rates. Insurance Groups (an insurer or holding company that owns two or more insurers) will often file different rates for the different insurers it utilizes in a given state. In this way, it can use lower rates for select insureds and higher rates for other insureds.

Standard Rates. These rates also include both the loss and expense components. These rates are utilized in administrative pricing states; these are states where rating bureaus file rates on behalf of all insurers that utilize the same approved rates.

Assigned Risk Rates. These are usually combined rates applicable to those insureds that are subject to an assigned risk insurance program. Such insureds are not able to purchase insurance from insurers within the voluntary insurance marketplace.

Rates can vary greatly between jurisdictions for several reasons, but are most impacted by applicable benefit levels and medical costs.

NCCI also has a Basic Manual Users Guide which provides additional guidance and information when using the Basic Manual. The Users Guide covers various topics, including coverage, terms and dispute resolution. Various state reference tables are also provided.

Experience Rating Plan Manual for Workers Compensation and Employers Liability Insurance

This manual outlines the rules related to experience rating (also see Chapter 10 for a detailed examination of the experience rating process). Experience rating is a refinement in the premium promulgation process. It compares an individual policyholder's three years of experience (payroll and loss history) against expected experience. The net result is a credit or debit.

These rules are grouped into five categories:

- General explanations

- Elements and formula

- Ownership changes and combination of entities

- Application and revisions

- Special rating conditions

Each category has subsections which address related issues. For instance, under "Special Rating Conditions," there are subcategories for employee leasing/professional employer organizations, separate state experience rating modifications and construction/contracting risks. There is also an Appendix section which includes standardized forms.

Retrospective Rating Plan Manual for Workers Compensation and Employers Liability Insurance

This manual outlines the rules, procedures, values and formulas which apply to retrospectively-rated plans (these plans are discussed in detail in Chapter 11). In basic terms, a retrospective rating plan establishes an initial premium upon which a workers compensation policy is issued. There is a premium adjustment after the policy expires based largely on audited standard premium, program factors and the losses which have been incurred or paid on a specified loss valuation date. Because the premium is not finalized until after a policy expires, these types of plans were coined with the "retrospective" designation.

This manual is similar to other NCCI manuals, in that there are specified categories of rules and subcategories. The four categories of rules are:

- General explanation

- Eligibility for the plan

- Operation of the plan

- Administration of the plan

There is also an appendix section which includes multiple tables addressing expected loss ranges, insurance charges, expense ratios, basic premium calculations and rating values.

Similar to the Basic Manual, NCCI publishes a User Guide for the Retrospective Rating Manual. This provides the reader with additional information and insights.

As noted in Chapter 11, retrospective rating plans have fallen out of favor with many large insureds that instead opt for less expensive deductible plans. Retrospective rating plans are mandatory with the assigned risk programs in some states (usually based on a premium size threshold).

SCOPES Manual

This manual provides general information and guidance for classifying operations for workers compensation rating purposes. The depth of the explanations in this manual is far greater than the classifications section of the Basic Manual. However, if there is a conflict between an explanation contained in the Scopes Manual and the Basic Manual, the Basic Manual prevails.

The SCOPES Manual is an indispensable source of information, particularly for insurance underwriters, premium auditors, brokers and agents. This manual describes both national and state specific classifications (known as state exceptions or state specials). Classifications are indexed by name, industry and code. It also contains classification examples. For education purposes, a copy of the pages describing the Clerical Office Employees NOC classification (code 8810) is marked as Appendix D. It is well worth noting that these pages identify the states that have exceptions to this description, the description itself and related operations that are not assigned to this classification. After reviewing these pages, the reader should have a good understanding of which employees should be assigned to this classification.

(According to NCCI, 35 states and the District of Columbia utilize the classification coding system in the Scopes Manual. In addition, eight states provide NCCI with state-specific information for inclusion in the Scopes Manual. While Scopes is used as a reference tool in these states, the rating authority in each state interprets and applies their rules; these states are: California, Indiana, Massachusetts, New Jersey, New York, North Carolina, Ohio and Wisconsin. The Scopes Manual does not apply in Delaware, Michigan, Minnesota, North Dakota, Pennsylvania, Washington, or Wyoming. See Appendix for the state-by-state summary).

To the casual observer, it would appear that the "Our Manuals" portion of Part Five gives insurers carte blanche to do anything they want, without fear of repercussion. This is not the case, however. Workers compensation insurance is highly regulated by each state. Note that the second sentence of this provision—"*We may change our* manuals *and apply the changes to this policy if authorized by law or a governmental agency regulating this insurance*"— recognizes that changes by insurers must conform to state laws and rating agency rules. For instance, Illinois has a law which allows policy holders to request and obtain premium-related corrections retroactively from insurers who incorrectly applied classifications, payrolls or other rating system factors.[2] This overrides conflicting rating rules established by rating bureaus or insurers. The Illinois statute is reproduced below for reference purposes:

> *Insurance companies shall apply correct classifications, payrolls and other factors of a rating system to compute premiums. If the application of incorrect classifications, payrolls or any other factors of a rating system results in the payment by an insured of premiums in excess of the premiums that would have been paid utilizing the correct applications of classifications, payrolls or other factors of a rating system, the insurer shall refund to the insured the excessive premium paid for the period during which the incorrect application of classifications, payrolls or other factors of a rating system were applied. This Section is intended to codify existing law and practice.*

When premium disputes arise between insurers and their policyholders, advisors to policyholders should recognize that resolution may come from understanding the manuals which an insurer uses and the state laws and regulations which govern the application of premium related variables.

Classifications

The second clause in the Premium section addresses rating classifications:

> *Item 4 of the Information Page shows the rate and premium basis for certain business or work classifications. These classifications*

were assigned based on an estimate of the exposures you would have during the policy period. If your actual exposures are not properly described by those classifications, we will assign proper classifications, rates and premium basis by endorsement to this policy.

Source: Workers Compensation and Employers Liability Insurance Policy, WC 00 00 00C, National Council on Compensation Insurance, Effective January 1, 2015 (refer to Appendix A).

Item 4 of the Information Page (refer to Appendix A) is the designated space within a standard workers compensation policy where the rating classifications are shown. On the preprinted WC 00 00 01 A Information Page, the space for inserting information in Section 4 is very limited. Typically, the insurer will insert a reference to another schedule (such as, "See Classification Schedule" or "See Schedule of Forms and Endorsements"). In any event, the classification schedule will list the rating classification descriptions, code numbers, estimated remuneration, rates and premiums. A sample appears below:

WORKERS COMPENSATION CLASSIFICATION SCHEDULE					
Insurance for this coverage provided by:					
INSURANCE COMPANY					
Policy Number WC 6554498-01					
ITEM 4.	**CLASSIFICATION OF OPERATIONS**		**PREMIUM BASIS**	**RATES**	
LOC.	Entry in the item, except as specifically provided elsewhere in this policy, does not modify any of the other provisions of this policy	Code No.	Total Estimated Annual Remuneration	Per $100 of Remuneration	Estimated Annual Premium
	ABC, Inc. FEIN # Xx-Xxxxxxx 6508 Main St. Anytown, USA 12345				
	Concrete or Cement Work–Floors, Driveways, Yards, Sidewalks & Drivers	$321	$1,000,000	14.24	$342,400.00

ITEM 4.	CLASSIFICATION OF OPERATIONS		PREMIUM BASIS	RATES	
	Contractor– Project Manager Construction Executive, Construction Manager or Construction Superintendent	$606	$90,000	4.92	$4,428.00
	Clerical Office Employees NOC	$810	$300,000	.38	$1,140.00

The purpose of the classification sytem is to group employers with similar operations into classes. This allows insurers to develop rates which are reflective of the anticipated loss experience for a specific type of operation. This is important to all stakeholders involved in workers compensation. If you are an insured with a very low hazard operation (such as an accounting office), you would not want to be charged the same workers compensation rates as higher hazard operations, such as concrete finishers or chemical manufacturers.

Classifications are divided into two types. These are referred to in the insurance industry as "basic classifications" (also referred to as the "governing" classification) and "standard exception classifications". Basic classifications describe the busness of an employer (as opposed to the occupation of each employee). For instance, a retail baker will be assigned to one classification (such as "Bakery"), while a breakfast bar manufacturer may be assigned to "Cereal or Bar Manufacturing." Both classifications involve baking, but the exposure to loss in a manufacturing environment versus a "mom and pop" local bakery is very different.

After the one governing basic classification is assigned, secondary classifications may be assigned when:

- the basic classification requires that certain operations or employees be separately rated;

- the insured may engage in construction or erection, farm, repair, or mercantile operations that require additional basic classifications;

- the insured operates more than one business in a state.

Standard exception classifications describe occupations which are common to many businesses. These are not included in a basic classification, unless the classification wording dictates otherwise. The standard exception classifications are (1) clerical office employees, (2) clerical telecomuters, (3) drivers, chauffers, messengers and their helpers, (4) salespersons or collectors-outside, and (5) automobile salespersons. So if an organization has clerical employees, such employees are subject to the clerical office employees classification and are rated separately.

There are over 600 different classifications used in the United States and the number is growing. A major reason why new classifications are developed is because of technology. A local "quick printing" shop has a far different loss exposure than a large scale commercial printer. It was because of the new technology asssociated with quick printers that a new classification was developed ("Quick Printing-Copying or Duplication Service-All Employees & Clerical, Salepersons, Drivers"). The rate difference between the "Quick Printing" and "Printing" (commercial printers) classifications can be significant. For instance, the state approved voluntary advisory 2016 rate per $100 in Illinois for quick printers is $1.87 compared to $4.03 for commercial printing operations (a difference of 215 percent).

There are many rules and nuances associated with classification procedures, but the following are worthy of special mention:

- The rules apply separately to each operating legal entity.

- If no basic classification describes the operations of an insured, the classification that comes closest to describing the operation should be assigned.

- Assignment of more than one basic classification is possible under certain circumstances, such as when an insured conducts operations involving construction, farming, employee leasing or a mercantile business.

The NCCI Basic Manual or equivalent manual should be consulted for specific rules and exceptions.

The Classifications provision in Part Five of the workers comp policy gives the insurer the right to modify one or more of the classifications, if it determines that an insured's operations are misclassified. There are occasions where operations are intentionally or unintentionally misclassified by a broker, agent or insured. The Classifications provision provides protection to the insurer.

In most states, changes or corrections of classifications are handled in the following general ways (exceptions exist, so consult the appropriate manual):

- A classification change due to a change in the insured's operations applies as of the date the operation changed.

- Corrections to classifications which favor the insured (premium reduction) apply retroactively to the inception date of the policy.

- Corrections to classifications which favor the insurer (premium increase) apply in different ways depending on when the correction is effective. If the change is effective during the first 120 days of the policy, then the change is applied retroactively to the inception of the policy; if after 120 days but before the final ninety days of the policy, then as of the day the insurer discovers the cause for correction; and if during the last ninety days of the policy, then only to the following renewal policy.

Conversely, an insured may feel that its operations are misclassified to its detriment. The insured can state its case to the insurer and come to a resolution. If the insurer and policyholder cannot resolve their differences, most rating bureaus and state funds provide some form of formal dipute resolution services. An insured can also seek an inspection and assignment of classification. If still not satisfied, most states have a formal appeals process established to handle disputes. This is usually handled by a state committee, internal review panel or appeals board.

There are many "grey areas" in classifying operations for workers compensation rating purposes. A business may be very unusual and not contemplated by any specific classification. Or a business may have several types of operations. And with the disparity between the rates applicable to differing classifications, the impact can be significant for all the stakeholders.

Policyholders rarely have access to the rating or classification manuals. Many times, they are not aware that such manuals exist or that there are so many classifications and rules. They usually rely on the expertise of brokers, agents, consultants, underwriters and premium auditors. The reality is that mistakes occur more often than many would like to admit.

Remuneration

The third clause in the Premium section addresses "remuneration:

Premium for each work classification is determined by multiplying a rate times a premium basis. Remuneration is the most common premium basis. This premium basis includes payroll and all other remuneration paid or payable during the policy period for the services of:

1. *all your officers and employees engaged in work covered by this policy; and*

2. *all other persons engaged in work that could make us liable under Part One (Workers Compensation Insurance) of this policy. If you do not have payroll records for these persons, the contract price for their services and materials may be used as the premium basis. This paragraph 2 will not apply if you* give us proof that the employers of these persons lawfully secured their workers compensation obligations.

Source: Workers Compensation and Employers Liability Insurance Policy, WC 00 00 00C, National Council on Compensation Insurance, Effective January 1, 2015.

This clause tells the insured what the basis is for calculating the premium. The premium is determined by multiplying a rate times a premium basis, which is most commonly "remuneration". The meaning of remuneration clearly includes payroll and all other remuneration paid or payable. Insurers rely on their manuals to sort out what remuneration is considered to be.

In its Basic Manual, NCCI substitutes the term "payroll" for "remuneration", but the meaning is the same. (This is because NCCI defines "payroll" to include money or substitutes for money.) NCCI further defines what is included and excluded in its meaning of "payroll".

Inclusions:

- Wages or salaries (including retroactive wages or salaries).

- Total cash received by an employee for commissions and draws against commissions.

- Bonuses including stock bonus plans.

- Extra pay for overtime work.

- Pay for holidays, vacations, or periods of sickness.

- Payment by an employer of amounts that would have been withheld from employees to meet statutory obligations for insurance or pension plans such as the Federal Social Security Act or Medicare.

- Payment to employees on any basis other than time worked, such as piecework, profit sharing or incentive plans.

- Payment or allowances for hand tools or hand-held power tools used by employees in their work or operations for the insured. These tools may be supplied directly by the employee or to the employee through a third party.

- The rental value of an apartment or house provided to an employee based on comparable accommodations.

- The value of lodging, other than an apartment or house received by an employee as part of their pay to the extent shown in the insured's records.

- The value of meals received by employees as part of their pay to the extent shown in the insured's records.

- The value of store certificates, merchandise, credits or any other substitute for money received by employees as part of their pay.

- Payments for salary reduction, employee savings plans, retirement or cafeteria plans (IRC 125) that are made through employee-authorized salary reduction from the employee's gross pay.

- Davis-Bacon wages or wages from a similar prevailing wage law.

- Annuity plans.

- Expense reimbursements to employees to the extent that an employer's records do not confirm that the expense was incurred as a valid business expense. (Exception: When it can be verified that the employee was away from home overnight on the business of the employer, but the employer did not maintain verifiable receipts for incurred expenses, a reasonable expense allowance, limited to a maximum of $30 per day, is permitted.)

- Payment for filming of commercials excluding subsequent residuals that are earned by the commercial's participant(s) each time the commercial appears in print or is broadcast.

Exclusions.

- Tips or other gratuities received by employees.

- Payments by an employer to group insurance or group pension plans for employees.

- Payments by an employer into third-party trusts for the Davis-Bacon Act or a similar prevailing wage law provided the pension trust is qualified under IRC Sections 401(a) and 501(a).

- The value of special rewards for individual invention or discovery.

- Dismissal or severance payments except for time worked or vacation accrued.

- Payments for active military duty.

- Employee discounts on goods purchased from the employee's employer.

- Expense reimbursements to employees to the extent that an employer's records confirm that the expense was incurred as a valid business expense.

- Reimbursed expenses and flat expense allowances (except for hand or hand-held power tools) paid to employees may be excluded from the audit only if all three of the following conditions are met:

  o The expenses are incurred for the business of the employer; (2) The amount of each employee's expense payments or allowances are shown separately, and (3) The amount of each employee's expense reimbursement is a fair estimate of the actual expenses incurred by the employee in the conduct of his/her work (As noted previously: When it can be verified that the employee was away from home overnight on the business of the employer, but the employer did not maintain verifiable receipts for incurred expenses, a reasonable expense allowance, limited to a maximum of $30 per day, is permitted.)

  o Supper money for late work

  o Work uniform allowances

  o Sick pay paid to an employee by a third party such as an insured's group insurance carrier that is paying disability income benefits to a disabled employee

Employer-provided perks such as:

- use of company-provided automobiles;

- airplane flights;

- incentive vacations (e.g., contest winners);

- discounts on property or services;

- club memberships;

- tickets to entertainment events.

Employer contributions to employee benefit plans (including contributions made by the employer, at the employer's expense that are determined by the amount contributed by the employee) such as:

- employee savings plans;

- retirement plans;

- cafeteria plans (IRC 125).

There are additional NCCI rules governing the following:

- Overtime payroll (the premium portion is excluded)

- Guaranteed wages (generally no portion is excluded)

- Premium pay (no portion is excluded if the extra compensation is for special hours or unusual work conditions)

- Payroll limitations, exceptions or exclusions (such as for executive officers, members of LLCs, partners and sole proprietors)

- Wages for time not worked (idle time and wages paid to key employees are generally included)

- Interchange of labor (special rules apply when employees perform duties involving two or more assigned classifications)

As with many things workers compensation-related, there are exceptions to the preceding meaning of "payroll", along with additional rules established in various states. When dealing with "remuneration" or "payroll" issues, the applicable insurer manuals in use should <u>always</u> be consulted.

Agents and brokers can provide a valued service by fully understanding how "remuneration" and "payroll" are applied in the rating of workers compensation premiums and educating their clients accordingly. Many times different forms of "payroll" are included in estimates or payroll audits because insureds do not know what should and should not be included. Besides possessing copies of the applicable manuals, another good resource for agents and brokers are the classification guides published by the Premium Audit Advisory Service (accessible via www.verisk.com, last visited February 1, 2016).

The second portion of the Remuneration clause deals with an insurer having the right to charge for nonemployees who provide services or products and have not secured their obligations under workers compensation laws. (Employers most commonly secure their obligations by purchasing workers compensation insurance or becoming a qualified self-insured entity.)

The reason this right is given to the insurer is that in most states a principal is responsible for payment of compensation benefits to employees of uninsured contractors. For example, if a building owner engages an uninsured roofer to conduct repairs, and an employee of the roofer falls off the roof and is injured, the building owner may be responsible for the employee's workers compensation wage benefits and medical expenses.

An insured can avoid additional premium charges if it can demonstrate the service provider(s) has workers compensation insurance. This can be evidenced through various documents, such as a certificate of insurance, certificate of exemption or a copy of an applicable workers compensation policy.

If an insured cannot demonstrate that its service providers have insurance, the insurer will rely on special rules in its manuals to charge additional premium. Under NCCI's Basic Manual, the premium for uninsured contractors will depend on whether or not payroll records exist for the applicable uninsured employees. If such records exist, actual payroll will be used, along with the appropriate classification(s). If records do not exist, the additional premium will be determined based on the subcontract amount applied to percentages for different types of work. The minimum percentages are: 33 1/3 percent for mobile equipment with operators; 50 percent for labor and material; 90 percent for labor only, and 100 percent for piecework.

To avoid controversy and potentially higher costs, insureds should secure and maintain certificates of insurance on all contractors and service providers. It should be part of an established process when contracting with others.

Premium Payments

The fourth clause in the Premium section addresses premium payments:

> *You will pay all premium when due. You will pay the premium even if part or all of a workers compensation law is not valid.*

> Source: Workers Compensation and Employers Liability Insurance Policy, WC 00 00 00C, National Council on Compensation Insurance, Effective January 1, 2015.

The premium payments clause notes that the employer named in Item 1 of the information page is required to pay all premium when due. In the event of multiple named insureds, the first named insured has the responsibility for the payment. This latter phrase is not in this particular clause, but, under the Conditions section of the policy, the first named insured is tapped as the representative of all insureds. So, that entity has the duty to make the premium payments to the insurer.

Additional provisions related to premium payments may be set forth in program rating agreements (e.g., retrospective or deductible plans). Also, there is a cancellation provision of the policy set forth in the Conditions section. This allows the insurer to cancel in the event of nonpayment. This section is commonly amended by state amendatory endorsements which tailor the cancellation provision to dovetail with state laws. Usually ten days advance written notice of cancelation is required in the event of nonpayment by the insured.

The second sentence of the premium payments clause requires the insured to pay the premium even if a workers compensation law is wholly or partially declared to be invalid. In the early days of workers compensation legislation, some states passed statutes which were elective in nature. Others passed legislation which limited compensation to specified hazardous employments. In the early 1900's there were several constitutional challenges to workers compensation laws. Things eventually settled down, and by 1920, 42 of the 48 states had workers compensation laws in place. Insurance companies do not want to return premium or argue with insureds over premium issues in the event some part of a workers compensation law is declared to be invalid; hence, the need for a premium payments provision.

Final Premium

The fifth clause in the Premium section addresses final premium:

The premium shown on the Information Page, schedules, and endorsements is an estimate. The final premium will be determined after this policy ends by using the actual, not the estimated, premium basis and the proper classifications and rates that lawfully apply to the business and work covered by this policy. If the final premium is more than the premium you paid to us, you must pay us the balance. If it is less, we will refund the balance to you. The final premium will not be less than the highest minimum premium for the classifications covered by this policy.

If this policy is canceled, final premium will be determined in the following way unless our manuals provide otherwise:

1. *If we cancel, final premium will be calculated pro rata based on the time this policy was in force. Final premium will not be less than the pro rata share of the minimum premium.*

2. *If you cancel, final premium will be more than pro rata; it will be based on the time this policy was in force, and increased by our short-rate cancelation table and procedure. Final premium will not be less than the minimum premium.*

Source: Workers Compensation and Employers Liability Insurance Policy, WC 00 00 00C, National Council on Compensation Insurance, Effective January 1, 2015.

The premium shown on the information page of the policy is an estimate. The final premium is determined after the policy ends by using the actual, not the estimated, premium basis and the proper classifications and rates that apply to the work covered by the policy. Since the premium basis (e.g., payroll estimate) may change during the policy period, an appropriate premium charge is more properly figured at the end of the policy period when the true exposures are known by the insured and insurer. If the final premium is more than the estimated premium paid by the insured, the difference must be paid to the insurer. If the situation is reversed, a refund will be made by the insurer to the first named insured.

The insured is informed here that the policy has a minimum premium, that is, a charge that will be paid regardless of the actual remuneration.

This minimum premium is the highest minimum premium for the rating classifications identified in the policy, and for which there is an actual exposure. This charge is made to cover the expenses that the insurer has incurred in underwriting and issuing the workers compensation policy. This seldom comes into play, except for small organizations with nominal payroll.

This clause also determines the amount of premium in case the policy is cancelled. If the insurer cancels the policy, the final premium is calculated on a pro rata basis, based on the time the policy was in force. If the insured cancels the policy, the final premium is based on the time the policy was in force plus the short-rate cancellation penalty (as calculated using the manuals of the insurer). A rule-of-thumb for the short rate penalty is 10 percent of the unearned premium.

The rating manual used by the insurer may make an exception for the short-rate cancellation penalty, if the insured retires from all business covered by the policy, sells the business, or completes all work covered by the policy.

Records

The sixth clause in the Premium section focuses on records:

> *You will keep records of information needed to compute premium. You will provide us with copies of those records when we ask for them.*

Source: Workers Compensation and Employers Liability Insurance Policy, WC 00 00 00C, National Council on Compensation Insurance, Effective January 1, 2015.

The insurer needs information to charge a proper premium. In order to do so, it will require specific records (discussed in the next section) from the insured. The insured is required to cooperate in this endeavor. This clause requires the insured not only to keep records, but also to provide copies of them to the insurer when asked. An insured will not be successful in avoiding addition premiums because it does not have records or fails to produce documents requested by the insurer.

Audit

The last clause in the Premium section addresses premium audits:

> *You will let us examine and audit all your records that relate to this policy. These records include ledgers, journals, registers,*

vouchers, contracts, tax reports, payroll and disbursement records, and programs for storing and retrieving data. We may conduct the audits during regular business hours during the policy period and within three years after the policy period ends. Information developed by audit will be used to determine final premium. Insurance rate service organizations have the same rights we have under this provision.

Source: Workers Compensation and Employers Liability Insurance Policy, WC 00 00 00C, National Council on Compensation Insurance, Effective January 1, 2015.

Depending on the premium size of a workers compensation policy and prior audit experience, a premium auditor may choose to:

- waive the audit;

- request a voluntary audit;

- conduct a telephone audit;

- conduct a physical audit.

When an insurer waives the audit the policy premium is not adjusted. With a voluntary audit a premium adjustment is made using payroll figures provided by the insured. A telephone audit is usually conducted when the insured's location is in a remote area or the auditor needs to ask additional questions. A physical audit consists of a visit to an insured's office location and a physical review of on-site records.

As part of an on-site audit, the auditor will typically review the scope of an insured's operations and locations, the form of the entity, payroll registers/journals, individual earnings records, IRS Form 941 (Employer's Quarterly Federal Tax Return), casual labor, independent contractors, executive payroll, overtime payroll, severance payments, rating classifications and insurance certificates. The auditor may complete an audit worksheet outlining his/her findings based on interviews and a review of documents.

The insurer and applicable rating organizations have the right to examine and audit all the records of the insured that relate to the policy. This specifically includes, but is not limited to, ledgers, journals, registers, vouchers, contracts, tax reports, payroll and disbursement records, and programs for storing and retrieving data. But requests from insurers may not be unreasonable or onerous. Likewise, the insured is responsible to cooperate with reasonable requests and to respond in a timely fashion.

This process will go smoothly if policyholders have records readily available for review, provide a comfortable and well lit space for the auditor and conduct an exit interview to review the preliminary results. This eliminates possible misunderstandings and problems.

The insurer and rating organizations may conduct audits during regular business hours during the policy period and within three years after the policy period ends. The information developed by the audits is used to determine the final premium.

There is a tendency to think that a premium audit is always performed after the policy period has expired. However, insurers have the right to perform an audit during the policy period. Mid-term audits are most frequently performed when the insurer suspects the operations are misclassified or the estimated payroll is incorrect.

Practical Information—Workers Compensation Rating Bureaus

Workers compensation rating bureaus provide a variety of functions depending upon the states involved and the scope of services they provide. In general, rating bureaus collect statistical data (such as payroll and loss information), promulgate rating classifications and rates, develop policy forms and endorsements and file information with regulators on behalf of their respective members. These bureaus may also develop rules for experience rating, retrospective rating, and other rating mechanisms.

The use of rating bureaus is a much more efficient way of handling these functions, compared to a system where each insurer self-performs these activities on their own. The data would be limited and the costs and human resources needed to perform the work would be substantial.

The leading workers compensation rating bureau is the National Council on Compensation Insurance (NCCI). NCCI's Basic Manual for Workers Compensation and Employers Liability Insurance has been approved for use in 37 states and the District of Columbia. Of these, 33 states are competitive rating jurisdictions (rates and rules are filed or adopted by insurers) and four are administrative pricing jurisdictions (rates and rules are filed by NCCI on behalf of the insurers). The administrative pricing states are Arizona, Florida, Idaho and Iowa.

There are fourteen states where the Manual does not apply. Of these, four have monopolistic state funds (North Dakota, Ohio, Washington and

Wyoming) and ten others utilize their own rating systems (California, Delaware, Massachusetts, Michigan, Minnesota, New Jersey, New York, Pennsylvania, and Wisconsin).

COMPETITIVE RATING JURISDICTIONS – NCCI		
STATE		
Alabama	Kentucky	North Carolina
Alaska	Louisiana	Oklahoma
Arkansas	Maine	Oregon
Colorado	Maryland	Rhode Island
Connecticut	Mississippi	South Carolina
District of Columbia	Missouri	South Dakota
Georgia	Montana	Tennessee
Hawaii	Nebraska	Texas
Illinois	Nevada	Utah
Indiana	New Hampshire	Vermont
Kansas	New Mexico	Virginia
		West Virginia

ADMINISTERED PRICING JURISDICTIONS – NCCI	
STATE	
Arizona	Idaho
Florida	Iowa

JURISDICTIONS WHERE NCCI BASIC MANUAL DOES NOT APPLY		
STATE		
California	New Jersey	Pennsylvania
Delaware	Louisiana	Washington
Massachusetts	New York	Wisconsin
Michigan	North Dakota	Wyoming
Minnesota	Ohio	

The rating bureaus are a wonderful source of rating and classification information. Insurance professionals would be well- served by obtaining the appropriate manuals in the state their policyholders have operations.

Treatment of Executive Officers, Sole Proprietors, Partners and LLC Members

Each state addresses the employment status of executive officers, sole proprietors, partners and limited liability company members. This information is summarized in Appendix C. Most states include such classes of individuals under their workers compensation laws. In some states, these classes may opt out of the system.

When such individuals are included for coverage, they are assigned to the classification that applies to the operations in which they are engaged. In other words, if a president of a roofing company is principally involved in roof installation, the officer will be properly assigned to the appropriate roofing classification.

The payroll of such individuals may be limited for reporting purposes. Each state sets minimum and maximum reporting thresholds for executive officers (executive officers are the president, vice president, secretary treasurer, and such other office appointed in accordance with the bylaws or charter of the employing entity). These limitations are set forth in the respective state rate pages. For example, the minimum reportable weekly payroll for an executive officer may be $1,000 a week. The maximum may be $2,000 a week, even if the officer is actually paid much more than that amount. Sometimes insureds can be very creative in using the payroll limitation applicable to officers. In one state, there was no applicable payroll limitation applicable to members of professional sports teams. As a result, one professional basketball team appointed each player as a team vice president and limited their weekly payroll to the amount stated in the state rate pages.

Partners or sole proprietors may be treated as employees or their payroll may be limited in state rate pages. Members of LLCs may be treated as officers, partners or sole proprietors, depending on state rules. In any event, any references to members or managers are collectively treated as "members". This is due to the variable terminology used in each state.

Other Rating Factors

There are numerous other rating factors utilized in promulgating workers compensation premiums. The manuals produced by rating bureaus will identify each of these factors and explain how they work and in what order these should be applied. The following table is a summary of the different rating factors incorporated in most state premium rating algorithms (step-by-step procedures for developing the premium).

Where an "X" appears, this means the element is included in the calculation. Each state will have their own algorithm, so specific state rating manual pages should be consulted.

Premium Elements Reference Table

	PREMIUM TYPE				
	Manual	Subject	Modified	Standard	Estimated or Final Annual Premium
Payroll divided by 100 × Rate	X	X	X	X	X
Supplementary Disease (foundry, abrasive, sandblast)	X	X	X	X	X
USL&HW Exposure for non-F-class	X	X	X	X	X
Waiver of Subrogation Factor		X	X	X	X
E/L Increased Limits Factor		X	X	X	X
E/L Increased Limits Charge		X	X	X	X
E/L Increased Limits Factor (Admiralty, FELA)	X	X	X	X	
E/L Voluntary Compensation Flat Charge		X	X	X	X
Experience Rating Modification			X	X	X
Supplemental Disease Exposure (Asbestos, NOC)			X	X	
Atomic Energy Radiation Exposure NOC				X	X

	Manual	Subject	Modified	Standard	Estimated or Final Annual Premium
Charge for nonratable catastrophe loading				X	X
Aircraft Seat Surcharge				X	X
Balance to Minimum Premium (State Act)				X	X
Balance to Minimum Premium (Admiralty, FELA)			X	X	
Premium Discount					X
Coal Mine Disease Charge					X
Expense Constant					X
Catastrophe Provisions					X

Source: Basic Manual Users Guide, F. Reference Tables, 2. Premium Elements Reference Table, National Council on Compensation Insurance 2016.

This table provides an understanding of the meaning of different premiums: manual, subject, modified, standard and final. These are common terms used in workers compensation, but not always understood by industry practitioners.

The table includes several elements that are unusual, such as rates/loadings for diseases and radiation. These will not be discussed here. However, other elements are worth identifying.

Waiver of Subrogation. This is a charge for the insurer's agreement to waive its rights of subrogation against specified third parties. The premium charge can be a flat amount, but is more typically a percentage total manual premium.

Employers Liability Increased Limits Factors/Charges. These charges are applied if an insured desires to increase the standard employers liability coverage limits to a higher amount. This usually consists of applying a percentage to the manual premium.

Experience Modification. This is a factor which is promulgated by the applicable rating agency or regulatory body. The modification is a mathematical formula which accounts for three years of payroll by classification and losses incurred. This factor can have a major impact on the ultimate premium charged. The factor is applied to the total subject premium.

Per Passenger Seat Surcharge. This is a charge associated with employees flying in owned or leased aircraft. The charge is set forth in the state rate pages and applies per aircraft passenger seat. There may be a maximum surcharge per aircraft.

Premium Discount. The relative expense of issuing and servicing a policy that has a large premium is lower on a percentage basis than for policies with a smaller premium. The premium discount is a percentage credit applied to total standard premium. Rating bureaus have tables that outline the percentage credit for different premium levels or such credits can be found in state rate pages.

Expense Constant. This is a charge to cover expenses that are common to all workers compensation policies regardless of size. The amount of the expense constant varies by state, but it usually falls within the range of $100-300 per policy.

Catastrophe Provisions. These are charges made for catastrophic loss exposures, such as terrorism. A rate is usually applied to the estimated payroll.

There are other premium elements applicable to one or more states, but not all states. Most of these involve premium credits. Some of these include:

- certified risk management programs (premium credit);

- certified workers compensation healthcare network (premium credit);

- coinsurance (premium credit);

- contracting programs (various program titles);

- deductible programs (premium credit);

- designated medical provider (premium credit);

- drug/Alcohol free workplace (premium credit);

- managed care arrangements (premium credit);

- merit rating (premium credit);

- safety programs (various program titles);

- schedule rating (premium credit/debit).

More information on these state pricing programs is available from the applicable rating bureau.

Endnotes

1. Workers Compensation and Employers Liability Insurance Policy, WC 00 00 00B, National Council on Compensation Insurance, Effective July 1, 2012.

2. Illinois Compiled Statutes 215 ILCS 5/462b (from Ch. 73, par. 1065.9b).

Chapter 10

Experience Rating

Introduction

Experience rating is a mechanism which better aligns insurance premiums to the loss expectancy and risk characteristics of insured organizations. Workers compensation manual rates incorporate the expected losses of many employers that comprise a given rating classification. For instance, a manual rate for Concrete or Cement Work will incorporate expected losses for all contractors who perform this type of construction work. However, the loss experience of individual contractors who perform this type of construction work will vary considerably from one to the next. The experience rating process addresses this variability.

In very general terms, the experience rating process incorporates three years of an organization's payroll and claims history. The historical payroll is applied to expected loss rates for that industry, resulting in the "expected losses" for the three-year term. The expected losses are then compared to the organization's actual losses for the same period. The net result is a modification factor. This factor has a direct impact on the workers compensation premium that will be charged. It will penalize organizations with poor loss experience (debit) and reward those with a positive claims history (credit).

There are several benefits of experience rating. These include the following:

- It customizes premiums to individual insureds based on their historical experience. This refinement more closely aligns charged premiums to the loss exposures of an individual employer.

- It provides an incentive to employers to improve their loss experience through proactive safety programs and quality claims management. Employers are able to exercise control over the frequency of accidents through effective loss control efforts. Employers also can impact how claims are handled, which helps to mitigate the financial impact of claims.

- It assists insurers in their risk selection and underwriting process.

- It serves as a benchmark or criteria item for selecting contractors by project owners.

Who Oversees Experience Rating Programs?

Experience rating programs are administered by workers compensation rating bureaus. These rating bureaus oversee the experience rating plans and experience modification calculations.

The NCCI experience modification plan applies in 39 jurisdictions (38 states and the District of Columbia). Independent experience rating plans apply in eight states: California, Delaware, Michigan, Minnesota, New Jersey, New York, Pennsylvania, and Wisconsin (Note: Minnesota, New York, and Wisconsin permit combination with NCCI states for interstate experience rating; Indiana, Massachusetts and North Carolina have independent rating organizations that issue their own intrastate experience rating modifications, but participate in NCCI interstate experience rating). In monopolistic state fund states, the NCCI plan applies only to employers liability and on an advisory basis.

Experience Rating States Breakdown

A. JURISDICTION WHERE THE NCCI PLAN APPLIES		
STATE		
Alabama	Kentucky	Rhode Island
Alaska	Louisiana	South Carolina
Arizona	Maine	South Dakota
Arkansas	Maryland	Tennessee
Colorado	Massachusetts	Texas
Connecticut	Mississippi	Utah
District of Columbia	Missouri	Vermont
Florida	Montana	Virginia
Georgia	Nebraska	West Virginia
Hawaii	Nevada	
Idaho	New Hampshire	
Illinois	New Mexico	
Indiana	North Carolina	
Iowa	Oklahoma	
Kansas	Oregon	

B. JURISDICTION WHERE THE NCCI PLAN DOES NOT APPLY		
STATE		
California	Minnesota	Pennsylvania
Delaware	New Jersey	Wisconsin
Michigan	New York	

C. JURISDICTION WHERE THE NCCI PLAN APPLIES TO EMPLOYERS LIABILITY ONLY AND ON AN ADVISORY BASIS (MONOPOLISTIC FUND STATES)	
STATE	
North Dakota	Washington
Ohio	Wyoming

This discussion centers on the NCCI plan, which provides the framework for experience rating in most jurisdictions. It should be noted that even within those states subject to the NCCI's experience rating plan, there are exceptions applicable to specified variables in certain states. These are referred to as "state exceptions."

The experience rating process is quite similar in non-NCCI states. When addressing experience rating in such states the appropriate manuals should be consulted. These manuals are available at the respective state websites.

General Points

There are several general items to consider about experience rating:

- Experience rating is prospective in nature. While an experience modification calculation incorporates historical data, the modification developed adjusts current premiums.

- Experience rating can substantially affect the amount of workers compensation premium that a business must pay. It provides a direct correlation between claims history and premium.

- Experience modifications generally are developed on an annual basis and are effective for a period of twelve months. Policies issued for a period no longer than one year and sixteen days are treated as a one-year policy. Policies issued for longer terms will be divided into consecutive twelve-month units for experience rating purposes.

- Only one experience modification is applied to a risk at any one time. That experience modification applies to all operations of the risk. A risk is defined as all entities eligible for combination under the plan, regardless of whether one or more insurance policies are used to insure them.

- The expected losses used to develop experience modifications are based on expected loss rates applicable to all insureds for a specified rating classification. For example, the expected losses for a machine shop operating in Florida would be compared with the expected losses for all machine shops in Florida.

- The loss experience used in an experience rating calculation is typically valued eighteen months after the effective date of a policy and annually thereafter, for a total of ten valuations. Such valuations usually occur six months prior to the effective date of a policy, assuming a common anniversary date has been maintained.

- Schedule rating usually is permitted in addition to experience rating.

Eligibility

Experience rating is mandatory for all eligible insureds who meet certain premium eligibility requirements. Eligibility is determined by the amount of qualifying premium that an insured generates. States vary in their premium thresholds. The following table includes premium eligible requirements for selected states governed by the NCCI experience rating plan.

Subject Premium Eligibility Requirements

STATE	TOTAL PREMIUMS 2 YEARS OR LESS	AVERAGE ANNUAL PREMIUMS MORE THAN 2 YEARS
Alabama	$10,000	$5,000
Alaska	5,000	2,500
Arizona	6,000	3,000
Arkansas	8,000	4,000
Colorado	8,000	4,000
Connecticut	11,000	5,500
District of Columbia	7,000	3,500

STATE	TOTAL PREMIUMS 2 YEARS OR LESS	AVERAGE ANNUAL PREMIUMS MORE THAN 2 YEARS
Florida	10,000	5,000
Georgia	10,000	5,000
Hawaii	5,000	2,500
Idaho	6,000	3,000
Illinois	10,000	5,000
Indiana	5,000	2,500
Iowa	7,500	3,750
Kansas	6,000	3,000
Kentucky	10,000	5,000
Louisiana	10,000	5,000
Maine	9,000	4,500
Maryland	10,000	5,000
Massachusetts	11,000	5,500
Mississippi	9,000	4,500
Missouri	7,000	3,500
Montana	5,000	2,500
Nebraska	6,000	3,000
Nevada	6,000	3,000
New Hampshire	11,000	5,500
New Mexico	9,000	4,500
North Carolina	8,000	4,000
Oklahoma	10,000	5,000
Oregon	5,000	2,500
Rhode Island	10,000	5,000
South Carolina	9,000	4,500
South Dakota	7,500	3,750
Tennessee	9,000	4,500
Texas	10,000	5,000
Utah	7,000	3,500
Vermont	8,000	4,000
Virginia	7,000	3,500
West Virginia	9,000	4,500

Source: NCCI, Experience Rating Manual, 2003 Edition (as Amended)

An insured qualifies for experience rating in an individual state when it meets the premium eligibility requirement in the state in which it operates. This is called an "intrastate rating." An insured qualifies for a multi-state rating ("interstate rating") when it meets the premium eligibility requirement in any state and develops experience in one or more additional states where the NCCI plan applies or where an independent state rating plan allows for a combination of states for an interstate rating.

A unity experience modification factor (1.00) may be applied to an insured for different reasons: (1) it does not qualify for experience rating, (2) it does not have adequate payroll/claims data available (such as a new business) or such data does not meet specified requirements, or (3) data could not be provided due to an ownership change.

Businesses may not cancel, rewrite, or extend a workers compensation policy in an attempt to avoid experience rating, or qualify for or avoid a change in their experience modifications. In essence, an entity may not take any action to evade the application of an experience modification. These rules are directed towards eliminating abuses by insureds that choose to restructure themselves for the sole purpose of avoiding the application of a debit experience modification.

The Mod Factor

Under the NCCI plan, an experience modification factor (which often is referred to as the experience mod, Emod, EMR or mod) of less than 1.00 means that the firm will get a credit on its premium. A mod greater than 1.00 means that a debit will apply. A 1.00 mod is referred to as a unity modification.

For example, a mod of .75 indicates that the insured organization will pay 25 percent less in premium than the average firm in its industry because of its better-than-average loss experience. A modification of 1.25 means that the organization will be subject to a 25 percent increase in premium because of its poor loss experience.

To illustrate the premium impact on a general contractor, refer to the table below. This contractor has total payroll of $4.8 million. If it is subject to a .75 modification it will pay an annual premium of $233,990. If this same contractor is subject to a 1.25 experience modification its premium will be $387,927. This is a difference of $153,937. With a 2 percent profit margin this contractor must increase its revenue by over $7.5 million to make up the difference.

Code	Classification	Impact of .75 Experience Mod			Impact of 1.25 Experience Mod		
		Payroll	Rate	Premium	Payroll	Rate	Premium
5213	Concrete Construction	500,000	29.10	145,500	500,000	29.10	145,500
5221	Concrete floor/ driveway	600,000	13.39	80,340	600,000	13.39	80,340
5403	Carpentry	200,000	22.28	44,560	200,000	22.28	44,560
5606	Executive Supervisors	1,000,000	4.92	49,200	1,000,000	4.92	49,200
8810	Clerical	2,500,000	.38	9,500	2,500,000	.38	9,500
	Subtotal	4,800,000		329,100	4,800,000		329,100
	Experience modification		0.75	(82,275)		1.25	82,275
	Subtotal			246,825			411,375
	Premium discount		0.052	12,835		0.057	23,448
	Total			233,990			387,927

A mod is based on three years of an organization's loss history. The most current year is omitted from the calculation. To illustrate, assume that an insured's policy is effective January 1, 2015 and is subject to experience rating. Also assume that it purchased annual policies for the previous four years. The mod that is effective January 2015, is based on the premium and losses from policy years January 1, 2012-13, January 1, 2013-14, and January 1, 2014-15. Experience from the January 1, 2015-16 policy year is not used because the loss experience is "green" and is not mature.

While three years of experience normally is used, up to three and three-fourths years of experience can be used in certain situations. There also are situations in which a newly organized business may apply for experience rating after being in business for only two years.

Anniversary Rating Date

The normal anniversary rating date is the effective month and day when experience modification and rate changes take effect. The anniversary rating date usually corresponds to the policy inception date. However, it may differ if prior policy years were longer or shorter than twelve months in duration. (Note: This does not apply to policies insured as part of a wrap-up/consolidated insurance program.) Experience mods are usually effective for twelve months and cannot be used for longer than fifteen months.

An insured cannot cancel an existing workers compensation policy before its normal expiration date in order to take advantage of a decrease in compensation rates or experience modification. Even if the policy was canceled and rewritten midterm, the lower rates and experience modification would not apply to the new policy until the insured's normal anniversary rating date.

Example 1

Meridian Manufacturers has an experience modification that is effective April 1, 2015. It applies to a policy with an effective date of April 1, 2015 or to any policy with an effective date up to July 1, 2015. If Meridian decides to change its policy renewal date from April 1 to July 1, so that it coincides with its fiscal year, the April 1 anniversary rating date is used for the entire fifteen months. At the end of the fifteen months (July 1, 2016), a new experience modification applies and the normal anniversary rating date changes to July 1.

In addition, rates that were in effect for the policy on April 1 will apply until July 1, 2015.

Example 2

The experience modification of Grix Construction Company is effective from February 1, 2015-16. Its normal anniversary rating date is February 1. It wants to change the policy renewal date to July 1, 2016, so that premium payments coincide with its fiscal year. To accomplish this, Grix buys a new policy for the term of July 1, 2015-16 and cancels the February policy. The February 1, 2015 modification applies until February 1, 2016. A new modification applies from February 1, 2016 until July 1, 2017. The new normal anniversary rating date begins July 1, 2016, when a new modification and rates also apply.

The previous two examples apply for single-policy risks. Other rules apply if more than one policy with varying effective dates are involved.

Why is this important? Credit and debit modifications can greatly affect the amount of workers compensation premium that a business has to pay. The experience rating procedure is designed so that an insured cannot unfairly escape poor loss experience. It also promotes safe workplaces by offering a financial incentive to companies that prevent worker injuries and effectively manage claims.

Mod Worksheet Input Data

How is information about individual businesses gathered? The mod calculation starts with the filing of unit statistical reports by insurers to the appropriate rating bureau. The "unit stat" cards used by insurers and rating bureaus are standardized and contain various types of data: policy and insurer information, classification codes, audited payrolls and premium, and loss information. This information is gathered eighteen months after policy expiration and annually thereafter (usually six months before the effective date of the experience mod) and must be reported by the insurers to the appropriate rating bureau(s) within two months thereafter.

The payrolls set forth in the unit stat cards are the audited payrolls by classification for each workers compensation policy.

The loss information includes the gross incurred loss amounts for each individual claim. This includes both payments and loss reserves for indemnity and medical losses. Some expenses are not to be included in the loss amounts. These include medical and legal expenses incurred for the benefit of insurers, unallocated loss adjustment expenses (insurer employees' salaries, overhead, and traveling expenses and independent adjusters and attorneys for performing claims investigations). Allocated Loss Adjustment Expenses (ALAE) are treated as part of the loss amounts. These are specific expenses associated with a single claim. ALAE includes the following types of expenses:

- Attorneys' fees associated with insurer staff or outside firms.

- Court costs and alternative dispute resolution fees. This includes the costs of expert testimony, medical examinations, witnesses and summonses, copies of documents, arbitration/mediation, surveillance and appeals bonds.

- Medical cost containment expenses, whether performed by insurer staff or outside firms. This includes costs associated with bill auditing, utilization reviews, accessing provider networks and medical fee review panels.

There are some exceptions to gross loss reporting as set forth in the applicable statistical plan. These may include subrogation recoveries, fully fraudulent claims, and noncompensable claims.

As previously mentioned, the loss information is typically valued six months prior to the effective date of the modification. For instance, let's assume that Horner Hat Co. has a worker compensation policy that is effective 1-1-16 and this policy is subject to experience rating. The insurers providing coverage to Horner Hat for the three years beginning 1-1-12, 1-1-13 and 1-1-14, will supply the rating bureau with stat cards which have the audited payrolls and incurred losses valued as of 7-1-15. The rating bureau will then create an experience modification worksheet based on this data.

The NCCI rules and requirements for reporting statistical data are set forth in its Statistical Plan for Workers Compensation and Employers Liability Insurance. Each non-NCCI state will have their own statistical reporting plans and manual, usually published by applicable state rating or advisory bureau. Each of these plans/manuals has common components addressing the following:

- Scope – Applicability and effective date of plan

- General Rules – Rules/guidelines for reporting data

- Premium/Exposure/Loss Data – Rules/guidelines on reporting data elements

- Subsequent Reports/Corrections – Rules/guidelines on correcting data

- Pension Tables – Factors for calculating pension benefits payable to claimants/dependents

Historically, these reports were filed manually by insurers. Increasingly, submissions by insurers are electronic and tailored to the data fields required by rating organizations.

General familiarity with how data reporting works is important for agents, brokers and insureds.

Besides obtaining a general understanding of the terms and data used, timing is an important issue. For example, an employee hurt his back at work and the injury was deemed as compensable. In the first few months following the accident, the insurance company paid medical bills of $20,000 and lost wages of $8,500. It established reserves of $45,000 for medical and $52,000 for wage loss indemnity. The insurer believed the employee would be off work for at least a year. However, initial treatment was successful, and he returned to work much earlier than expected. It is important for the reserved amounts to be reduced to reflect this return to work before the unit statistical report is filed. As such, many agents, brokers and insureds perform a detailed claims review about two months before the stat cards are due. (More information on claims management is contained in Chapter 12.)

Making the Mod Calculation

Upon receiving the statistical data for an organization, the NCCI calculates and issues the workers compensation experience modification worksheet, which is effective on the normal anniversary rating date. The worksheet is usually issued about thirty to sixty days in advance of the normal anniversary date.

At times the issuance of a final modification may be delayed due to lack of data. In these cases a contingent or tentative modification may be used. Once the final mod is issued, it will be endorsed onto the workers compensation policy. The effective date of the new mod is governed by the rules of the applicable rating bureau and state insurance laws and regulations.

A sample experience rating worksheet for fictitious insured Happy Hotel Co. is located in Appendix B. This is the standard format which NCCI uses to produce its worksheets. Other rating bureaus use similar formats for their standard worksheets.

When a worksheet is received, elements such as payroll and actual incurred losses should be reviewed for accuracy. If payroll is understated or losses are overstated the mod will be higher than what it should be. Conversely, if payroll is overstated or claims are understated the mod will be artificially low. If errors are found a request for recalculation should be made.

The Mod Worksheet

It is beyond the scope of this book to go into intimate detail on the formulas and nuances associated with the mod calculation, so only a basic overview is presented. However, it is very important to understand the different terms and elements associated with the worksheet, and how they work together.

The experience mod worksheet is divided into two separate parts. The first page is the Summary Page. The second page (and such additional pages as required) is the Data Input Page. The Data Input Page is the starting point in the experience rating calculation process, so we will begin our review there.

The table below is a reproduction of the second page of the Happy Hotel Co. experience modification worksheet located in Appendix B, except arrows and numeric references have been added to bring attention to specific components in the worksheet. Each component will then be briefly discussed.

Data Input Page Table

WORKER'S COMPENSATION EXPERIENCE RATING

Risk Name: Happy Hotel Co.[1]   **Risk ID:** 123456789[4]

Rating Effective Date: 07/15/2015[2]   **Production Date:** 09/04/2015[3]   **State:** Florida[5]

Carrier: Any | **Policy No.** WC 2011 | **Effective Date:** 7/15/2011 | **Expiration Date:** 7/15/2012

Code [6]	ELR [7]	D-Ratio [8]	Payroll [9]	Expected Losses [10]	Exp Prim Losses [11]	Claim Data [16]	IJ [15]	OF [14]	Act Inc Losses [13]	Act Prim Losses [12]
8810	.10	.43	983,795	984	423	281937585 [17]	05	F	1,834	1,834
9052	1.57	.45	3,172,676	49,811	22,415	171953685	06	F	421	421
9058	1.11	.49	1,375,693	15,270	7,482	784942730	06	F	2,075	2,075
9807 ADDITIONAL PREMIUM				0	0	181672485	06	F	2,878	2,878
						NO. 10[18]	06	*	6,410	6,410
						041807485	09	F	34,024	15,500
						415021730	09	F	51,140	15,500

Policy Total: 5,532,164 | **Subject Premium:** 127,892 | **Total Act Inc. Losses:** 98,782

Carrier: Any   Policy No. WC 2012   Effective Date: 7/15/2012   Expiration Date: 7/15/2013

Code	ELR	D-Ratio	Payroll	Expected Losses	Exp Prim Losses	Claim Data	IJ	OF	Act Inc Losses	Act Prim Losses
8810	.10	.43	1,050,397	1,050	452	NO. 2	05	*	2,834	2,834
9052	1.57	.45	3,244,353	50,936	22,921	13201781	05	F	3,632	3,632
9058	1.11	.49	1,476,697	16,391	8,032	13201088	06	F	3,946	3,946
9807	ADDITIONAL PREMIUM			0	0	NO. 9	06	*	6,375	6,375
9841	DRUG FREE CREDIT			-3,419	-1,570					

Policy Total: 5,771,447   Subject Premium: 147,599   Total Act Inc. Losses: 16,787

Carrier: Any   Policy No. WC 2013   Effective Date: 7/15/2013   Expiration Date: 7/15/2014

Code	ELR	D-Ratio	Payroll	Expected Losses	Exp Prim Losses	Claim Data	IJ	OF	Act Inc Losses	Act Prim Losses
8810	.10	.43	1,050,397	1,050	452	NO. 2	05	*	2,834	2,834
9052	1.57	.45	3,244,353	50,936	22,921	13201781	05	F	3,632	3,632
9058	1.11	.49	1,476,697	16,391	8,032	13201088	06	F	3,946	3,946
9765	WORKPLACE SAFETY C			-01,281	-589					
9807	ADDITIONAL PREMIUM			0	0					
9841	DRUG FREE CREDIT									

Policy Total: 5,411,877   Subject Premium: 152,847   Total Act Inc. Losses: 90,862

[1] **Risk Name**: Named insured.

[2] **Rating Effective Date**: Effective date of the mod.

[3] **Production Date**: Date the worksheet was produced.

[4] **Risk ID**: Identification number assigned to the named insured.

[5] **State**: The state of operations; if multiple states "Interstate" will appear.

[6] **Code**: The classification code(s) appearing on the premium audit.

[7] **ELR**: Expected loss rate per $100 of payroll. Note these are different for each code. These rates are updated annually by the rating bureau.

[8] **D-Ratio**: This is the "discount ratio." It is the percent applied to expected losses to obtain expected primary losses. This factor is updated annually by the rating bureau.

[9] **Payroll**: Audited payroll for each classification code.

[10] **Expected losses**: Expected ultimate losses; Formula is (7) X [(9)/100)].

[11] **Expected Primary Losses**: The portion of expected losses that are used in full value in the mod formula; Formula is (8) X (10).

[12] **Actual Primary Losses**: The portion of actual incurred losses that are used at full value. In Florida, this is the first $15,500.

[13] **Actual Incurred Losses**: The gross incurred amount for each claim (payments and reserves).

[14] **OF**: "O" = claim is open; "C" = claim is closed.

[15] **IJ**: Codes for different types of injury.

[16] **Claim Data**: Lists the claim file number for each incurred claim over $2,000.

[17] **28193785**: Claim file number for this particular claim.

[18] **No. 10**: The number of individual claims below $2,000 (grouped together). In this case these are all "medical only" claims (injury code 6), that total $6,410.

The Data Input Page is fairly straight forward. The objective here is to calculate/display expected losses, expected primary losses, actual incurred losses and actual primary losses. These figures are then transferred to the Summary Page.

The Summary Page draws data from the Data Input Page, adds factors and follows the stated formula to arrive at the experience rating factor. This page has some new terms and factors.

(The following table is the first page from the Happy Hotel Co. experience modification worksheet located in Appendix B. Arrows and numeric references have been added to aid the discussion.)

Summary Page Table

WORKERS COMPENSATION EXPERIENCE RATING								
Risk Name: Happy Hotel Co. Risk ID: 123456789								
Rating Effective Date: 07/15/2012 Production Date: 03/02/2012 State: FLORIDA								
State	Wt.[1]	Exp Excess Losses[2]	Expected Losses[3]	Exp Prim Losses[4]	Act Exc Losses[12]	Ballast[11]	Act Inc Losses[10]	Act Prim Losses[9]
FL	.17	117,598	154,582	36,984	228,310	33,975	290,909	62,599
(A) Wt	(B)	(C) Exp Excess Losses (D – E)	(D) Expected Losses	(E) Exp Prim Losses	(F) Act Exc Losses (H – I)	(G) Ballast	(H) Act Inc Losses	(I) Act Prim Losses
.17		117,598	154,582	36,984	228,310	33,975	290,909	62,599

	Primary Losses	Stabilizing Value[5]		Ratable Excess[13]	Totals
Actual[6]	(I) 62,599	C * (1 – A) + G 131,581		(A) * (F) 38,813	(J) 232,993
Expected[7]	(E) 36,984	C * (1 – A) + G 131,581		(A) * (C) 19,992	(K) 188,557
	ARAP	**FLARAP**	**SARAP**	**MAARAP**	**Exp Mod**
Factors[8]		1.24			(J)/(K) 1.24 **[14]**
Rating reflects a decrease of 70% medical only primary and excess loss dollars where ERA is applied.[15]					

[1] **WT**: This is a weighting factor which is applied to Actual Excess Losses (12) and Expected Excess Losses (2). It is also part of the Stabilizing Value (5) and Ratable Excess (13) formulas. The percentage is based on

the amount of Expected Losses. As Expected Losses increase, so does the percentage.

[2] **Excess Losses**: This is Expected Losses (3) less Expected Primary Losses (4).

[3] **Expected Losses**: This is an input from the Data Input page.

[4] **Expected Primary Losses**: This is an input from the Data Input page.

[5] **Stabilizing Value**: This is a combination of a portion of the Expected Excess Losses (2) and the Ballast (11). This adds stability to the mod formula.

[6] **Actual**: This is the numerator line of the mod formula.

[7] **Expected**: This is the denominator line of the mod formula.

[8] **Factors**: These are factors applied to specified assigned risk programs. Most of these factors are applicable to assigned risk policies with debit modifications.

[9] **Actual Primary Losses**: This is an input from the Data Input page.

[10] **Actual Incurred Losses**: This is an input from the Data Input page.

[11] **Ballast**: This is part of the Stabilizing Value formula and is added to both the Actual and Expected line items. It limits the effect of any single loss. The ballast amount varies depending on Expected Losses (as Expected Losses increase so does the Ballast).

[12] **Actual Excess Losses**: Actual incurred losses (10) less actual primary losses (9).

[13] **Ratable Excess**: The portion of excess losses (both actual and expected) that are subject to the mod formula.

[14] **Experience Modification**: The "Actual" line sum divided by the "Expected" line sum. In this case the mod is .96. This insured will essentially pay 4 percent less for workers compensation insurance than its competitors.

[15] **Rating Reflects a Decrease of 70 percent Medical Only Primary and Excess Loss Dollars**: NCCI caps the value of medical-only claims (Injury Code "6") to 30 percent of the incurred amount.

As respects the NCCI experience rating plan, the Expected Loss Rates, Discount Ratios, Weighting Values, Ballast Values and Accident Limitations are contained in the "Table of Expected Loss Rates and Discount Ratios Applicable to All Policies." These values are updated annually for each state and will have a specific effective date.

The experience mod formula is set forth in Exhibit 2. A simpler way to summarize this is:

$$\frac{\text{Actual Primary Losses + Stabilizing Value + Ratable Actual Excess Losses}}{\text{Expected Primary Losses + Stabilizing Value + Ratable Expected Excess Losses}}$$

The numerator of the ratio above, which represents the Happy Hotel Co. experience, is divided by the denominator, which represents expected experience for the class (in this case, all hotels in Florida). The mod is rounded to two places. The mod for Happy Hotel is .96. The net result for Happy Hotel is that it will pay about 4 percent less for workers compensation premium than its competitors.

A few general points on experience rating are worthy of mention. These are:

- Each claim that goes into the mod calculation is divided into a primary and excess portion. Actual Primary Losses reflect an insured's claim frequency. The maximum primary value for each loss used in the calculation varies by state. In the case of Happy Hotel Co.'s mod, the maximum value is $15,500. Thus, if Happy Hotel Co. has two losses—one valued at $84, 262 and one valued at $4,172—the actual primary losses used are $19,672. This represents $15,500 of the first claim and all of the $4,172 claim. This captures the frequency of losses, regardless of severity. Actual excess losses are total losses minus actual primary losses. In both cases, incurred losses (paid and reserve amounts) are used.

- The NCCI caps the value of medical-only claims—in which there is no lost work time—at 30 percent of the actual primary and excess portions of the individual claim. Therefore, a medical-only claim valued at $20,000 would contribute only $4,650 ($15,500 × 30%) to the actual primary losses and $1,350 to actual excess losses ($4,500 × 30%). The impact of medical only claims has clearly been reduced by this limitation.

- Actual excess losses are weighted so that only a portion are used in determining both actual and expected excess losses.

- Experience rating focuses more on the frequency of losses than on the severity. The Ballast value helps to achieve this goal. It increases as expected losses increase to offset the effect of a single large loss.

- The losses that go into the calculation are subject to limits that are set by the NCCI. There is a maximum amount that may be included for: 1) an accident involving one person; or 2) an accident involving two or more individuals. The maximum values vary by state, but an example would be a per claim limit for one person of $106,500 and a multiple claim accident limit of $213,000. Depending on the state, there may be additional limitations applicable to employers liability, L&HWCA or occupational disease claims.

- NCCI maintains a maximum debit modification formula. The formula places a maximum cap on experience mods. About 2 percent of insureds are subject to this cap.

Applying the Mod

Experience mods apply to the premium that an organization develops by using an insurer's rates in force on the effective date of the mod. In most states, the following portions of premium are *not* subject to experience modification:

- Loss constants

- Expense constants

- Policy minimum premium

- Premium under the National Defense Projects Rating Plan

- Seat surcharge for aircraft operation

- Premium under atomic energy classifications

- Large deductible credits (credit portion)

- Coal mine disease charges for risks subject to the Federal Coal Mine Health and Safety Act

- Premium developed under three-year fixed rate policies

- Nonratable elements of manual rates

- Assigned risk surcharges

- Debits and credits under schedule rating

- Premium discounts based on premium size

- Terrorism Risk Insurance Act (TRIA)- certified losses

- Catastrophe (other than TRIA)

- Miscellaneous state surcharges and assessments

The mod does apply to the other areas of premium. Once the modified premium is calculated, it is adjusted for other credits, debits, surcharges, premium discounts, and expense constants, etc.

The definitive source for what elements the experience modification is applied to in a given state is the premium algorithm. The algorithm is most commonly found in the workers compensation manuals published by rating bureaus. NCCI includes rating algorithms in its Basic Manual For Workers Compensation and Employers Liability Insurance. The NCCI algorithm applicable to Illinois is located in Appendix B.

Recalculation and Revisions

A classification of a business may be revised if a mistake has been made or for other reasons established by the appropriate rating organization. When this happens, the experience modification is recalculated, with past payrolls reassigned to the correct classification. This could result in either a higher or lower mod, depending on the relative rate of the new classification compare to the rate of the old classification.

There are times where the reported payroll must be revised. Corrections are generally required to be done within three years of the expiration of the affected policy. NCCI allows revision to the current and up to two preceding experience rating modifications. However, this period may be amended by state insurance laws or regulations (see Chapter 9 for additional information).

When losses are retroactively revised, the mod will also be revised. However, the recalculation as a result of changes in losses is generally only done for one of three reasons: clerical error, payment recovery, or no payment made. Modifications cannot be retroactively changed simply because reserves were set too high when they were initially calculated.

When a recalculation results in a lower mod, the change is made retroactively to the policy inception date or anniversary rating date (if different than the policy effective date). The application of a higher recalculated mod varies depending on how long a policy has been in effect or the length of time since the anniversary rating date.

If an increase occurs during the first ninety days of a policy period, it is applied retroactively to the inception date. After the first ninety days, the increase is applied on a pro-rata basis from the date the insurer endorses the policy with the new modification. If the increase is recalculated within the first ninety days after the anniversary rating date (if different from inception date) it applies retroactively to the anniversary rating date. If recalculated more than ninety days after the anniversary rating date, the mod is applied on a pro-rata basis from the endorsement date.

However, a higher recalculated mod is applied retroactively to inception date if the recalculation is caused by:

- the employer failing to comply with audits or because of other faults caused by an agent or employer, including modification avoidance;

- retroactive reclassification of a risk;

- termination of an insured's employee leasing arrangement under a master policy;

- change in ownership or combinability status; or

- Appeals Board or judicial decision.

One Risk or Two?

Company mergers and acquisitions present special situations for experience rating. After a merger, the acquired business's historical loss experience usually is transferred to the acquiring owner and excluded from the experience of the prior owner.

For example, Fabulous Footware purchases Trendy Dry Cleaners, a five-year-old company that has a modification of 1.50 because of poor claims experience. Fabulous Footware has had good loss experience and is benefiting from a modification of .75. Trendy's experience is reassigned to Fabulous. The combination of Fabulous's good experience and Trendy's poor experience results in a new modification of 1.05. The revised modification must be applied to all of Fabulous's operations, even though the types of operations differ from one another.

If Fabulous were not experience rated before the acquisition, an experience modification would be calculated using all of both company's experience. Fabulous now would have a modification that would apply to both operations.

But what if Fabulous doesn't want to be penalized for Trendy's losses? Can Fabulous keep Trendy a separate operation and thereby avoid a combined modification?

The NCCI experience rating plan, as well as those of other jurisdictions, in most instances require that only one modification be used for all operations of a risk. A risk is defined as either a single entity or two or more entities which qualify for combination under the plan. Two or more entities are to be combined only if:

1.   the same person, group of persons, or corporation owns more than 50 percent of each entity; or

2.   an entity owns a majority interest in another entity, which in turn owns a major interest in another entity. In this case, all the entities are combinable regardless of how many there are.

Therefore, if the owners of Fabulous, or the corporation itself, own more than 51 percent of Trendy, only one modification is used. Majority ownership is based on a majority of issued voting stock, a majority of the owners, partners or members if no voting stock is issued, a majority of the governing board participation of each general partner in the profits of a partnership or ownership interest held by an entity as fiduciary. Limited partnerships are not considered when determining majority interest.

Changes of ownership also may result from:

•   sale or transfer of all or a portion or an entity's ownership interests;

•   sale or transfer of an entity's physical assets to another firm that takes over the business;

•   formation of a new entity after an existing entity is dissolved; or

•   voluntary or court-mandated establishment of a trustee or receiver.

In these cases, the experience of the prior business usually transfers to the surviving or new business. However, the prior business's loss experience may not be transferred to the new owner if the rating organization confirms all the following: 1) there is a completely new owner; 2) there is a change in operation that results in a reclassification of the governing code; and 3) the material change in ownership includes a change in the process and hazard of the operation.

When ownership changes, the insurance company reports the details of the change to the appropriate rating organization. The information may be submitted in narrative form on the insured's letterhead and signed by an officer of the company. Or, the information may be reported by using a form entitled the Confidential Request for Information (ERM-14). Often an insurer will request a completed ERM-14 form from an insured when there is a question of whether entities should be combined for experience purposes. A copy of this form is reproduced in Appendix B.

Recent Development—Rating Split Point Change

NCCI recently changed its nationwide experience rating plan. This change relates to the "split point" used. Split point is the dollar value that splits a loss into two components: the primary and excess portions. Recall earlier in this chapter that the first $5,000 of each loss is considered as primary, with the remainder being excess.

NCCI changed the split point because the $5,000 amount previously used was too small to be effective. NCCI contends that the average cost of a claim in 1988 was $2,527. The average cost in 2011 rose to $8,887. The result was that experience rating has become less responsive. (The $5,000 split point was not changed for over twenty years.)

In its Circular CIF-2011-14 and subsequent filings, NCCI proposed changing the split point amount as follows:

- $10,000 for the first year (2013)

- $13,500 for the second year (2014)

- $15,500 for the third year (2015)

- Indexed for claim cost inflation for the third year and future years (Note: Most NCCI states will use $16,000 for 2016

But how does this change impact insureds? What can they expect? According to NCCI, the change results in the following:

- At the state level, this is "revenue neutral" (the increased mods for some insureds will offset the decreased mods for others).

- Those employers with credit mods experience larger credits.

- Employers with debit mods experience higher debits.

- The average experience mod across all employers is unchanged.

NCCI in the following table projects the changes in mod distribution for the first year (Note: A change in mod from 1.10 to 1.20 would be a change of 10 points).

Change in Mod Points	Organizations (%)
11 or more	7.0%
+5 to +10	6.5%
+2 to +5	4.3%
–2 to +2	35.8%
–2 to –5	38.3%
–5 to –10	8.1%
–10 or more	0.0%

In addition to the change in the split point, NCCI changed the maximum debit modification formula. The modification, which is advertised as negligible on an overall state level, impacts 2.7% of insureds, as opposed to 1.9% under the current formula.

The effective dates of the filings in the various states are set forth in the table below.

NCCI Filing #-1402 – Revisions to the Experience Rating Plan Primary/Excess Split Point Value and Maximum Debit Modification Formula Filing Status

State	NCCI	Non-NCCI	Mono-polistic	"Split Point" Filing Effective Date	Approved	Notes
AL	x			March 1, 2013	x	
AK	x			January 1, 2013	x	
AZ	x			January 1, 2013	x	
AR	x			July 1, 2013	x	
CA		x				
CO	X			January 1, 2013	x	
CT	x			January 1, 2013	x	
DC	x			November 1, 2013	x	

State	NCCI	Non-NCCI	Mono-polistic	"Split Point" Filing Effective Date	Approved	Notes
DE		x				
FL	x			January 1, 2013	x	
GA	X			March 1, 2013	x	
HI	X			January 1, 2013	x	
ID	x			January 1, 2013	x	
IL				January 1, 2013	x	
IN		x		January 1, 2013	x	Independent bureau that uses NCCI for ratemaking and most rules.
IA	X			January 1, 2013	x	
KS	X			January 1, 2013	x	
KY	X			October 1, 2013	x	
LA	X			May 1, 2013	x	
ME	X			January 1, 2013	x	
MD	x			January 1, 2013	x	
MA		X		TBD		Independent rating bureau that follows NCCI.
MI	x			January 1, 2013	x	
MN		x				
MS	X			March 1, 2013	x	
MO	X			January 1, 2013	x	4-year implementation with $7,500 first year split point.
MT	X			July 1, 2013	x	
NE	X			February 1, 2013	x	
NV	X			March 1, 2013	x	
NH	x			January 1, 2013	x	
NJ		x				
NM	x			January 1, 2013	x	
NY		X		October 1, 2013	X	Approved first year $10,000 split point, other years TBD.
NC		x		April 1, 2013	x	Independent rating bureau that follows NCCI.

State	NCCI	Non-NCCI	Mono-polistic	"Split Point" Filing Effective Date	Approved	Notes
ND			X			Monopolistic state
OH			x			Monopolistic state
OK	x			January 1, 2013	x	
OR	X			January 1, 2013	x	
PA		x				
RI	X			June 1, 2013	x	
SC	X			July 1, 2013	x	
SD	x			July 1, 2013	x	
TN	x			March 1, 2013	x	
TX	X			July 1, 2015	X	See Texas Commissioner's Order 3708
UT	X			December 1, 2013	x	
VT	X			April 1, 2013	x	
VA	X			April 1, 2013	x	
WA			x			Monopolistic state
WV	X			November 1, 2013	x	
WI		X		October 1, 2013		Follows NCCI
WY			x			Monopolistic state

Schedule Rating

Schedule rating is sometimes confused with experience rating. Perhaps this is because both rating mechanisms focus on the risk characteristics of an individual organization. Because of misunderstandings between the two different forms of rating, schedule rating is discussed here.

As noted previously, schedule rating may be used in addition to experience rating. The NCCI and other rating bureaus administer the schedule rating plans. This discussion focuses on the NCCI model.

Schedule rating credits or debits are applied after the experience modification, but before the premium discount and loss constant. The maximum credit or debit is 50 percent. The goal of schedule rating is to reflect characteristics of a particular organization that are not reflected in experience rating. NCCI rules require that schedule rating be applied to filed and approved rates without deviations. Deviations are discounts that are filed by insurers and applied to rates before the premium is calculated.

Schedule credits or debits are assigned for specific reasons. These are listed below, along with some examples of each.

- *Premises/work environment*. Drug-free workplace, controlled hazards, good housekeeping, industrial hygiene, ergonomic designs and administrative controls.

- *Classification peculiarities*. Caused by technology, employee distribution or assignment.

- *Medical facilities*. On-premises first aid, emergency plans, return-to-work programs and managed care.

- *Safety devices and equipment*. Guarding, personal protection, inspection, maintenance and training.

- *Employees*. Selection, training, experience, motivation, supervision and controls.

- *Management cooperation*. Commitment to safety and loss control, cooperation with insurer and rating bureau.

- *Management safety organization*. Employee involvement, accident investigation/analysis and active safety committee.

Insurers report the total dollar amount of schedule credits and debits they apply annually to the NCCI. Schedule credits and debits that are applied to an organization must be backed up by evidence contained in the insurer's underwriting documentation. If an insured corrects a situation that led to a debit to the insurer's rating, it may be removed effective with the date that correction documentation was received by the insurer.

Thus, in addition to the effect of an experience modification, an insured's workers compensation premium may be subject to a 50 percent increase or decrease based on schedule rating. This is very important to employers that have operations in states where schedule rating is allowed.

Summary

Experience rating embodies a simple goal within a complex process. It is designed to encourage safe working conditions by providing a financial incentive to reduce worker injuries. Organizations that succeed with this reap a financial reward through a lower than average experience modification. Businesses that fail to do so are penalized with a higher than average modification. Experience rating directly affects an organization's competitive economic stance.

As noted in the previous chapter on premium, the rates that are used for workers compensation coverage often are fairly consistent across classifications. However, businesses can directly control their premiums by preventing and managing claims to earn a lower experience mod. In addition, they can institute safety and employee training programs that enable them to qualify for schedule rating, another source of potentially lower premiums.

The opposite also is true. Both experience and schedule rating penalize businesses that fail to institute programs to prevent and manage claims. These businesses are forced to pay higher premiums for coverage that is mandated by law.

Chapter 11

Financial Plans

Introduction

Workers compensation programs are priced very differently depending upon the plan structure. Nonetheless, no matter what type of plan is involved, the costs can be segregated between "fixed" and "variable". Fixed costs remain constant unless the payroll (or other rating basis) changes. These are the costs that will be incurred regardless of loss experience. For instance, under a guaranteed cost program, the entire premium is fixed. Variable costs are inherent to loss sensitive programs. These costs vary depending on the amount of sustained losses. Examples of variable costs are claims amounts and claims handling charges. Claims handling charges are usually a percentage of the claims or a set fee per claim.

Both fixed and variable costs must be considered when choosing a financial plan. By segregating costs into these two elements, it will be easier to understand and compare the ultimate costs of different plans.

When evaluating the costs of financial plans the insurance industry uses many different terms, which at times can be confusing. It may be helpful to review the Other Rating Factors section in Chapter 9. This sets forth the meanings of different premium/cost related components and terms. In this chapter different types of premiums are referenced, including the following:

Manual Premium. Estimated payroll multiplied by applicable rates.

Subject Premium. This is Manual Premium adjusted to include additional cost elements, such as waivers of subrogation and voluntary compensation coverages, employer's liability increased limits and credits for small deductibles. This type of premium is commonly referenced in retrospective rating plans.

Modified Premium. This is Subject Premium multiplied by the applicable experience rating modification.

Standard Premium. This is Modified Premium adjusted to include additional rating components, such as contracting class premium adjustment programs, disease and radiation exposures, non-ratable catastrophe loadings and aircraft seat surcharges.

Final Premium. This is Standard Premium adjusted to include other factors, such as premium discount, coal mine disease charges, expense constant, terrorism, and catastrophe charges.

As reinforced many times throughout this book, these definitions and rating elements may differ by state or by insurer. When in doubt, consult the state approved rating algorithm and applicable rating plan agreements, or discuss with the insurer.

There are two forms of financial plans: guaranteed cost and loss sensitive.

Guaranteed cost plans charge a premium that is fixed, regardless of the loss experience incurred. Naturally, the premium is adjusted based on an audit of the actual payroll for the policy year. The entire risk of workers compensation losses is transferred to the insurer. However, if an insured is subject to experience rating, its claims experience will impact future modifiers.

Loss sensitive plans are those where the final cost is not known at the inception of the insurance policy. The ultimate cost is largely predicated on the dollar amount of claims arising from insured accidents happening within the policy year. The timing of the premium adjustment(s) and other terms of the loss sensitive plan are usually spelled out in rating agreements that are acknowledged and entered into by both parties.

The far extreme from guaranteed cost workers compensation is self-insurance. With a self-insurance plan, an entity self-assumes the financial consequences of claims. Some self-insured entities elect to purchase excess insurance, which is often referred to as "stop loss" insurance. This can apply to individual claims and/or all claims during a specified period (usually annually). Most states require that self-insurers become approved and post collateral (usually a surety bond or letter of credit) to secure their financial obligations. The approval process can be arduous at times.

In a self-insured program, the fixed costs are much lower than with a guaranteed cost program. These include the premium for stop loss coverage, assessments, and cost of collateral, taxes and service fees. These may be as low as 15 percent of the standard premium. The remaining costs are associated with claims, both adjusting and payment. The ultimate cost of a self-insured program can be very different than initially anticipated due to the financial impact of claims.

Market conditions, account size, and claims history affect the type of financial plans available to insureds. When the market is soft, a greater variety of financial plans may be offered, even when an insured's loss history is poor. When the market hardens, however, fewer options are offered and loss history may have a greater impact on the type of financial plan available. In addition, smaller organizations may not be eligible for certain financial plans; they may only be eligible for a fully insured, or guaranteed cost, program.

Between the two extremes of guaranteed cost and self-insurance are a number of other methods of financing the workers compensation exposure. This chapter examines these in terms of the level of risk transfer, cash flow, fixed costs, ultimate costs and collateral required.

Types of Financial Plans

The types of financial plans that will be discussed are:

- guaranteed cost;

- dividend;

- incurred and paid loss retrospective rating; and

- large deductibles.

Self-insurance and captive plans will not be discussed because these are individually designed and beyond the scope of this book.

The form at the end of this chapter highlights some of the major differences among seven types of financial plans.

Many workers compensation experts use premium size guidelines when deciding what type of financial plan a business should seek. Very small businesses with workers compensation premiums of $25,000 or less may not be offered alternatives other than a guaranteed cost or dividend plan. Since there is no down side to a dividend plan for an insured, it is attractive to small businesses. Adverse market conditions may cause insurers to refrain from offering dividend plans to all but the best insureds, however, so businesses may be forced to purchase a guaranteed cost program.

NCCI regulations permit insurers to offer incurred loss retrospective plans to organizations with premiums of $25,000 or more. Individual insurers may have different eligibility criteria. Since there is a risk of paying more with a retro plan, businesses need to be sure they understand and can financially assume that risk. Most organizations do not voluntarily consider retro plans if their premiums are less than $100,000.

As businesses grow in size and sophistication, the types of financial plans they are offered also become more diverse and complex. Larger businesses should be sure that they have adequate safety and claims management systems and procedures in place before choosing a plan that imposes substantial financial risk. Financial stability also is considered by insurers before offering a workers compensation plan that has attractive cash flow.

Some professionals use a premium of $500,000 to $1,000,000 as the viable threshold for a business that desires to self-insure, depending on the state(s) involved. This is only a rule of thumb, but it is wise to remember that a certain premium size is necessary to support the management programs that are required with self-insurance and to also satisfy state eligibility requirements.

Both the qualitative and quantitative aspects of a program should be considered when choosing a plan. Qualitatively, an organization may desire a specific financial program because it affords a desired level of autonomy or a greater opportunity to influence claims adjusting. An insurer is more likely to customize claims handling processes and activities for an insured that is retaining more risk. The quantitative aspects are the expected costs for any given financial plan.

The way in which worker injuries are managed can greatly impact both current and future workers compensation costs. Because of this, close attention must be paid to cost and program management when trying to understand and select an appropriate workers compensation program.

The various types of plans differ greatly in the relative level of risk transfer, fixed costs, cash flow, collateral required, autonomy of the insured and administration effort required by the insured.

As illustrated in the table below, guaranteed cost programs generally include the most insurance risk transfers and least risk. Cash flow management is low or non-existent. At the other end of the spectrum is self-insurance, which features the least insurance, best cash flow management and lowest fixed costs. In exchange for these advantages, a self-insured organization has the most risk, highest collateral requirement and intense program administration. So the decision on the most appropriate plan for an insured will depend on multiple factors.

Attributes of Financing Plan Alternatives

Plan Alternatives	Plan Attributes					
	Risk Transfer	Fixed Costs	Cash Flow	Collateral Required	Autonomy of Insured	Administration by Insured
Guaranteed cost	High	High	Low	None	Low	Low
Dividend	High	High	Low	None/low	Low	Low
Incurred loss retro/large deductible	Varies	Low	Moderate	High	High	High
Paid loss retro/ large deductible	Varies	Lower	Higher	High	High	High
Self-insurance	Low	Lowest	Highest	Highest	Highest	Highest

Guaranteed Cost Plans

A workers compensation policy with a fixed or guaranteed cost premium is the most conservative and the easiest to understand. Such programs are the most stable in terms of cost. An organization that chooses a guaranteed cost plan knows the ultimate cost at policy inception because the policy premium is the cost. The premium varies only as a result of changes in the payroll or experience modifier. It does not vary directly as the result of loss experience and cannot be increased retrospectively.

The guaranteed cost premium is the "final premium" (see definitions stated earlier). This includes the application of an experience modification, if an organization qualifies for experience rating. (Premiums and related calculations are discussed in Chapter 9. Experience rating is discussed in Chapter 10).

Guaranteed cost programs should not necessarily be thought of as the highest cost or the least desirable. In many states guaranteed cost programs may be eligible for significant premium credits or discounts. These reductions to premium may include:

- certified risk management programs;

- certified workers compensation healthcare network;

- coinsurance;

- contracting programs (various program titles);

- deductible programs;

- designated medical provider;

- drug/Alcohol free workplace;

- managed care arrangements;

- merit rating;

- safety programs; and

- schedule rating.

While guaranteed cost plans can be highly desirable to an insured organization, these are not for everybody. If an organization desires more autonomy, an alternative plan may be more appropriate.

Dividend Plans

Dividend plans are designed to reward an insured if claims are less than anticipated. The prospect of a potential dividend acts as an incentive for an organization to prevent and manage worker injuries. The dividend may be based on the loss experience of a particular group to which the insured belongs or of the individual insured. With group dividend plans, the claims experience of the entire group is compiled. If the insurer has made a profit on the group, a dividend may be declared. In like fashion, individual dividends are determined based on the amount of losses the individual organization incurs.

Dividends are never guaranteed. They are payable only upon declaration of an insurer's board of directors. If declared, these are paid at various intervals after the policy expires, sometimes in a lump sum and sometimes in a series of payments. Dividends usually are not computed earlier than six months after a policy expires. The details on how and when a dividend is payable is usually provided to an insured as part of the original proposal or by an endorsement in the policy.

Dividend plans usually come in three varieties: fixed, sliding scale and retention.

Fixed Plans

A fixed or flat dividend, if declared, is usually payable six to twelve months after a policy expires. These are most often used with affinity or group insurance programs. Affinity programs are designed around a type of business. For example, a trade group of manufacturers, grocery stores, schools, or other business type may develop a workers compensation group program that is open to association members. Since the group represents a large amount of premium, insurers may be willing to offer a dividend plan to its members. Even though an insured receives the benefit of a possible dividend, it will not have to pay additional premium—aside from additional premium that may be developed with changes in payroll or experience modification. An exception exists for assessable insurance policies issued by a mutual insurance company or reciprocal.

Dividend plans work because insureds are rewarded when the insurer makes an underwriting profit on a homogeneous group of organizations. Since the insured does not risk having to pay more premium in the event of adverse losses, the potential return is lower than with individual loss-sensitive plans. There is a trade-off between risk and potential benefit.

For example, an association of manufacturers may go to one insurer to purchase workers compensation insurance. Individual group members are underwritten separately, and the amount of premium for each is reviewed as a whole to provide the insurer with an incentive to write the coverage. Individual workers compensation policies are issued to each group member, and each pays its own premium. After the policies expire, the claims experience of all members is combined to determine whether an underwriting profit was made. If so, the insurer may declare a dividend. However, if claims costs are higher than a predetermined expected amount, a dividend will not apply.

Group or affinity programs often are used when coverage is difficult to obtain, especially when the premium of individual group members is relatively low. An insurer may not be interested in insuring a small individual manufacturer that generates only $15,000 of premium. However, if a number of manufacturers solicit coverage as a group, the combined premium often is large enough to interest insurers. Insurers are often able to develop customized industry-specific safety and claims management programs. This improves risk awareness and often results in better overall loss experience.

There are times when an insurer will offer a dividend to an entire group that is computed based on the experience of the group as a whole, as well as individual dividends to members that are computed on the experience of the member. In these types of programs, a group member is eligible to receive two dividends.

Insurers will sometimes offer fixed dividends to individual insureds that are unrelated to any group. This is simply a pricing tool used by insurers to attract insureds. These are most common in states that do not allow merit rating or schedule rating credits.

Sliding Scale Plans

The next type of dividend plan is tied directly to the underwriting results of individual insureds. Instead of relying on group experience, an individual organization stands on its own claims experience for purposes of dividend calculation. These are called sliding scale dividend plans. These plans contain a "scale" or schedule that set forth a range of incurred loss ratios (incurred losses divided by audited premium). There is also a corresponding schedule of dividends (also expressed as a percentage of audited premium). Like fixed dividends, the amounts must be approved each year by the insurer's board of directors.

To illustrate such a dividend program, let's assume that Spring Products, Inc. has a workers compensation policy that is subject to the sliding scale dividend schedule below. The audited premium for January 1, 2015-16 is $100,000; the incurred losses are $30,000. Therefore, the incurred loss ratio is 30 percent. Consulting the dividend schedule below, Spring Products is entitled to a 25 percent dividend ($25,000).

Spring Products, Inc. Sliding Dividend Schedule

Incurred Loss Ratio Range	Dividend Percentage
0-10%	35%
11-20%	30%
21-30%	25%
31-40%	20%
41-50%	15%
51-59%	5%
60+%	0%

Sliding scale dividend plans are usually written for one year. Losses are valued at a predetermined date, such as at six months after policy expiration. If the loss ratio is less than a predetermined percentage, a dividend may be paid. The amount of the dividend "slides" with the loss ratio, subject to a maximum possible dividend. For example, the greatest dividend that Spring Products, Inc. could achieve is 35 percent of the audited premium ($35,000).

Retention Plans

Some dividend plans are based on mathematical formulas, as opposed to ranges of combined loss ratios. Some insurers use simple formulas. One such formula is:

Dividend = Audited premium – retention percentage

With this plan ("Retention Plan #1"), the insurer determined the percentage of premium it needed to cover all its expenses and profit was 34 percent, leaving 66 percent of the premium to pay losses. The unused premium amount becomes a dividend for the insured. In the case of Spring Products, it would have received a dividend of $31,000 under this plan [($100,000 – $34,000) – $35,000].

Other retention plans have more complicated formulas. Under one such plan the insurer expected a loss ratio of 65 percent. It determined that it would return to the insured 50 percent of the savings for loss ratios less than 65 percent, not to exceed 30 percent. We will refer to this as Retention Plan #2. Its formula:

Dividend = 50% × (65% – actual loss ratio) × audited premium

In the case of the previous scenario for Spring Products, the dividend would be 21 percent or $17,500 [50% × (65% – 30%) × $100,000].

Taking our analysis a step further, let's compare the three different dividend plans at various loss levels. Based on the table below, Retention Plan #1 is the most cost effective plan at all loss levels. Absent service considerations, if an insured were evaluating the three plans, they would select Retention Plan #1.

Comparison of Dividends: Sliding Scale and Retention Plans

Incurred Losses	Sliding Scale Dividend Plan	Retention Plan # 1	Retention Plan # 2
$5,000	$35,000	$61,000	$30,000
$15,000	$30,000	$51,000	$25,000
$25,000	$25,000	$41,000	$20,000
$35,000	$20,000	$31,000	$15,000
$45,000	$15,000	$21,000	$10,000
$55,000	$5,000	$11,000	$5,000
$65,000	$0	$1,000	$0

Sliding scale and retention plans may contain nuances regarding how these operate. Some plans have annual adjustments for up to three years, instead of one year. Some insurers have "claw back" provisions, whereby they can recover dividends previously paid, if losses deteriorate. Others apply loss conversion and/or loss development factors to incurred losses. However, there are too many of these nuances to cover here.

These plans are popular because insureds can benefit from better than expected losses, without the threat of additional premium if losses are worse than expected. These plans are not often available to insureds with poor or fluctuating loss histories because no risk, and only an opportunity to gain, is transferred to the insured.

There are scores of these types of plans in use by insurers. Since the terms of the plans differ, it is wise to obtain a complete description of how the plan operates before committing to a program.

Retrospective Rating Plans

Retrospective rating rewards organizations that have favorable losses and penalizes those with above average losses. The premium for expired policies is adjusted annually as claims develop and mature. Workers compensation claims often have long "tails". An accident may occur during the policy term and remain open for several years—until the worker is completely healed and back to work or is placed in some type of permanent disability program. Claims experience, both good and bad, affects the ultimate cost of these plans.

Under a retrospectively rated plan, an insured is affected by losses in two ways. First, its retrospective policy premium is adjusted upward or downward based on claims experience for that policy year. Second, its future experience modifier is impacted positively or negatively, depending on how actual loss experience compares with expected losses. This double benefit or penalty occurs because experience rating is used in conjunction with retro rating. However, the impact of the experience modifier is less with a retro policy than with a guaranteed cost policy. The effect of the modifier is largely limited to the fixed cost portion of the premium and specified program rating parameters. The modifier does not directly affect the variable costs.

There are two basic types of retro plans:

1. Incurred loss

2. Paid loss

There are numerous hybrid combinations of plans. However, only these two types are discussed in this book. The information on incurred loss retro rating is based on the National Council on Compensation Insurance (NCCI) retro rating system. States that do not follow the NCCI issue their own retro plan rules and regulations. However, for practical purposes, the NCCI program provides a general context that may be applied to non-NCCI states. In addition, the discussion will focus on the NCCI one-year incurred loss retro plan, even though three-year and multiple lines plans also are available.

A retro plan utilizes a simple concept. An insured pays an agreed upon premium during the policy term. The premium is used by the insurer to issue the policy, operate the program, and pay for claims and adjusting. Six months after policy expiration, claims are reviewed. If the program operating costs (fixed) and claims costs (variable) are lower than the amount paid in, the insured receives a retrospective return premium (credit). If the costs are higher than the amount paid, the insured is billed a retrospective additional premium. Retro plans are evaluated six months after the end of the policy period (eighteen months from policy inception) and in twelve-month intervals thereafter. For an annual policy, the evaluation dates would be eighteen, thirty, forty-two, fifty-four months, etc., after policy inception. The initial adjustment may occur after or in conjunction with the premium audit adjustment.

With an incurred loss plan, both paid and reserved claims are included when the retro premium is calculated. Up to a pre-designated level, the insured is responsible for its own claims. This can lead to improved loss prevention and claims management, which usually translates into lower overall costs. Insureds often seek an incurred loss plan because it offers an opportunity to substantially lower the ultimate premium (when claims experience is favorable).

Conversely, insurers may be willing to offer only a retro plan to insureds with poor claims experience for the same reason: the insured ultimately is charged for its losses. The possible gain of a lower premium is balanced against the risk that claims will be adverse, which would result in a higher premium. For example, various state assigned risk plans impose mandatory incurred retro rated plans for larger insureds.

Organizations qualify for a one-year retrospective rating plan if their estimated modified standard premium is at least $25,000. Even though a minimum $25,000 of modified standard premium is the NCCI threshold, not many insureds or insurers would be interested in such plans at that level. Also, if a retro plan includes other commercial liability lines of insurance, the appropriate ISO or other applicable retro rating manual should be consulted.

Retrospective Rating Formula

The retrospective rating premium formula, without elective elements, is as follows:

Retrospective Premium = [Basic Premium +

(Losses × Loss Conversion Factor)] × Tax Multiplier

The retro premium is subject to minimum and maximum premiums.

The basic factor (BF) is the percentage of standard premium that is needed to issue the policy and operate the program. It includes insurer administrative costs, producer commission, loss control service costs, insurance charges and profit. This factor does not include premium taxes or claims adjustment expenses, as these costs are charged separately. The basic factor usually ranges from 15-35 percent of standard premium, depending upon the amount of standard premium, the amount of insurance being provided and other factors in the plan. The basic factor multiplied by the standard premium develops the basic premium.

The loss conversion factor (LCF) is a percentage that represents the insurer's cost to adjust claims. It usually ranges from 8-15 percent of losses. At times, adjusting costs are represented by a flat dollar amount per type of claim instead of a percentage. For purposes of this discussion, a percentage LCF is used. The LCF is added to the total value of claims, which are referred to as converted losses. The LCF reflects general claims adjusting costs. Unusual adjusting costs, such as special surveillance and expert witness testimony, are allocated to specific claims. These are called allocated loss adjusting expenses (ALAE). ALAE can be treated differently in the retro formula and is a subject of negotiation between insurer and insured. It can be part of incurred losses, in which case the LCF is adjusted to exclude ALAE. The alternative is for ALAE to be added to the converted losses.

The tax multiplier (TM) is the average cost of licenses, taxes, fees, and assessments that insurers must remit to individual states. In general, tax multipliers fall in the range of 4-6 percent of retro plan premium.

Retrospective premiums are limited by minimum and maximum premiums. The retro premium can never fall below the minimum premium, regardless of how favorable the loss experience is. This is because the insurer must be able to recover its program costs. The maximum premium ensures that the risk is not subject to unlimited losses. The insured may choose to buy coverage that limits individual losses in addition to the overall program cost. This is called purchasing a loss limitation or loss limit.

Retro plans are not eligible for insurer premium discounts. This is because premium discounts are used to lower the expense portion of the guaranteed cost premium. Since retro plan operating expenses are covered by the basic premium, operating costs are, in theory, already minimized.

The basic premium and loss conversion factors, as well as the minimum and maximum premiums, are established through negotiation between the insured and insurer. A change in the minimum premium, maximum premium and LCF retro variables impact the basic premium. The following table illustrates these relationships.

Impact of Retro Factors on Basic Premium

Plan Factor	Impact on Basic Premium
Minimum Premium	
Increase	Decrease
Decrease	Increase
Maximum Premium	
Increase	Decrease
Decrease	Increase
Loss Conversion Factor	
Increase	Decrease
Decrease	Increase

Regardless of the retro factors agreed upon, it is important to monitor the financial implications of a retro plan through the entire time it remains open.

Excess Loss Premium

An insured may elect to purchase excess loss coverage (loss limitation). Excess loss coverage limits the amount of loss that will be included in the retro premium calculation.

Excess loss coverage stabilizes retro plans by dampening the effect of large losses. For example, three employees are seriously injured in an industrial accident. The total cost of all three injuries exceeds $1 million. If a $100,000 per accident loss limit (including ALAE expenses) were purchased, only the first $100,000 of all claims arising from the one accident would be included in the retro adjustment. If a $100,000 per claim loss limit was chosen, the first $100,000 cost of each claim, or $300,000, would be included in losses used in the retro adjustment.

Losses above the loss limitation are not subject to retrospective rating. The excess loss premium does not fluctuate with losses. It is simply a separate premium included in the retrospective premium formula. The workers compensation retrospective rating endorsement, which is attached to the policy, designates the subject and non-subject premiums separately.

How a Retro Works

The following illustrates how a retro plan works by discussing four policies, all of which are written on one-year retrospective plans. Each of the policies has:

- modified standard premium of $100,000;

- maximum premium of $140,000; and

- minimum premium of $70,000.

Figure 1 illustrates how the first adjustment of each policy, made at six months after expiration, generates different results for each policy.

Figure 1

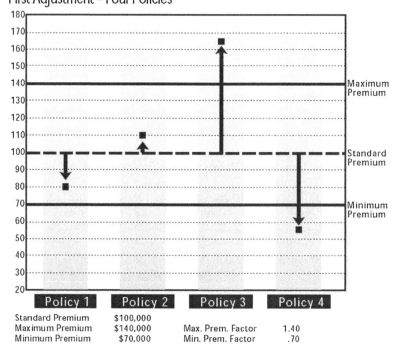

In these policies, the entire modified standard premium of $100,000 was paid to the insurance company during the policy term. Thus, retro adjustments were made on the basis of a premium pay-in of $100,000.

As discussed previously, workers compensation claims often take a significant amount of time to mature and develop to maximum potential. Over a period of years a claim may increase or decrease in value as the worker undergoes continuing treatment or returns to work. Consequently, the losses that are used in subsequent retro calculations may differ significantly from those used for the first adjustment.

As shown in Figure 1, the first adjustment for Policy 1 resulted in a retro premium of $80,000. Therefore, $20,000 was returned to the insured. The first adjustment for Policy 2 produced a retro premium of $110,000, so the insured was billed $10,000 additional premium. Policy 3 generated a premium of $166,000 at the first adjustment because of several large claims. Since the program includes a maximum premium of $140,000, the insured was billed only $40,000. Policy 4 would generate a return premium of $45,000 if there was no program minimum premium. Lower than expected claims produced a retrospectively adjusted premium of only $55,000. However, the insured only received a return premium of $30,000, because $70,000 is the minimum premium.

However, the premium for each of these policies is adjusted annually using updated losses. To illustrate this, refer to Figure 2, which charts the first four retro adjustments that are issued at intervals of eighteen, thirty, forty-two, and fifty-four months after policy inception.

Figure 2

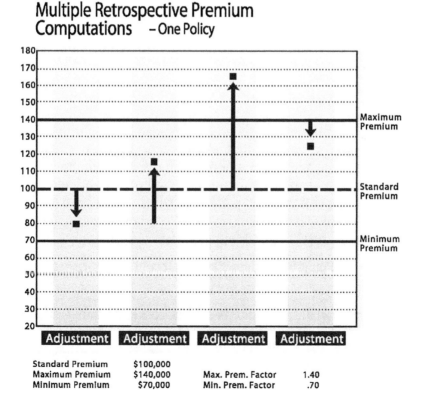

Policy 1 generated a $20,000 return premium at the first adjustment. At the end of thirty months (second adjustment), the retro premium was recalculated at $115,000 because several claims deteriorated. The insured is not only required to pay the difference between the standard premium ($100,000) and the retro premium ($115,000), but it also must repay the $20,000 return it received at the first adjustment. Thus, the premium billing at thirty months is for $35,000. At the end of forty-two months, claims continue to deteriorate, and the retro premium increases to $165,000. However, the insured is only billed $25,000 because the $165,000 exceeds the maximum $140,000 premium. The fourth computation produces a retro premium of $125,000, because several claims were resolved at costs lower than anticipated. The insured therefore is returned $15,000 ($125,000 less $140,000 paid to date).

These adjustments continue until all claims are closed or the insured and insurer mutually agree to close the plan. It is not unusual for retro programs to remain open for five or more adjustments.

Optional Retro Premium Components

The basic retrospective premium formula discussed previously does not include two optional elements that may be added separately to a retro plan. They are excess loss premiums (ELP) and retrospective development factors (RDF).

As discussed previously, the excess loss premium is a charge if the insured elects a loss limitation. To calculate this, an ELP factor is applied to standard premium and the loss conversion factor. Many retro plans include the ELP as part of the basic premium, so a separate charge for ELP may not appear in retro calculations.

The purpose of the retrospective development premium is to smooth out some of the fluctuations that often occur between the first and subsequent retro adjustments; it stabilizes the retro premium over time. This reduces the likelihood that the insured will receive a large premium return at the first calculation, which likely will have to be repaid to the insurer at subsequent calculations. The premium is calculated by applying a RDP factor to the standard premium and LCF.

If both the ELP and RDF elements are elected the retrospective rating formula is:

Retro Premium = [Basic Premium + Excess Loss Premium + Retrospective Rating Development Premium + (Losses × LCF) × Tax Multiplier

As mentioned previously some insurers incorporate the ELP into the basic premium.

Audit vs. Retro Calculation

The terms "premium audit" and "premium calculation and adjustment" often are confused, but they are decidedly different calculations. The premium audit is calculated apart from the retro premium computation and adjustment, because these numbers are needed in order to calculate the modified standard premium. Recall that the initial premium used at the inception of the policy is merely an estimate. This is the amount paid to the insurer before or during the policy term. The actual modified standard premium is determined at the premium audit. If the payroll is more than estimated, an additional premium is charged; if less than estimated, a refund is made. This audited modified standard premium then is used as the pay-in amount for the first retro adjustment. While the calculations are technically separate, in practice, some insurers perform the calculations at the same time.

Retro Policy Cancellation

If an insured goes out of business, a one-year retro plan is cancelled as follows:

1.   The modified standard premium is calculated on a pro rata basis.

2.   The retrospective premium then is calculated using the pro rata modified standard premium.

The minimum and maximum premium factors are applied to the pro rata modified standard premium. If the minimum and maximum factors were .50 and 1.50 respectively, they would be multiplied against the modified standard premium to develop the dollar amount of the minimum and maximum premiums on the pro rata cancellation.

However, insureds who cancel a retro plan for reasons other than going out of business are penalized to discourage them from exiting a retro plan that is not going well. The process in this case is:

1.   The premium for the policy is calculated on a short-rate basis.

2.   The retrospective premium is calculated using the short-rate premium.

The short-rate is calculated by taking the partial premium for the period the plan was in effect, extending it for a full year, and then multiplying the result times the short-rate factor. The short-rate premium is used as the minimum premium. In addition, the annualized standard premium, rather than the short-rate premium, is used as the basis for computing the maximum premium. This serves as an additional deterrent to canceling the policy under adverse loss conditions.

Retrospective Rating Forms

Insureds usually sign an election form indicating that they are aware of selecting a retro rating plan. An election form typically contains the following:

- Name of insured

- Date plan takes effect; formula factors (basic premium, minimum premium, maximum premium, loss conversion factor, tax multiplier, and retrospective development factor if applicable)

- Loss limitations and excess loss premium factor if applicable

- Signature of insured

- Date election form signed

- Policies covered under the plan

Retrospective rating is included in a policy by attaching a retrospective endorsement. (These endorsements are described in Chapter 6.)

Incurred Loss vs. Paid Loss Plans

The main difference between incurred loss and paid loss plans is the type of claims included in the calculations. With an incurred plan, incurred losses are utilized in determining the retro premium. With a paid loss plan, paid losses are utilized. The major benefit of a paid loss plan for an insured is improved cash flow.

With a paid loss plan, the insured pays the insurer a deposit premium and establishes a claims fund at the beginning of the year. The deposit premium is similar to the basic premium in an incurred loss plan; it is designed to cover insurer expenses and profit. The claims fund is established so that the insurer can pay claims as those come due. The insured is required to replenish the claims fund as the insurance company uses it to pay claims (usually monthly or quarterly). Since the insured has the benefit of holding onto its funds longer, the insurer requires collateral.

Collateral is required as a financial guarantee that future claims will be funded. The collateral often is in the form of a letter of credit or cash escrow account. Surety bonds were once prevalent as a form of collateral with retros, but bonds are less common because surety bond companies restricted availability.

The amount of collateral is usually updated annually by the insurer. In theory, the amount of collateral should decline as claims mature and eventually close out.

Large Deductible Plans

In most states, insureds are able to utilize smaller deductibles to retain greater risk and obtain premium credits. Deductibles may apply to medical payments, indemnity payments or both. With few exceptions, the range of deductibles is between $100 to $25,000, with most states allowing an upper limit of $5,000 or less. The NCCI Benefits Deductible Endorsement, WC 00 06 03, (described in Chapter 6) is utilized in many states to specify the amounts, terms and conditions of the selected deductible.

While these "small deductible" programs are beneficial, particularly to small and medium size organizations, a significant need developed in the late 1980's and early 1990's for alternative programs. Larger organizations cried out for higher deductible plans that would be simple to administer and reduce costs. Cost reductions were achievable though significant reductions of residual market charges and premium taxes.

Insurers responded by developing programs that met the needs of industry. Individual states for the most part did not stand in the way of these new alternatives. State regulators understood that the ultimate payment of benefits and medical expenses to injured workers was not based on the financial security of individual insureds, but rather on the financial security of the insurer. This is because the insurer is responsible for the payment of deductible claims and then seeks reimbursement from the insured. This is in contrast to self-insurance, where the self-insurer assumes the financial obligation of making certain workers are compensated for their injuries and medical expenses are paid.

This is not to say that state regulators are not involved in large deductible plans. Many states specify requirements such as minimum premiums and deductibles and to what the deductibles may apply. The requirements vary more than one would anticipate, but insurers are very aware of the requirements and structure their programs accordingly.

It is safe to say that since the mid-1990's large deductible programs have become increasingly popular, at the expense of retro and self-insurance programs. The large deductible programs are much easier to administer and are very flexible.

Many insurers now actively market large deductible plans to their new customers and existing policyholders. The deductible usually ranges from $100,000 to $1,000,000 per accident. Aggregate coverage for losses falling within the deductible layer is routinely available.

The implementation of a large deductible plan is similar to the paid loss retrospective rating plan discussed previously. The insured pays a deductible premium and arranges for an escrow account with funds adequate to pay the deductible portion of expected claims for a sixty to ninety-day period. Additionally, the insured is billed every month for actual payments (or incurred amounts if an "incurred" deductible plan applies) that fall within the deductible layer. The amount of collateral required is based on estimated losses and the insured's financial condition.

As with a paid loss retro plan, the initial pay-in of a deductible plan is substantially less than the full estimated standard premium.

Advantages of a large deductible program include the following:

- Superior cash flow.

- Greater flexibility and ease of use compared to retro plans or self-insurance.

- Avoidance of regulatory restrictions associated with self-insured plans.

- Possible reduction of fixed costs and taxes.

- Immediate benefit from favorable loss experience.

- Availability of insurer claims and safety services.

- In some cases, the insured retains investment income associated with cash collateral and escrow funds.

There also are negative features to large deductible plans. These include:

- Potential higher costs if loss experience is adverse.

- Letters of credit may be difficult to obtain or expensive for highly leveraged companies.

- Additional administration associated with complying with claims handling regulations.

- May be difficult to change insurers due to collateral considerations.

Deductible Program Design Considerations

In designing a deductible program, the following should be considered:

Paid vs. Incurred Approach. Similar to retros, these programs can be structured to apply on a paid or incurred basis. The paid basis will have better cash flow, but higher collateral. The incurred basis will involve higher payments on the front end.

Deductible Form and Amounts. Deductibles can be tailored to also include ALAE, in part or in whole. The actual amounts of the deductibles (per accident and aggregate) must be decided upon.

Tailored Services. Loss prevention, claims management protocols and managed care services must be agreed upon. These are usually provided by the excess insurer, but can be unbundled under certain situations.

Claims Escrow Fund. This is the amount that is kept on hand at a bank for the insurer to pay claims from. Insurers usually require two-three months of expected losses on hand.

Collateral Form and Amount. Most insurers deal exclusively with letters of credit. Others are more creative and allow alternate forms of collateral. There is significant variability of how a collateral amount is determined amongst insurers. The amount, and how it is periodically adjusted, is a very important consideration.

Deductible Program Documents

The insurer and insured organization enter into contracts that outline the responsibilities of the parties and how the agreed upon program works. These may include documents with many different titles, such as Deductible Agreement; Deductible Reimbursement Agreement; Reimbursement, Indemnification and Security Agreement; Indemnity Agreement; Finance Agreement; Claim Fund Agreement; and Aggregate Loss Cost Agreement.

These agreements will generally cover the following items:

- Responsibilities of the parties

- Program description

- Program structure

- Defined terms

- Payment terms

- Loss fund

- Collateral

- Services

- Program termination.

These agreements are not standardized. Each insurer uses their own forms and differences do exist between insurers. Those considering large deductible programs are advised to obtain appropriate counsel when evaluating the applicable agreements.

Collateral Issues

The amount of collateral required by an insurer and how it is adjusted is a mystery to many. And yet it is a very important item to those that have paid loss retros, large deductibles and self-insurance programs.

Financing plans that allow an insured organization to hold insurance premiums that would otherwise be paid to the insurer are known as "cash flow plans". Cash flow plans allow the insured to retain the loss portion of the insurance premium amount. The remaining fixed costs portion funds insurer expenses and related costs.

Claims paid by the insurer are drawn from an escrow account (bank account) initially funded by and then replenished periodically (usually monthly) by the organization. This loss fund holds only a small amount of the total loss dollars that will ultimately be required to satisfy all claim obligations.

Under retros and large deductible plans, the insurer is essentially assuming the credit risk of its insured. To guarantee that the insured will continue to replenish the loss fund, and to secure total expected ultimate loss amounts, the insurer requires that, at the program's inception, the organization provide them with collateral (usually a letter of credit). The collateral remains in place until all claims have been paid and closed (or as otherwise set forth by the rating plan documents). The amount of collateral grows with each additional year of a loss sensitive program. This is because the financial obligations grow in concert with unpaid claims.

Things become murky when an insurer tries to quantify those obligations. Should the collateral amount be based on the aggregate deductible amount, expected ultimate losses, first year losses or what? There is no one approach that is accepted by insurers or regulators.

Many insureds believe they are powerless when it comes to establishing and adjusting collateral with insurers. But that does not need to be the case. Through proactive involvement the insured can have a meaningful voice in the process.

Initial Calculation

In setting the amount and terms of the initial collateral the insurer considers the following factors:

- The insured's creditworthiness.

- Five years of historical loss experience and ratable exposures.

- Calculation of expected losses (at given retention levels).

It is important to note here that the insured and its insurance broker can influence the amount of collateral that the insurer will require, by providing appropriate information and addressing some key factors. These are set forth below.

Financials

- Provide the most recent audited and interim financials.

- Provide a brief overview of the trends and expectations.

- Provide plenty of time for the insurer to become familiar with the credit profile.

Loss Information

- Provide accurate up-to-date historical loss experience. If needed, provide longer than the normal five-year requirement.

- Provide explanations of any large losses, especially if these are considered to be "one time" events and not to be repeated.

- It is very helpful for the insured's insurance broker to independently calculate the expected losses as a check on the calculations of the insurer.

Rating Plan Documents

- Become familiar with how collateral is treated and adjusted. With a new program, collateral builds for five to seven years.

- The language of these agreements is typically one-sided (in favor of the insurer) and is not usually negotiable. However, some insurers will make modifications if there is a good reason to do so.

Initial Insurer Calculation

When an insurer has all the necessary information it needs, it will calculate the expected losses at a given retention level. The insurer reviews rating exposures and loss data for at least five years. It takes the incurred claims amounts and applies loss development factors (to account for incurred but not reported claims and the development of known claims) and trend factors (to account for inflation). These are compared with trended rating exposures to arrive at an "expected loss rate." This rate is applied to the projected exposure (payroll) to arrive at expected ultimate losses. The insurer will then determine the collateral needed. The range is usually between (a) ultimate expected losses and (b) ultimate expected losses less expected payments at eighteen months after program inception.

Various aspects of the calculations sometimes cause controversy:

- What losses did the insurer use when conducting its analysis?

- Why did the insurer use the loss development factors it did? (These factors vary considerably between insurers.)

- What percentage of ultimate claims does the insurer require to be collateralized? 100 percent of expected losses? Expected ultimate losses less actual paid losses at policy expiration? Or what?

Ongoing Management

Collateral amounts are evaluated by insurers on an annual basis and adjusted accordingly. This review is done as part of the renewal process. There is an opportunity for the insured's management to review and request an adjustment to the amount of collateral required, if warranted.

The process for recalculating collateral is very similar to the process used in the initial calculation of the collateral. Recently valued historical loss information will continue to be required with an increasing emphasis on the loss information developing from the year or years subject to the cash flow plan. The claims that make up this loss information should be reviewed carefully well before that data is made part of the renewal process. Claims that have the potential to impact the amount of current and future collateral should have a clear plan for closure. Re-evaluation of the credit profile is also undertaken.

As before, both the insured and the broker can be influential in negotiating the collateral amount.

The recommended steps are:

1. The insured, broker and insurer claims adjusters should meet periodically to review large claims and determine a strategy leading to closure for each.

2. Ninety days prior to renewal, the broker should prepare a report for the insurer that:

    *   shows the results of the most recent claims review;

    *   summarizes the loss experience in a clear, meaningful way;

    *   includes projections for ultimate losses for each policy year; and

    *   includes a projection of a reasonable collateral amount.

3. Provide up-to-date financial information, expanding beforehand in those areas where the insurer may have questions.

4. Prepare a short summary of business and financial expectations.

5. Provide all of the above to the insurer no later than forty-five days before the program renewal date.

6. Meet with the insurer to present specific concerns and desired outcomes, and supply answers to any questions the insurer may have.

Chapter 12

Cost Management Issues

Introduction

Workers compensation is much more than an insurance policy. It is a system that balances on the premise that injured workers will be taken care of regardless of fault. In exchange, workers give up the right to sue their employers for these injuries. With few exceptions, states require most employers to either carry workers compensation insurance or become qualified workers compensation self-insurers. Until 2013, Texas was the only state to allow employers to decline to carry coverage (referred to as "nonsubscribers"). Oklahoma passes legislation effective February 1, 2014, to allow qualified employers to become nonsubscribers. Other states permit exceptions for very small organizations or specific types of organizations.

Workers compensation costs directly affect the bottom line of all American businesses. Controlling this bottom line cost gives employers a financial incentive to prevent worker injuries from happening and to manage those that do.

Financial incentives obviously are not the only reason for promoting a well-run workers compensation program. No amount of insurance will ever pay for the cost of lost worker productivity and experience that is incurred when an employee is injured on the job. No amount of insurance will ever adequately compensate a family for the loss or permanent disability of a father or mother.

However, financial incentives do present a measurable reason to maintain safe workplaces. The system financially rewards those organizations that are able to prevent accidents or decrease the severity of claims with lower premiums. The system penalizes those that fail to do so.

The rewards and penalties can be great. In Chapter 10 we illustrated the difference in premium for a contractor with a .75 modification vs. a 1.25 modification. With a 1.25 mod the contractor would be paying 66 percent more for its workers compensation premium compared to if it were subject to a .75 mod. As premiums grow, the financial incentives become more prominent.

Much of the historical effort with claims management focused on the indemnity (lost time) part of the claim; that made sense as that was the largest claims component. However, the medical costs portion now exceeds the indemnity part. According to NCCI lost time claims statistics for accident year 2010, the indemnity part was $21,900 and the medical portion was $26,900. In fact, the medical part has exceeded the indemnity portion for all accident years beginning with 2002 and the gap is widening as time goes on. As medical inflation continues seemingly unabated, some project that the medical costs will amount to two-thirds of all claims costs by 2019.

This chapter focuses on concepts and programs that encourage employers, their managers, and their employees to aggressively manage workers compensation claims. The critical element in all of them is a commitment by senior management. Absence of this commitment may not doom the programs to failure, but it certainly makes them less likely to succeed.

This chapter does not attempt to address workplace safety engineering; that subject is well beyond the scope of this guide. It does, however, present ideas on how claims can be managed so that workers recover and return to work as quickly as possible.

Managing Overall Costs

Many insured organizations blame insurers, claims adjusters or the "workers compensation system" for losses and high insurance costs. But the reality is that organizations can do a lot to shape their own destiny and control costs.

Some things that they are able to do, which are all discussed in greater depth later in this chapter, are:

- Have rigorous procedures in place to notify promptly the insurer of accidents and claims. Early notification provides a significant payback in reducing costs.

- Collaborate with the insurer and jointly craft claims handling instructions. These instructions set forth the responsibilities of the parties and ensure uniformity of handling.

- Maintain a formal return-to-work program. Studies are uniform in their conclusions: return- to-work programs reduce costs for the employer and foster better health and peace of mind for the injured worker.

- Fully understand the managed care services provided by the insurer and the costs for these services.

- Remain cognizant of the impact that ADA and FMLA may have on the handling and disposition of workers compensation claims.

- Maintain a safety incentive program in an effort to change employee behavior and attitude towards safety.

- Implement a cost allocation system that assigns costs to individual operating units based on their contribution to the cost of risk of the organization.

Above all, the insured organization must have an active role in the claims management process from beginning to end. If it truly wants to control its costs, it does not have the luxury of abrogating its responsibilities to insurers or their vendors. Involvement and communication are paramount.

Timely Notice of Accident

The time period between an accident occurring and reporting the injury to an insurer or TPA is called "lag time". Studies have concluded that the longer the lag time, the greater the claims costs and frequency of litigation. One of the earliest studies on lag time was released by Kemper Insurance in 1994.[1] This study showed a direct correlation between delays in reporting claims and ultimate claims costs.

In 2000, Hartford Insurance completed a lag time study involving over 53,000 permanent partial and temporary total claims occurring between 1996 and 1999.[2] The study measured the average cost of total loss payment segregated by when claims were originally reported. The results were eye opening. Claims reported in the second week following injury cost 18 percent more than claims reported in the first week. Claims reported in the third and fourth weeks cost on average 30 percent more than claims reported in the first week. Claims reported thereafter resulted in 45 percent greater settlement amounts. For accidents resulting in back injuries, the average cost of claims reported after the first week was 35 percent greater compared to those reported in the first week.

Late reporting also impacts the likelihood and costs of litigation. According to one expert, 22 percent of claims reported within ten days are litigated, compared to 47 percent when reporting occurs thirty-one days and later following injury.[3] According to one insurer, delaying notification of a claim by just three days increases the chances of attorney involvement by 50 percent.[4]

Why are the benefits of prompt claims reporting so dramatic? Some of the reasons include:

- early medical intervention results in more effective treatment;

- return to work can be considered and planned for;

- injured workers feel better and recover more quickly;

- reduced costs: medical, legal, administrative and lost time.

A best practice for organizations of all sizes is to report at least 65 percent of claims within twenty-four hours of injury and 90 percent of all claims within seventy-two hours. This one simple step can produce costs savings for employers and healthier workers. With a multitude of reporting methods used by insurers (fax, internet, call centers and nurse intake calls), there is no excuse for late reporting by employers.

Claims Handling Instructions

It is important for employers and insurers to be on the same page as to how workers compensation claims will be handled. Often insurers and their insureds reduce these handling procedures to writing in a claims handling instructions document. These instructions create common expectations and service consistency. The instructions can be very simple or elaborate depending on needs. Such instructions will often address the following areas:

Designated Adjusters. Many employers want specific adjusters assigned or designated to handle all the claims arising from their operations. They feel that by getting to know the employer's philosophies better, return to work opportunities, etc., claims handling quality increases.

Three Point Contact within Twenty-four Hours. The claims adjuster makes contact with the injured employee, employer and treating physician within twenty-four hours after receiving a notice of injury. Early intervention promotes employee health and recovery. This procedure also promotes information flow between the parties.

Investigation. A thorough investigation of the circumstances surrounding an accident is very important. Not all injuries are compensable under state workers compensation laws. The claim adjuster should determine compensability early on in the claims handling process. Subrogation potential against negligent third parties is also evaluated.

Action Plans. The adjuster is the quarterback for determining the strategies to be employed in bringing a claim to ultimate resolution. This means having an action plan for each claim.

Medical Management. This involves the effective use of medical providers and use of managed care techniques. The treatment plan must be known and reviewed. Especially with lost time cases, nurse case managers are often employed to direct the medical care for an injured employee.

Disability Management. The key to disability management is to return an injured employee back to work and to accommodate physical restrictions. The claims adjuster must be knowledgeable about light/modified duty opportunities with the employer.

Litigation Management. This involves when, how and what legal counsel will be engaged in claims that are litigated. Sometimes these instructions will identify specific law firms to be used.

Reporting. Some employers like to know when claims are reserved at higher levels or when larger claims may be settled. Dollar thresholds are established as a means to trigger communication between the adjusters and the insured.

Claims Review Meetings. Particularly with loss sensitive programs, insured organizations often find it beneficial to meet periodically with the adjusters either telephonically or face-to-face to review claims.

Loss Runs. Employers often desire loss runs on a monthly or quarterly basis, depending on how many claims they normally experience. Larger organization will also want to come to an understanding with the insurer on how the loss runs will be organized (by entity, state, location, etc.) and delivered (hard copy, digital, web portal, etc.).

The scope of the claims service instructions will have a lot to do with the size and sophistication of the insured organization. With small organizations having guaranteed cost policies, the activity may consist of obtaining an understanding from the insurer of how claims will be handled. With large, sophisticated organizations possessing loss sensitive rating plans, the instructions will be more elaborate. No matter what size the organization, communication is the key to success.

Return to Work Programs

Return-to-work programs (also called RTW, modified work, transitional duty or light-duty) are designed to return employees to the job as soon as possible—even with physical restrictions. For example, an assembly line worker may be able to perform all the tasks making up his normal job, with the exception of lifting items weighing more than ten pounds. A light-duty program could modify the job so that another worker lifted heavier items, or the affected employee could be placed in another area where lifting is not required.

Statistics on the likelihood of returning to work after being off work for a set amount of time are sobering. The longer a disabled employee is off work the lesser the chance of the employee returning to work. According to the July 2004 edition of *The Risk Report*, the chances of an employee ever being able to return to their pre-injury job is:

• After four weeks of disability	90 percent
• After eight weeks of disability	75 percent
• After twelve weeks of disability	50 percent
• After six months of disability	20 percent
• After one year of disability	2 percent

There is considerable evidence that supports the creation and use of RTW programs. Studies overwhelmingly conclude that such programs benefit both employers and employees alike. Some of the benefits for employers are:

- Reduced costs (both direct and indirect)

- Reduced administrative work

- Improved employee retention

- Increased productivity and organizational performance

- Better employee relations

- Employees also receive benefits:

- Job security

- Income continuity

- Maintenance of employee benefits and seniority

- Reduced stress

- Better health and satisfaction, shortened recovery time

- Heightened self-esteem and morale

The steps in creating a return to work program will vary between organizations, depending on many factors, including the organization's culture, management support and attitudes, availability of alternate jobs, regulatory requirements, etc. Organizations must create a plan that is customized to their needs and any external requirements. However, most RTW plans include four core components. These are: (1) assessing job tasks, (2) identifying alternate duty jobs, (3) educating health care providers, and (4) making offers to employees.

When returning employees to modified work, employers need to exercise care that the job truly falls within the confines of any physical restrictions placed on the employee by the treating physician. One way to do this is to write specific job descriptions for each position—regular and light-duty—so that physicians have a clear picture of the physical demands of the work. The physical demands of each job must be known, such as lifting, standing, reaching, environmental conditions, etc. Another way is to videotape individuals performing specific jobs and to submit the tapes to the physician so it can be determined whether the restricted employee can accomplish each task. Once the physician determines and communicates the medical restrictions applicable to the injured employee, the employer can review various jobs that are open, or can be created or modified, that comply with the restrictions.

RTW programs are important because injured workers are more likely to successfully return to regular employment if they are not off work for extended periods of time. This is particularly important when experienced, skilled employees are injured. Employers need to monitor the physical restrictions, however, so that employees can be moved progressively through various work-hardening positions.

Managed Care Services

As mentioned earlier, the medical cost component of workers compensation costs has exceeded the indemnity portion since 2002. As a result, medical cost containment has received a lot of attention from insurers and insureds alike. Compared to health insurers, workers compensation insurers were slower to establish cost containment mechanisms.

Managed care services are provided by insurers directly as part of their claims services or through contracted vendors (collectively referred to as "insurer" in this chapter). These services can be segregated into two areas: (1) bill review and (2) specialized services addressing utilization and case management.

Bill Review

The goal of the medical review process is to identify variances between the medical bills (including pharmacy and medical equipment) received and the costs that should actually be charged. When bills are received by the insurer these are typically scanned and digitized. The bills are run through specialized billing software that identifies variances between the charges made and scheduled fees (in a scheduled fee state), usual and customary fees, and negotiated fees under HMO, PPO or other contracts. This software also isolates improper billing practices, such as upcoding, unbundling and unrelated services. Some bills, such as from out-of-network providers, must be further reviewed by staff and repriced as appropriate.

For complex bills, coding specialists perform in-depth reviews for modifier inaccuracies (there are specialized codes for each procedure performed by medical providers and health care institutions). Nurses may also review questionable billing practices and documentation.

Insurers keep very detailed records about the savings they achieve for each function or service provided. Examples of these categories include "fee schedule savings" (charges by medical providers are higher than allowed by state fee schedules or usual and customary amounts), "exclusion savings" (the service is not covered under applicable workers compensation laws), "duplicate bill savings" (elimination of duplicate bills), "foreign HMO/PPO savings" (savings achieved with out-of-network HMOs/PPOs), "medical review unit savings" (repricing and negotiation), or "denied or negotiated savings" (amounts denied or negotiated further).

Medical Case Management

The goals of medical case management are twofold: (1) to achieve the best ultimate medical outcome for the injured worker and (2) reduce costs for the employer. Case management can include a variety of customized services, including the following:

Action Plans. Nurse case managers assess the needs of injured workers and work with health care providers to review possible treatments and implement a medical plan. The case managers are usually well versed with return-to-work opportunities.

Utilization Review. This addresses the necessity of medical treatments and appropriateness of procedures; this review includes pre-certification, during treatment and extended services.

Physician Review. This involves the review of a physician by a peer (usually board certified in the same specialty).

Independent Medical Exams. With some cases it is appropriate for an injured worker to undergo separate testing and obtain second opinions from health care professionals. This may be particularly appropriate once the employee has reached maximum medical improvement and a determination must then be made as to any remaining permanent partial disability.

Cost of Managed Care Services

Insured organizations utilizing loss-sensitive plans need to question insurers on the scope of the managed care services contemplated and how the insurer will charge for these services. All too often the charges are buried in the fine print of proposals or not disclosed at all.

Most insurers charge a percentage of "savings" associated with medical bill review and network discounts (HMO, PPO, medical provider network, health care network, managed pharmacy programs, medical equipment programs, etc.). The charges often appear in insurer billings as part of "allocated loss adjustment expenses" (ALAE). The percentage that is charged can vary widely between insurers, but is usually 20-30 percent of savings.

Some insurers take a hybrid approach to charging for these services. They may make a flat charge for each medical bill that is reviewed and charge a percentage of network savings. This approach almost always ends up saving money for insured organizations.

Occasionally billing abuses occur that give insurers a bad name. For instance, an insurer may receive a $25,000 chiropractic bill, determine that it is not compensable and decline payment, and then charge the insured 27 percent of the savings. This same chiropractor submits another bill for $35,000. The adjuster disallows the bill and charges another 27 percent of the savings. This goes on for some time until the insured organization pays the insurer tens of thousands of dollars of medical expenses for a single claimant. Another example involves bills in scheduled fee states. Some insurers view adjustments of medical costs to the allowable fees as part of their normal adjusting and do not charge extra for the service. Others charge the same percentage of savings that they do for other medical cost reductions. For large organizations, this could be a sizable difference in ultimate costs. The lesson here is that an insured organization must come to a common understanding with its insurer on how they will be charged for these valuable services.

Medical case management services may be partially included in claims handling charges already being made, or these may be charged for separately. Separate costs usually are based on hourly rates of specialists, such as nurse case managers, medical advisor peers, medical directors and medical consultants. Utilization reviews are usually charged based on a flat rate per review.

Organizations should consider the following when reviewing managed care services and costs:

- Medical bill review services are not a commodity. The scope and quality vary by insurer and vendor.

- Obtain data from the insurer as to the savings it has historically achieved for each service performed.

- Flat fees are often more appropriate than fees based on a percentage of savings.

- Fully understand what services are charged for as part of normal claims processing and what will be charged for separately.

- Determine the maximum cost of services for a single injured worker and/or multiple workers injured in the same accident.

- For case management services, obtain the applicable hourly rates for professionals and utilization reviews.

ADA and FMLA Implications

Some insurance industry professional operate under the misconception that, since exclusive remedy provisions in workers compensation laws bar employees from suing their employers, employers are not subject to Americans with Disabilities Act (ADA) or Family and Medical Leave Act (FMLA) related claims. This is untrue. The workers compensation system is not directly linked to the ADA or FMLA. However, both the ADA and FMLA have implications for injured workers and their employers. How these laws overlap and apply in situations where there is an injured worker entitled to compensation creates uncertainty for employers.[5]

The ADA prohibits private employers with fifteen or more employees from discriminating against a "qualified individual" with a "disability". A qualified individual is a person with a disability who can perform the essential functions of a job with or without "reasonable accommodation." Employers must make reasonable accommodations to allow a qualified worker who has a known disability to perform a job. A reasonable accommodation is an adjustment to a job or work environment that will enable a qualified applicant or employee with a disability to perform the essential job functions. A person has a disability if he or she (1) has a physical or mental impairment that substantially limits one or more major life activities, (2) has a record of such impairment, or (3) is regarded as having the impairment.

Reasonable accommodations apply on an individual basis because the requirements of each job and the extent of disability are different. Examples of reasonable accommodations include the following:

- Modifications to training programs

- Reassignment to a vacant position for which the person is qualified

- Modifications to the job or work schedule

- Providing interpreters or readers

- Telecommuting

Employers are not obligated to provide a reasonable accommodation if it creates an undue hardship. This may be due to cost or if the accommodation would be disruptive of or alter the operation of an employer's business.

FMLA applies to (1) all public agencies and elementary or secondary private or public schools (regardless of the number of employees) and (2) private employers with 50 or more employees (in 20 or more work weeks in current or preceding year. Employers must allow eligible employees to take up to twelve weeks unpaid leave in the event of (1) birth, adoption or foster care of a child, (2) serious health condition of the employee, spouse, son, daughter or parent, or (3) a qualifying exigency arising from active duty in the armed forces by a spouse, son, daughter or parent of the employee. A leave of up to twenty-six weeks is allowed in the event a covered military service member is recovering from an injury or illness sustained while on active duty.

To be eligible for a leave, an employee must have worked (1) for the employer for at least twelve months (as of the date the leave commences), (2) at least 1,250 hours during the twelve months period, and (3) at a worksite that employs at least fifty people or within seventy-five miles of that worksite.

Workers compensation is regulated by the states. Each state has its own set of rules and regulations covering compensability, benefits and settling claims. When adjusting workers compensation claims, one must be cognizant of the potential impact that ADA and FMLA (federal laws) may have. The key is to look at the requirements of each of the applicable laws separately, and meld an approach that complies with all the requirements. Sometimes this is easier said than done.

For example, let's assume Tom Smith, an assembly line worker, works for Acme Parts Company. Tom suffers a serious shoulder injury that requires surgery. Ultimately, Tom is left with a significant decrease in motion that limits his ability to perform a major life activity. He is no longer able to perform his job because of the amount of lifting required. Tom is protected under ADA if Acme has 15 or more employees. In that case, Acme needs to provide an accommodation, if the position can be modified or if a vacant position is available, provided there is no undue hardship to Acme. Under FMLA, Tom's medical condition qualifies him to be covered, provided Acme has 50 or more employees. Tom may take a medical leave. Acme may voluntarily pay Tom during this period, but it is not required to do so. If Tom is able to resume his old duties, Tom would have a right to be reinstated to his old job. The applicability of workers compensation would depend on state laws. If the claim is compensable, Tom's medical expenses would be paid and he would be entitled to wage loss (indemnity) payments. If Tom is able to return in a light or modified duty capacity and Acme has such work available, Acme may be required to place him in such a position. If Tom refuses the position he may lose his indemnity benefits. But if Tom is still eligible under FMLA, Acme will be unable to terminate his employment.

One can appreciate the complexity of the handling of claims subject to multiple laws. If two or more employees are involved in a single accident, the complexity increases even further. The key is to recognize that workers compensation claims handling can't be done with blinders on. The process must encompass compliance with federal laws in addition to state workers compensation laws.

Safety Incentive Programs

Some organizations believe that incentive programs designed around accident-free work days can lead to a safer workplace. They hear of others having significant success. This is also bolstered by research. Paul Goodrum and Manish Gangwar published an article entitled "Safety Incentives: A Study of Their Effectiveness in Construction" in the July 2004 edition of *Professional Safety*. One of the conclusions of their three-year study was that, for those organizations that had a safety incentive program in 2000, the mean time lost-time incidence rate from 1999 to 2001 decreased by 44.16 percent.

When a safety incentive program is desired, it can be structured in a number of ways. It usually awards employees with gifts as safety improvements are made or accident history improves. Programs can also apply on a departmental or location basis.

For example, a manufacturer's experience modification is 1.60 because of poor loss history. This means that the organization is paying

60 percent more for workers compensation insurance than its competitors. The organization decides that it must improve its loss experience. It implements a safety incentive program to encourage managers and employees to avoid accidents. The plan is structured with individual departments grouped into safety teams. Each team member is given a lunch certificate for each month in which he or she is accident free. Each employee receives a larger certificate if no one in the team is injured. For each accident-free quarter worked, larger awards are presented. Individuals that work an entire year without an accident receive $300.

The above incentive plan is "injury" based. The reward criteria are based on the number of injuries or illnesses. An alternative form of incentive plan is "behavior" based. Under this type of plan the criteria for rewards are changes in behavior. Examples include are safety suggestions, reporting "near misses" and attending safety presentations.

Detractors of incentive plans focus largely on injury based plans. The main concerns are twofold: (1) the focus is not on long-term improvement, and (2) workers may not report accidents in order to achieve a reward. For many years OSHA has warned employers of the drawbacks of injury based plans. As a result of the criticism in safety circles, there has been some movement away from injury based plans to those that focus on changing behavior.

Regardless of the types and specifics of such programs, these do highlight senior management's commitment to safety, which is a major key to safety improvement over time.

Premium/Cost Allocation Systems

A workers compensation cost allocation system serves three purposes. First, it is a tool used in the budget process. Second, it serves as an incentive to control costs. Third, it assigns costs to individual operating units based on their contribution to the cost of risk of the organization. If an organization has three operating units and one of those units is responsible for 60 percent of historical workers compensation claims, it makes sense that it would be allocated a much greater cost than the remaining two units. If it is not allocated higher costs, its behavior will not change. Rather, the behavior will be perceived as acceptable.

There are several methods that can be utilized to allocate workers compensation costs (fixed and variable) across operating units. Two will be discussed here: (1) pro rata and (2) loss based.

With a pro-rata allocation program, all the costs are treated as fixed. These costs are allocated based on a specified measure, such as payroll or standard premium. No safety or claims management incentive is built into this type of system because the allocations are not sensitive to claims.

With loss based programs, the allocation is based in whole or part on an expected loss calculation. This calculation usually utilizes three to five years of losses. A word of caution: If a business unit experienced a shock loss within the loss years used to determine the allocation, it will probably be necessary to use a lesser amount for the one claim. This will help to moderate large changes in allocations from year-to-year.

The table below is a sample allocation method used by a construction company. This contractor has three divisions. For each division, the losses are limited to $100,000 maximum for any one accident. The sum of three years of losses is divided into three years of payrolls to arrive at a loss rate for each $100 of payroll. This is referred to as the "expected loss rate". This rate is applied to estimated payroll to arrive at expected losses. This is done for each division. The organization then allocates the fixed costs based on a pro-rata share of payroll (instead of losses). It feels that payroll is a good measure of loss potential and chose that measure.

Sample Allocation Calculation #1

	Division 1	Division 2	Division 3	Total
Total losses 2013-2015	$ 600,000	$ 100,000	$ 400,000	$ 1,100,000
Total payroll 2013-2015	12,000,000	9,000,000	6,000,000	27,000,000
Loss rate per $100 payroll	5.00	1.11	6.67	4.07
Estimated payroll 2016	4,000,000	3,000,000	2,000,000	9,000,000
Expected losses	200,000	33,000	133,000	366,000
Fixed costs	32,000	24,000	16,000	72,000
Cost allocation for 2016	232,000	57,333	149,333	438,667

To illustrate how a slightly different methodology can impact how costs are spread, we utilize the same raw information in the calculation above, except the fixed costs are allocated based on the expected losses that each division bears to the total. The fixed costs are spread based on losses rather than exposure (payroll). This makes a fairly significant difference, particularly for Division 2. This is reflected in the table below.

Sample Allocation Calculation #2

	Division 1	Division 2	Division 3	Total
Total losses 2013-2015	$ 600,000	$ 100,000	$ 400,000	$ 1,100,000
Total payroll 2013-2015	12,000,000	9,000,000	6,000,000	27,000,000
Loss rate per $100 payroll	5.00	1.11	6.67	4.07
Estimated payroll 2016	4,000,000	3,000,000	2,000,000	9,000,000
Expected losses	200,000	33,000	133,000	366,667
Fixed costs	39,273	6,545	26,182	72,000
Cost allocation for 2016	239,273	39,879	159,515	438,667

The point of this is that allocation systems can be created in many ways and modified still further. The key is to have a system that best fits the needs of the organization.

Summary

The value of effectively managing a workers compensation program cannot be underestimated. The idea of creating a safer workplace should be the defining goal of all employers. The workers compensation system provides financial incentives to do just that—through experience and schedule rating and optional financial plans.

What should never be overlooked, however, are the hidden costs of employee injuries—the cost of finding and training replacement workers, the cost of losing experienced employees to injury, and the cost of lowered morale after a serious workplace accident. Cost management programs can heighten awareness of the vital importance—to both management and labor—of preventing and managing employee injuries.

Endnotes

1.   On-the-Job Injuries Being Reported Sooner: Delays Mean Higher Costs (1994), Kemper Insurance Media Release.

2.   Glen-Roberts Pitruzzello, "The High Cost of Delays", NCCI Summer 2000 Issues Report.

3.   Tom Lynch, "The Cost of Lag Time", Workers Comp Insider, January 15, 2004 (http://www.workerscompinsider.com/2004/01/the-cost-of-lag.html last visited September 18, 2012).

4.   Loss Control Insights, "Prompt Reporting of Workers' Comp Claims Pays Off In Many Ways", Fireman's Fund Insurance Company, 2005.

5.   Some of the comments in this section are based on a Special Report entitled "The Leave Maze- Managing FMLA, ADA, and Workers' Compensation Issues", published by Business and Legal Reports (2010).

Chapter 13

Issues in Workers Compensation

Introduction

Several issues have found their way into the courtroom for decisions on whether injuries fall within the workers compensation system or not. Is workers compensation the exclusive remedy for injured workers? Who is to provide coverage for leased workers? What does "in the course of employment" mean? Are mental injuries suffered by employees compensable?

This chapter focuses on such issues. The discussions do not exhaust the subject matter, but they do present a solid base of information for those who work within the workers compensation system.

Exclusive Remedy

The workers compensation system stood for many decades as the sole recourse of employees injured on the job. This exclusive remedy provided injured employees with scheduled medical and lost-wage benefits in exchange for their giving up the right to sue the employer. The statutes provided immunity to employers from common law actions brought by employees seeking payment for injuries arising out of and in the course of employment. However, since the case of *Duprey v. Shane*, 249 P.2d 8 (Cal. 1952), (a workers compensation and medical malpractice case in which the employee injured in the course of employment was also treated by her employer, a doctor, and who was allowed to circumvent the workers compensation exclusive remedy based on negligence), various legal doctrines have eroded the exclusive remedy concept and the seemingly clear-cut insurance situation. For example, common law suits against employers have been successfully brought on the basis of dual capacity, intentional tort, and third-party-over doctrines.

Dual Capacity

The *dual capacity* doctrine holds that an employer normally shielded by the exclusive remedy rule may be liable for additional damages for committing a wrongful act that is not related to the role of employer.

This occurs when the employer is judged to occupy a second capacity in which the exposure is common to the public in general.

A classic illustration of a potential dual capacity situation is that of a soda-bottler's delivery man injured by an exploding bottle during the stocking of a merchant's shelves. The soda-bottler employer is responsible for workers compensation for its employee, the delivery man. He also could be held responsible as the manufacturer of the bottle if the injured delivery man, as a member of the general public, decided to pursue a products liability action against the manufacturer. The decisive test of this doctrine, then, is not how separate or different the second capacity of the employer is from the first. It is concerned with whether the second capacity of manufacturer generates obligations unrelated to those flowing from the first, that of an employer.

Currently, courts in a majority of states generally reject the dual capacity doctrine. See, for example, *State v. Purdy*, 601 P.2d 258 (Alas. 1979) and *Billy v. Consolidated Machine Tool Corp.*, 412 N.E.2d 934 (N.Y. 1980). Furthermore, some state legislatures have forbidden or limited the possibility of dual capacity lawsuits through statutory law. For example, the California legislature largely abrogated the dual capacity doctrine by amending the labor code in 1982. Also, see *Suburban Hospital v. Kirson*, 763 A.2d 185 (2000), in which the Court of Appeals of Maryland declared that "the dual capacity theory was not compatible with Maryland law".

Note that in *Patton v. Simone*, 1992 WL 183051, the Superior Court of Delaware, New Castle County, remarked that, while the dual capacity doctrine has been rejected in a majority of jurisdictions, a new theory of liability has arisen called the dual persona doctrine. Under this concept, an employer may become a third person, vulnerable to tort suit by an employee if, and only if, he possesses a second persona to his status as employer that by established standards the law recognizes it as a separate legal person.

The court quoted from 2A Larson Workmen's Compensation Law § 72.81 (1982) that "dual persona is distinguished from dual capacity in that the former is recognized as a person other than the employer, whereas the latter is a person acting in a capacity other than that of employer. Thus, the question becomes not one of activity or relationship, rather it becomes one of identity."

It should be noted that in order to clearly address dual capacity (or dual persona) lawsuits, both the workers compensation form and the general liability form were revised. The part two section of the workers compensation policy—employers liability insurance—specifically provides that damages claimed against the insured in a capacity other than as an employer may be paid. The current commercial general liability form specifically excludes bodily injury to an employee whether the insured is liable as an employer or in any other capacity. Thus these two forms make it as clear as possible that injury to an employee is to be handled under the workers compensation and employers liability policy regardless of whether dual capacity is claimed or not.

Intentional Tort

As stated by the United States District Court, W.D. Michigan, Southern Division, in *Barnes v. Sun Chemical Corporation*, 2015 WL 4878865, "an intentional tort shall exist only when an employee is injured as a result of a deliberate act of the employer and the employer specifically intended an injury. An employer shall be deemed to have intended to injure if the employer had actual knowledge that an injury was certain to occur and willfully disregarded that knowledge. The issue of whether an act was an intentional tort shall be a question of law for the court".

In many jurisdictions, injuries caused by an employer's intentional actions have been ruled not to arise out of the course of employment. Furthermore, public policy does not permit an employer immunity from civil actions when the employer intended to injure or otherwise harm an employee. However, the question of intentional tort versus the exclusive remedy of the WC system is still subject to judicial rulings. Some examples are illustrated below.

The issue before an Illinois appellate court was whether exclusive remedy bars a suit against the employer of a pizza delivery man when the employer knew with substantial certainty that the delivery man would be attacked while making a delivery. That court decided to allow such suits if it can be shown that the employer had a specific intent to injure or cause injury to the employee. The claimants could not show that intent, so the case was dismissed. However, the point was made that the exclusive remedy of the workers compensation system could be bypassed under certain conditions. The case is *Bercaw v. Domino's Pizza, Inc.*, 630 N.E.2d 166 (Ill. App. Ct. 1994).

Similarly, in *Limanowski v. Ashland Oil Company*, 655 N.E.2d 1049 (1995), the appellate Court of Illinois, First District, First Division, said that an employee seeking to avoid the exclusive remedy provisions of the workers comp act and to recover against his employer on an intentional tort theory, must prove by a preponderance of the evidence that the employer specifically intended to injure him.

In *Fricke v. Owens-Corning Fiberglass Corp.*, 571 So.2d 130 (La. 1990), a Louisiana court indicated that it is not necessary for the employer to intend to inflict actual damage or that actions be malicious. Intending to inflict either a harmful or offensive contact without the employee's consent was enough to constitute intent.

In *Gulden v. Crown Zellerbach Corp.*, 890 F.2d 195 (9th Cir. 1989), employees who had been ordered to clean up a PCB spill without protective clothing claimed the employer intended to injure them. A federal court of appeals decided that a jury could conclude that the intention to injure was deliberate where the employer had an opportunity to weigh the consequences and choose among courses of action. Therefore, allegations of intentional injury could not be dismissed by summary judgment on the basis of the state's workers compensation law. The employees sued based on tort liability. Similarly, in *Richie v. Rogers Cartage Co.*, 626 N.E.2d 1012 (Ohio Ct. App. 1994), an Ohio appeals court decided that a lawsuit by an employee against an employer could not be summarily dismissed if the question of company intent existed. The court said that there had to be a trial to determine whether the employer committed an intentional wrong.

In *Pursell v. Pizza Inn, Inc.* 786 P.2d 716 (Okla. Ct. App. 1990), employees alleged that their supervisors deliberately sexually battered and harassed them at work. After hearing the case, the court decided that such allegations of willful, intentional, or even violent conduct by the employer took the case out of the exclusive domain of workers compensation.

The Supreme Court of Oklahoma clarified this point in *Parret v. Unicco Service Company*, 127 P.3d 572 (2005). A widow of an employee who was electrocuted while replacing emergency lights at a tire company brought an action against the employer and the tire company. The court stated that specific intent to harm the employee was not required for an employer's conduct to be actionable in tort, but rather, an employee's claim fell outside of the exclusive remedy provisions of workers compensation if the injuries were the result of actions that the employer knew were substantially certain to cause injury.

In order for an employer's conduct to amount to an intentional tort for purposes of removing the claim from the exclusive remedy provision of workers comp, the court said that the employer must have desired to bring about the worker's injury, or acted with the knowledge that such injury was substantially certain to result from the employer's conduct. Furthermore, an employer's knowledge that the injury was substantially certain to follow from its conduct may be inferred from the conduct and all of the surrounding circumstances. The court did, however, state that mere allegations of intentional conduct will not circumvent the exclusive remedy provision; the worker must allege facts that plausibly demonstrate that the employer's conduct was intentional under the substantial certainty standard. (Note that this case was superseded by statute in 2010.)

The substantial certainty standard discussed by the Supreme Court of Oklahoma has been considered by other courts. In *Ramos v. Town of Branford*, 778 A.2d 972 (2001), the Appellate Court of Connecticut stated that the substantial certainty standard is a subset of the intentional tort exception to the exclusivity provision of the WC act, and whereas the intentional tort test requires that both act producing the injury and specific injury to the employee must be intentional, the substantial certainty standard requires showing that the act producing the injury was intentional or deliberate and resulting in injury from the standpoint of the employer or was substantially certain to result from the employer's acts or conduct. The same court in *Sorban v. Sterling Engineering Corporation*, 830 A.2d 372 (2003), said that to satisfy the substantial certainty test for determining whether an employee can maintain a civil action against the employer under the intentional tort exception, the employee must show that a reasonable person in the position of the employer would have known that the injury or death suffered by the employee was substantially certain to follow from the employer's actions.

The intentional tort exception to the exclusive remedy doctrine is not universally accepted in all jurisdictions, and the debate will continue. Court decisions will vary from one jurisdiction to another, and employers should be aware of decisions not only in the area where their company is domiciled but in all areas where they conduct business activities. Responsible employers also should realize that many states' workers compensation laws provide the right to bring tort action against an employer for injuries resulting from the employer's willful, deliberate conduct (often with the proviso, however, that the employee must prove that the employer committed a tortuous act with the belief that the injury was substantially certain to occur).

Third-Party-Over

The *third-party-over* doctrine involves the injured employee suing a third party, who subsequently is able to bring an action against the employer. For example, the employer may have contractually assumed the obligations and liabilities of the third party. For example, Coastal Manufacturing Co. hires M&J Maintenance Co. to do maintenance work. M&J agrees to hold Coastal harmless and to indemnify it for injury to M&J workers. An M&J employee is injured when an overhead crane runs into his scaffolding. The employee files for workers compensation benefits from M&J. In addition, he sues Coastal for negligence in operating the crane. Coastal turns the lawsuit over to M&J because the maintenance company had agreed to indemnify Coastal. M&J ends up paying workers compensation benefits, defending the lawsuit, and paying the lawsuit settlement.

The following court cases deal with the third-party-over doctrine.

In *Oliver v. N.L. Industries*, 566 N.Y.S.2d 128 (1991), the Supreme Court, Appellate Division, Fourth Department, New York ruled in a case where the employee filed an action to recover damages for personal injuries he sustained when he was struck by molten metal extruded from a die casting machine during the course of his employment. In ruling that the lawsuit against the employer could proceed, the court decided that an employer that independently assumed the obligations and liabilities of a third-party tortfeasor could not avail itself of the exclusivity provisions of the workers compensation law.

In another New York case, the same court ruled that a subsidiary was not immune from liability on the grounds that it no longer existed as a corporate entity as a result of a merger. In *Preston v. APCH*, 930 N.Y.S.2d 722 (2011), the employee was killed as a result of an accident at the plant where he was working. The employer company merged with another company after the accident and the new company sought to dismiss any action against it. The court decided that the exception to the exclusivity provision of the workers compensation law permitted the administrator of the worker's estate to bring an action against the employer when the accident occurred prior to the merger since the new company independently assumed the assets, obligations, and liabilities of the employer in the merger.

The Superior Court of Pennsylvania handled a case where an employee brought a personal injury action against the employer after he suffered an amputation of the left arm and other injuries in an on-the-job accident. In this case, the court discussed the dual capacity doctrine and the dual personal doctrine. The dual personal doctrine allows an employer to become a third person vulnerable to a tort action by an employee if the employer has a second identity, so completely independent and unrelated to its status as an employer in its second capacity as a separate legal person; the question, said the court, is not one of activity or relationship, but one of identity. For the dual personal doctrine to apply, as required to prevent an employer from asserting statutory immunity under the workers comp act, the duties of the employer under its other personal must be totally separate from and unrelated to those of the employment. This case is *Soto v. Nabisco*, 2011 PA Super 249 (2011).

The dual personal doctrine was also discussed by the Supreme Court of South Carolina in *Mendenall v. Anderson Hardwood Floors*,

738 S.E.2d 251 (2013). In this case, the personal representative of the estate of an employee that died after a work-related accident filed a wrongful death and survivor action against the employer's successor in interest. The defendants sought dismissal of the action based on the exclusivity provision of the state workers comp act. The Supreme Court held that, in a matter of first impression, the dual personal doctrine is an exception to the exclusivity provision of the workers comp act. Furthermore, the court said, under South Carolina law, whether the dual personal doctrine applies in a particular case turns on whether the duty claimed to have been breached is distinct from those duties owed by virtue of the employer's persona as such.

Note that the employers liability section of the WC policy specifically pays for damages for which the insured is liable to a third party by reason of a claim or suit by that third party. The commercial general liability forms specifically apply the workers compensation exclusion to any obligation to share damages with or repay someone else who must pay damages. However, this exclusion does not apply to liability assumed by the insured under an insured contract. Using the example of Coastal and M&J, M&J's general liability form will defend and pay if necessary because of the exception to the exclusion. M&J's employers liability insurance (part two on the workers compensation policy) will not apply since liability assumed under a contract is not covered.

Other Possibilities

It is safe to say that the exclusive remedy rule of workers compensation will continue to be the subject of repeated assaults. The following discussion is not the final word on this issue, but it does offer some examples of arguments being made pertaining to the preemption of exclusive remedy.

In *Kerans v. Porter Paint Co.*, 575 N.E.2d 428 (Ohio 1991), the claimant alleged that she was sexually molested on five separate occasions by a coworker and that Porter Paint did nothing to discipline or reprimand the coworker. Kerans sued based on sexual harassment. Porter Paint made a motion for judgment without trial based on the exclusive remedy of workers compensation. The Ohio trial court granted the company's motion, but on appeal, the Ohio Supreme Court stated that the workers compensation statute did not provide the exclusive remedy for claims based on sexual harassment. The Court decided that workers compensation provides coverage for economic losses resulting from accidents. The court said that workers compensation does not adequately compensate for psychological and emotional damages resulting from sexual harassment; sexual harassment did not usually result in economic loss, but in loss of dignity and self-esteem. Therefore, workers compensation was not the exclusive remedy for the damages suffered by a claimant based on sexual harassment.

Another example is *Bunger v. Lawson Co.*, 696 N.E.2d 1029 (Ohio 1998). Bunger was working late and was robbed. She claimed psychological injury and post-traumatic stress and sought workers compensation benefits. The state industrial commission said no. When the issue went to trial, a lower court declared that she was not entitled to workers compensation benefits because she had not suffered physical injury. In addition, she had no right to sue because the condition arose during the scope of employment. The Ohio Supreme Court reversed the finding of "no right to sue" and declared that "workers compensation does not foreclose an employee who has suffered purely psychological injuries from pursuing a common law remedy". The court reasoned that psychological injuries were not included within the definition of injury in the state workers compensation law. Therefore, such injuries could not be included in any grant of employer immunity (under the exclusive remedy rule) from a lawsuit for an injury suffered by an employee.

The Supreme Court of Ohio revisited the issue of compensability of psychological or psychiatric injuries in *McCrone v. Bank One Corp.*, 839 N.E.2d 1 (2005). In that case, an employee sought workers compensation benefits for purely psychological or psychiatric injuries suffered as a result of a pair of bank robberies in which neither the employee nor any third person was physically injured. The court found that the purely psychiatric injuries were not compensable under workers compensation and so, the exclusive remedy argument was not applicable.

The Supreme Court of Ohio continued its discussion of psychological injuries and workers compensation in the 2013 case of *Armstrong v. John R. Jurgensen Company*, 990 N.E.2d 568 (2013). Here, the claimant was involved in a fatal auto accident while working as a dump truck driver and then sought workers comp benefits for post-traumatic stress disorder (PTSD). The Supreme Court held that for a mental condition to be compensable under the workers comp law, a causal connection must exist between the claimant's physical injury and the claimant's mental condition. The court concluded that competent, credible evidence existed in this case to support the finding that the claimant's physical injuries did not cause his PTSD and so, workers compensation exclusivity was not available.

Another example is *Errand v. Cascade Steel Rolling Mills, Inc.*, 888 P.2d 544 (Ore. 1995). In this case, the Oregon Supreme Court allowed a lawsuit against an employer by an employee to proceed as an exception to the exclusivity rule of the workers compensation system. The court decided that the state law made workers compensation the exclusive remedy for "compensable injuries," and that where an employee's injuries have been determined not to fit into that category, the exclusivity status of workers compensation does not apply. (Note that this ruling was superseded by

ORS 656.018 [1995], whereby the state legislature stated that workers compensation is the exclusive remedy for work-related injuries, even if the claim itself is not compensable.)

In *Kerans*, the Ohio Supreme Court equated a workers comp claim with economic loss and declared that sexual harassment resulted in more than mere economic loss; therefore, workers compensation was not the exclusive remedy. In *Bunger*, the Court said that psychological injury was not bodily injury as defined by law; therefore, the workers compensation system was not the proper forum to seek compensation. In *Errand*, the injuries suffered by the employee did not fit into the definition of compensable injuries under the state workers compensation law. These cases illustrate that "bodily injury" is subject to court interpretation. If alleged damages are deemed to either not include bodily injury or extend beyond the statutory meaning of that term, a court may rule that workers compensation is not the claimant's sole path of recovery.

Exclusive remedy might also be breached when the claimant denies that the injury occurred *in the course of employment*. If the claimant was injured outside the course of employment, there is no causal connection between the injury and employment. A tort claim, then, based on negligence against the employer may be applicable. Some examples of this are *Middlekauff v. Allstate Insurance Co.*, 439 S.E.2d 394 (Va. 1994); *Williams v. Martin Marietta Energy Systems, Inc.*, 651 N.E.2d 55 (Ohio Ct. App. 1994); and *Copeland v. Boots Pharmaceuticals*, 916 P.2d 277 (Okla. Ct. App. 1996).

Uninsured motorists (UM) benefits can also be used as an avenue of attack against the exclusivity rule of the workers compensation system. In *Conzo v. Aetna Insurance Co.*, 705 A.2d 1020 (Ct. 1998), the issue was whether an employee injured in the course of employment while occupying the employer's car is entitled to collect UM benefits from the employer. The employee had already collected workers compensation benefits and then sought UM benefits. The state Supreme Court allowed the employee to collect from both sources. Note that this is a minority position at this time.

For another view on this point, see *Heller v. Pennsylvania League of Cities and Municipalities*, 32 A.3d 1213 (2011), wherein the Pennsylvania Supreme Court held that an exclusion of underinsured motorists coverage benefits for anyone eligible for workers compensation benefits violated public policy and is unenforceable.

Finally, another erosion in the exclusive remedy doctrine involves the preempting of state workers compensation laws by federal laws. The theory used is that the employer, through its actions or inaction, has violated a federal law, and the injured employee has a right to sue for any damages suffered based on that federal law. For example, migrant farm workers, injured while riding in their employer's van, received workers compensation benefits under Florida law and then sued in federal court. They argued that their injuries were caused in part by the employer's violation of motor vehicle safety provisions of the Migrant and Seasonal Agricultural Worker Protection Act. The employer claimed workers compensation as the exclusive remedy. The case went all the way to the United States Supreme Court. The case, *Adams Fruit Co., Inc., v. Barrett*, 494 U.S.638 (1990), ended when the Supreme Court affirmed that the federal migrant protection act does preempt state law. Therefore, workers compensation is not the sole remedy.

Note that Congress moved to overrule this decision by amending the federal law; see 29 U.S.C. §1854. However, other federal laws might be used to ignore the exclusive remedy idea behind workers compensation. Other examples of federal laws that should be considered are the Employment Retirement Income Security Act (ERISA), the Americans With Disabilities Act (ADA), and the Family and Medical Leave Act (FMLA).

Mental Stress Claims

Coverage under workers compensation insurance applies to bodily injury by *accident* and bodily injury by *disease* (including resulting death). The agreement does contain two stipulations: 1) bodily injury by accident must occur during the policy period; and 2) bodily injury by disease must be caused or aggravated by conditions of employment, with the employee's last exposure to those conditions occurring during the policy period.

The workers compensation policy does not define bodily injury. This can, and often does, lead to disputes over the question of coverage for mental stress claims. Is mental stress compensable under the law?

Generally, workers compensation cases involving emotional or mental conditions can be divided into three groups:

1. Mental stimulus resulting in physical injury.

2. Physical trauma resulting in mental injury.

3. Mental stimulus resulting in mental injury.

Most jurisdictions and workers compensation boards have no problem awarding benefits under the first two groupings because the employee is disabled by an injury that is associated with a physical manifestation.

In cases of mental injury as a result of mental stress, decisions vary from jurisdiction to jurisdiction. For example, courts in Illinois, Mississippi, and Texas have decided mental injury caused by mental stress is a compensable injury. Courts in Kansas, Wyoming, Ohio, and Wisconsin have denied workers compensation benefits for such injuries. (See the Ohio case mentioned previously, *Armstrong v. John R. Jurgensen Company*, wherein the Ohio Supreme Court noted that, consistent with the plain language of R.C. 4123.01, mental conditions are compensable under the workers compensation system only when a physical injury causes them.)

The most substantial factor found in those cases denying compensation without bodily injury is the difficulty of proving injury. Because mental injury is vague, shadowy, intangible, and could be within the control of the sufferer, it was feared that the disability could too easily be simulated. It is as if the courts were saying they could not comprehend a method to objectively value a claim based on mental pain without any accompanying physical injury to evaluate. Therefore, such claims had to be denied.

Jurisdictions that permit compensation for mental injury claims without accompanying bodily injury emphasize that the difficulty of formulating appropriate legal tests does not justify denying the claims. For example, in *NPS Corp. v. Insurance Co. of North America*, 517 A.2d 1211 (N.J. Super. Ct. App. Div. 1986), the New Jersey appeals court held that emotional distress and mental anguish caused to an employee by sexual harassment from a fellow employee constituted bodily injury. The court stated that New Jersey has come to recognize that mental and emotional distress is just as real as physical pain and that its valuation is no more difficult. Within that framework, the court disagreed with the defendant's argument that bodily injury necessarily entails some physical or corporeal harm caused by the application of external violence. The court said, "We are unable to separate a person's nerves and tensions from his body since, clearly, emotional trauma can be as disabling to the body as a visible physical wound".

(Note that though the *NPS* case was never overruled, the Supreme Court of New Jersey disagreed with the finding and held that "in the context of purely emotional distress without physical manifestations, bodily injury is not ambiguous. Its ordinary meaning connotes some sort of physical problem". This case is *SL Industries, Inc. v. American Motorists Insurance Company*, 607 A.2d 1266 [1992].)

The Colorado Court of Appeals added something to consider when determining whether mental stress can be listed as compensable under the workers comp system. In *Public Service of Colorado v. Industrial Claim Appeals Office of the State of Colorado*, 68 P.3d 583 (2003), the court said that the causes of a workers comp mental impairment and the commonality of those causes are questions of fact. And, when multiple stressors are alleged for the workers comp mental impairment, the determination of the causes of the impairment must include a separate analysis of each event to ascertain whether the claim is based in whole or in part upon facts or circumstances common to all fields of employment.

The dispute over whether bodily injury must be present in order to recover under workers comp for a mental injury claim will not be settled soon. At this time, a majority of authorities hold that bodily injury does not include mental stress and so, mental stress claims standing alone are not going to be compensated under workers comp laws. (In the *SL Industries* case noted above, the New Jersey Supreme Court listed numerous cases from other jurisdictions holding that bodily injury requires some physical component.)

However, if there is a discernible trend in this field, it is toward recognition of WC benefits for mental injury due to stress and tension. The reasoning: mental injury may be brought about in the same manner as stress causes a heart attack or other physical condition. For example, see *Irvin Investors v. Superior Court in and for the County of Maricopa*, 800 P.2d 979 (1990), wherein the Court of Appeals of Arizona, Division 1, declared that psychological injury to an employee was a mental condition caused by unexpected, unusual, or extraordinary stress related to employment, and thus, was compensable under the workers compensation laws of the state.

There is another aspect to consider. Since the workers compensation policy applies to injury by *accident*, can mental stress be equated with accident for recovery under the policy? Mental stress severe enough to cause disability generally does not develop overnight. If it is a gradual process over a long period, can it be termed an accident? The workers compensation policy does not define the word. However *Black's Law Dictionary* does offer the following: with reference to workers compensation acts, an accident is an event that takes place without one's foresight or expectation; an undesigned, sudden, and unexpected event.

Many insurance terms are subject to differing judicial interpretations, "accident" is no exception. The general principle is that impairments, even physical ones, developing in imperceptible stages as a result of particular work over an appreciable period of time are not compensable as accidental injuries. This principle has been adhered to in cases that decline compensation for a mental disability claim. For example, in *Lawson v. Employers Insurance of Wausau*, 330 F.Supp. 321 (E.D. Tenn. 1971), a federal court decided that a general mental breakdown resulting from overwork or long employment at a particular type of activity was not a compensable accident. The court stated that the employee's anxiety and hypertension did not disable the employee within the meaning of the state workers compensation law.

Other jurisdictions have ignored the general principle upheld in *Lawson* and granted compensation, equating a gradual deterioration of mental stability with an accident. The Supreme Court of Arizona in *Fireman's Fund Insurance Co. v. Industrial Commission*, 579 P.2d 555 (Ariz. 1978) held that an employee who suffered a mental breakdown as a result of constant work pressures did sustain a personal injury claim arising out of and in the course of her employment. The court agreed that the mental breakdown resulted from a gradual buildup of stress and tension at work and was sufficiently unanticipated to be called unexpected. It therefore was accidental within the meaning of the statute providing compensation.

The differing court decisions on compensation for impairments that develop over a period of time are reduced to disagreeing about whether accident means only a sudden, one-shot trauma or whether the word can encompass gradual trauma.

Arising Out of and In the Course of Employment

In order for workers compensation benefits to apply under the employers liability insurance section of the policy to, bodily injury to an employee must arise *out of and in the course of employment*. Aside from the issue of just what bodily injury includes, another point of contention can be just what arising "out of and in the course of employment" means. Since neither the various states' laws nor the policy define this phrase and the workers compensation policy itself does not offer a definition, the courts have taken on the task of clarifying the meaning.

"The test of the right to participate in the workers compensation fund is ... whether a causal connection existed between an employee's injury and his employment either through the activities, the conditions, or the environment of the employment". This is a quote from an Ohio state Supreme Court decision, *Bralley v. Daugherty*, 401 N.E.2d 448 (Ohio 1980). It points out that an employee must be injured as a result of employment before workers compensation or employers liability insurance will kick in; that is, the employment has to cause the injury. If a causal connection between the injury and the employment is disputed, such disputes are decided on a case-by-case basis.

In *Appeal of Griffin*, 671 A.2d 541 (N.E. 1996), Griffin was injured in a fight with coworkers and filed for benefits. The compensation board decided his injuries did not arise out of and in the course of employment, so Griffin appealed to the court. The New Hampshire Supreme Court stated that the injury did arise out of and in the course of employment. The court found that Griffin was driving his coworkers back from a meal and that the fight started with a quarrel about his driving. The driving was work-related and the fight was about the driving; thus, the injuries were work-related.

In this case, the Court explained the "arising out of and in the course of employment" requirements as follows: to meet the scope of employment test, the claimant must prove that the injury arose out of employment by demonstrating that it resulted from a risk created by the employment, and that the injury arose in the course of employment by demonstrating that it occurred within the boundaries of time and space created by the terms of employment, and that it occurred in the performance of an activity related to employment.

In *Williams v. Martin Marietta Energy Systems, Inc.*, 651 N.E.2d 55 (Ohio Ct. App. 1994), an Ohio appeals court decided that an injury suffered by an employee during a blood drive did not arise out of and in the course of employment. The employer had no control over the attempted drawing of blood from Williams. The employee's participation in the blood drive was not a regular incident and condition of employment and so the injuries suffered by the employee were not compensable.

In *Copeland v. Boots Pharmaceuticals*, 916 P.2d 277 (Okla. Ct. App. 1996), Copeland was a traveling sales rep. While on sales calls, she stopped for the night in a hotel. Copeland was bitten by a spider in the hotel and filed for workers compensation benefits. After benefits were denied, Copeland appealed. The appeals court in Oklahoma decided her injuries did not arise from her employment. The court said that the injuries did not stem from an employment-related risk. There was no connection between her job and the risk of encountering spiders; it was a personal risk and not a business risk.

In *Ganus v. St. Bernard's Hospital*, 457 S.W.3d 683 (2015), the Court of Appeals of Arkansas handled a case where the WC claimant sought benefits after she injured her right knee in a fall on her way to a cafeteria at the hospital at which she worked. The administrative law judge determined that the injury arose out of and in the course of employment and granted WC benefits. The hospital appealed and the appeals court noted that the employee was on a personal errand to retrieve food for her own benefit, that she was on a break and thus relieved of her work responsibilities, and that she specifically left her patient in the hands of another employee before she went to retrieve her lunch. Therefore, the court ruled that substantial evidence supported the determination that the claimant was not performing employment services at the time of her injury. The court held that in a workers compensation case, the test for whether an employee was performing employment services at the time of injury is whether the injury occurred within the time and space boundaries of the employment, when the employee was carrying out the employer's purpose or advancing the employer's interest directly or indirectly.

In *Legacy Health Systems v. Noble*, 283 P.3d 924 (2012), the WC claimant fractured her ankle while walking across a slippery parking lot on an errand to deposit a personal check. The Court of Appeals of Oregon reviewed the facts of the incident and offered a thorough analysis of the "arising out of and in the course of employment" requirement for WC benefits. The court stated that a workers comp claimant bears the burden of establishing the compensability of her injury, and specifically, the requisite connection between the injury and her employment. In determining whether an injury to a claimant occurs in the course of employment, a court has to look at the time, place, and circumstances of the injury. Furthermore, a workers comp injury is deemed to arise out of employment if the risk of the injury results from the nature of the work or when it originates from some risk to which the work environment exposes the claimant. The determination of whether a workers comp claimant's injury arose out of her employment depends on an assessment of the nature of the claimant's work and work environment in conjunction with the risk of harm that resulted in the injury. In sum, the court said that the focus of the court in determining whether a claimant's injury arose out of and in the course of her employment is on whether the claimant established a causal connection between her injury and her employment, that is, whether the injury resulted from a risk connected to either the nature of her work or her work environment. (In this instance, the court ruled that the claimant's fractured ankle due to walking across a parking lot to deposit a personal check did not arise out of her employment as required to constitute a compensable injury.)

Couch on Insurance makes the following observations on the subject. In *8 Couch on Insurance*, §115.70, it is stated that the words "in the course of employment" refer to the time and place of an accident and the circumstances under which it occurs. In 9A *Couch on Insurance*, §135:3, it is stated that an employee is "in the course of employment" where he or she is engaged in the furtherance of the employer's business, or doing a duty he or she was employed to do; moreover, a temporal and spatial nexus to the employment must be established.

Relationship to Employment

There are some activities engaged in by employees that raise the question whether such activities are related to employment. Examples are recreational and social activities (such as the company softball team or picnic), coming and going, horseplay and fights, and alcohol or drug consumption.

Many employers sponsor picnics, sporting events, and in-house physical fitness facilities where employees may get hurt. If such activities are paid for and supervised by the employer for the purpose of generating or improving the employer-employee relationship, an injury sustained by an employee can be considered to be in the course of employment. A general rule enunciated by Professor Larson (*Larson, Workmen's Compensation, §2201*) can be seen as a reliable guide: recreational or social activities are within the course of employment when they occur on the premises during a lunch or recreation period as a regular incident of the employment; or, the employer, by expressly or impliedly requiring participation, or by making the activity part of the services of an employee, brings the activity within the orbit of the employment; or, the employer derives substantial direct benefit from the activity beyond the intangible value of improvement in employee health and morale that is common to all kinds of recreation and social life.

For a discussion of this general rule, see *Ostrowski v. WASA Electrical Services*, 960 P.2d 162 (1998). In that case, the claimant sought WC benefits relating to injuries he sustained in a fight at a drinking party held after office hours. The Intermediate Court of Appeals of Hawaii stated that to determine whether the employee's participation in social or recreational activities is incidental to job duties, courts should consider whether: the activities occur on the employer's premises during lunch or recreation period as a regular incident of employment; or whether the employer, by expressly or impliedly requiring participation or by making the activity part of the services of the employee brings the activity within the orbit of employment; or whether the employer derives substantial direct benefit from the activity beyond the intangible value of improvement in the employee health and morale that is common to all kinds of recreation and social life.

In general, injuries sustained by an employee while coming to and going from work are not considered employment-related. There are exceptions to this rule, which usually apply when the employee is doing some work-related activity during the travel or if the employer controls the site where the injury occurred, such as a company parking lot. For an example of judicial thinking on the subject, see *Kuebel v. Black & Decker, Inc.*, 643 F.3d 352 (2011). In this case, the United States Court of Appeals, Second Circuit, ruled that even if the employee's at-home activities were integral and indispensable to his principal activities, they do not render the entirety of his commute time compensable. (It's true that this case involved a claim under the Fair Labor Standards Act, but the judicial thinking can be applied to workers comp claims.)

As for injury during horseplay or fights, the circumstances dictate whether the injury is sustained in the course of employment. If an employee is on the job and gets hurt because of the horseplay of another person, that injury is usually compensable. On the other hand, if the employee perpetrating the horseplay gets hurt, that usually is not considered work-related. The situation is similar when it comes to a fight. The instigator of the fight usually is not entitled to workers compensation benefits, but the injured victim can be depending on the circumstances. If the fight is personal (for example, a political disagreement), the injury cannot be said to occur in the course of employment. If the fight is business related (for example, an argument over possession of a tool), the injury may be considered in the course of employment and be compensable.

The Virginia Supreme Court handled an appeal of a workers compensation proceeding that revolved around the issue of whether an innocent victim of horseplay at work could recover workers comp benefits. In *Simms v. Ruby Tuesday, Inc.*, 704 S.E.2d 359 (2011), the Court said that horseplay occurs naturally in every workplace environment, and if the horseplay results in someone being hurt, that injury is compensable under the state workers compensation system. The Court also cautioned that while an injury caused by horseplay can be seen as being causally connected to the workplace and as arising out of employment, an innocent nonparticipating employee who is injured generally stands a better chance of recovering benefits that those who are injured while actually taking part in the horseplay.

Finally, standing alone, alcohol or drug consumption is not usually sufficient to defeat recovery of workers compensation benefits if the user is injured at work. If the worker is rendered incapable of doing his or her job due to alcohol or drug intake and is injured while under the influence, that injury is not generally considered to have occurred in the course of employment. The employee, in effect, abandoned the job through voluntary action and the injury is not considered to be in the course of employment. On the other hand, if the employee has consumed alcohol or drugs but can still function on the job and is injured, for example, at his station, that injury is in the course of employment and workers compensation benefits apply.

The Supreme Court of Montana received a workers comp benefits appeal pertaining to a worker being injured after smoking marijuana. This case is *Hopkins v. Uninsured Employers' Fund*, 251 P.3d 118 (2011). The Court decided that while drug consumption may preclude WC benefits if it is the leading cause contributing to the injury, there was no evidence in this instance to show that the worker's use of marijuana was such a major contributing cause of his injuries. Therefore, Hopkins was injured in the course of his employment and was entitled to workers comp benefits.

Some states may have legislated differently in regard to alcohol or drug consumption and compensability, and each state workers comp law should always be reviewed on this subject.

Workplace Violence

According to a January 2012 NCCI study entitled "Violence in the Workplace", work-related assaults are less frequent today than twenty years ago. However, such assaults result in more severe injuries compared to other causes, and are more likely to result in fatalities.

State workers compensation statutes govern if injuries caused by assaults are compensable. One might think that since assaults are intentional acts, that compensability would be doubtful, but that it not necessarily the case. Courts generally find for employees who are injured due to the increased risks of their profession. This includes (1) the duties are dangerous (policeman or prison guard), (2) the work environment is dangerous (night bartender in a high crime area), or (3) street risks (assaults on employees whose work involves travel on streets or highways).

Courts often look for a causal connection between a person's employment and the origin of the risk. For instance, it is likely that injuries caused by assaults that are inherent to the workplace (assaults by or upon supervisors, arguments over performance or violence related to labor disputes) would be compensable. On the other hand, assaults caused by private quarrels, wholly outside of the workplace, are generally not compensable. Assaults caused by a neutral force, such as random attacks by lunatics or drunks, may or may not be compensable, depending on the facts and circumstances of the employment.

The following cases illustrate how some courts have dealt with workers compensation coverage associated with injuries suffered as a result of physical assaults.

The case of *Marielo Paredes and Efren Carpio v. Ralph J Maiello DDS, Inc. and State Compensation Insurance Fund*, Case No. ADJ7168050 (2012), Workers Compensation Appeals Board, State of California, illustrates how the causal connection between employment and the assault comes into play. The husband of Marielo Paredes entered the offices of Ralph Maiello DDS, and shot four employees, including his wife, who later died. Mr. Paredes suspected his wife was having an affair with a co-worker. The workers compensation insurer denied coverage. The petitioner advanced several arguments, but the administrative law judge ruled that the decedent's death did not arise out of employment; rather, it arose from a personal matter and had nothing to do with Ms. Paredes work at the dentist office. This decision was affirmed by the Workers Compensation Appeals Board.

The court upheld compensation in *International Staff Management and Legion Insurance Company v. Takisha Stephenson*, 46 So.3d 367 (2010), Court of Appeals of Mississippi. Takisha Stephenson left work for the day, but was told she was wanted back inside her workplace. Upon reentering, she was shot by Reginald Davis, a former co-worker. In the weeks preceding the incident, Davis harassed and threatened Stephenson and her family. Stephenson survived the attack but was seriously injured. A dispute ensued regarding the compensability of Stephenson's injuries. Stephenson's employer took the position that Davis's motives for shooting Stephenson were purely personal and emanated from an alleged relationship between the two. Eventually, the administrative law judge ruled that Stephenson's injuries were suffered in the course and scope of her employment. The judge felt it was doubtful that any relationship between Davis and Stephenson was the sole cause of her injuries.

Kristina Wait v. Travelers Indemnity Company of Illinois, 240 S.W.3d 220 (2007), involved a "telecommuting" employee who suffered injuries in her home. Kristina Wait had an approved home office out of which she worked. While making lunch in her kitchen during a work day, a visiting neighbor assaulted her and she suffered severe injuries. She sought worker compensation benefits and argued that (1) the injuries arose from her employment because her at home work arrangement placed her in a position that allowed the assault, and (2) the injuries occurred in the course of her employment, as she was engaged in a permissible incidental activity (eating in her kitchen was akin to a worker eating in the company cafeteria). The Supreme Court of Tennessee ruled that Wait's injuries did occur in the course of her employment. It reasoned that the injuries were sustained during her lunch break at her work place. However, the court also found that her injuries did not arise out of her employment. The court concluded there was no causal connection between her employment conditions and the injuries she suffered, because there was no evidence that the person that committed the assault was part of the employment relationship or had any business with the employee. Therefore, the Supreme Court affirmed the lower court's ruling.

In *Padilla v. Twin City Fire Insurance Company*, 324 S.W.3d 507 (2010), the surviving spouse of an employee brought an action against the employer, seeking WC death benefits arising out of a fatal shooting of the employee on the work premises. The Supreme Court of Tennessee held that to be compensable under the WC law, an injury must both arise out of the work, referring to the cause or origin of the injury, and occur in the course of employment, referring to the time, place, and circumstances of the injury.

The court then addressed various types of assault. Assaults with an inherent connection to employment are compensable. Assaults stemming from inherently private disputes imported into the employment setting from the claimant's domestic or private life and not exacerbated by the employment are not compensable. Assaults resulting from a neutral force such as random assaults on employees by individuals outside the employment relationship can be compensable under WC, depending on the facts and circumstances of the employment.

In this instance, the court ruled that the fatal shooting of an employee on the work premises was a neutral force assault. The court held that the WC law does not require or permit a presumption of compensability for injuries sustained in a neutral force assault during employment. WC compensation due to a neutral force assault depends on the facts and circumstance of the employment, and here, the facts and circumstances did not serve as the necessary causal connection between the employment and the fatal shooting. WC benefits were denied.

(Note that the Supreme Court of Tennessee discussed the "street risk" doctrine in this case. The purpose of this doctrine is to provide the necessary causal connection between the employment and the injury when the employment exposes the employee to the hazards of the street for purposes of WC claims.)

The United States District Court for the Western District of Pennsylvania handled a case where the employees brought an action against the employer based on tort claims for battery and intentional infliction of emotional distress. The employer moved to dismiss the tort claims by asserting the claims were pre-empted by the state workers comp law. This case is *Hancuff v. Prism Technologies and Assemblies*, 357 F.Supp.2d 828 (2005).

In discussing the case, the court said that, for purposes of the WC act exception permitting tort claims for employee injuries caused by the intentional conduct of a third party for reasons personal to the tortfeasor and not directed against the employee as an employee or because of his employment, the court recognizes the rebuttable presumption that an injury is work-related where it occurs on the employer's premises. The critical inquiry in determining the applicability of the third-party attack exception is whether the attack was motivated by personal reasons, as opposed to generalized contempt or hatred, and was sufficiently unrelated to the work situation so as not to arise out of the employment relationship.

Employment of Minors

State employment laws govern minors. The scope of coverage under workers compensation and employers liability insurance for minors employed contrary to law varies by state. Therefore, it is not practical to apply general statements to particular cases.

When a *legally* employed minor is injured in the course of employment, the workers compensation system functions the same as in any employee injury situation. That is, the injured minor is eligible for all benefits prescribed by the state's workers compensation law, to be paid by the employer's workers compensation insurance. However, when *illegally* employed minors are injured in the course of employment, employers may find themselves in difficult situations regarding insurance coverage, particularly when the employer has knowingly permitted the illegal employment.

Note that a provision of the workers compensation policy makes clear that the insured is responsible for any payments *in excess of regular workers compensation benefits*, including penalties imposed because of injury to any person knowingly employed in violation of the law. Therefore, if an employer allows a minor to work in a situation that the law limits to adult workers, and the minor is injured, the employer will pay any penalties imposed upon him or her by the state. The workers compensation insurer will pay only the standard benefits. Some states impose a 50 percent increase in benefits (including Arizona, California, and Missouri). Illinois requires a 50 percent increase for minors under sixteen. Other states require *double* compensation (or 200 percent), as in Alabama and Ohio. In Arkansas, double compensation is required unless the minor misrepresented his age in writing to the employer. Mississippi and New Jersey mandate double compensation except for students fourteen and over who are employed between semesters or who are involved in on-the-job training. Rhode Island requires a tripling (300 percent) of benefits. In Wisconsin, double compensation is mandated for minors employed without a permit, and triple compensation is required when minors are employed in prohibited work.

The employers liability section of the policy excludes coverage of bodily injury to an employee hired in violation of the law if the employer or his executive officers actually know of the violation. The employers liability section also excludes punitive or exemplary damages because of bodily injury to an employee employed in violation of law. So, if the injured minor is allowed to sue the employer for personal injuries in lieu of seeking workers compensation benefits, any punitive damages will be paid by the employer and not the workers compensation insurer.

In a small number of states, including Oklahoma and Vermont, statutory workers compensation benefits are not extended to illegally employed minors. However, the employer is not relieved of financial responsibility. On the contrary, the minor is allowed to sue the employer at common law and the workers compensation policy need not respond. Common law actions may also be initiated against an employer by the parents of an illegally employed injured minor.

New Jersey and Illinois, for example, extend benefits to illegally employed minors by statute, but also give the injured minor the option of statutory benefits or suing the employer at common law. The employers liability section (part two) of the workers compensation and employers liability policy applies to liability of the employer under such circumstances. This is subject to two important exceptions: 1) punitive or exemplary damages because of bodily injury to an employee hired in violation of law; and 2) bodily injury to an employee while employed in violation of law with the "actual knowledge" of the employer or an executive officer.

It is important to note, however, that this second exclusion has been held unenforceable in at least one jurisdiction. In *National Grange Mutual Insurance Co. v. Schneider*, 392 A.2d 641 (N.J. Super. Ct. Law Div. 1978), the insurer relied on this exclusion in denying employers liability coverage to a meat market where a thirteen-year-old (hired knowingly without a work certificate even though he was too young to obtain one) severely injured an arm in a meat grinder. The claim was entered under the employers liability part of the policy because the minor had exercised the option given to illegally employed minors in New Jersey to sidestep the workers compensation's exclusive remedy provisions and bring suit at common law. Because the damages would have been covered had the minor brought claim under the workers compensation part of the policy, the court held it was against public policy for the insurer to be allowed to exclude coverage under the employers liability insurance. "The reformers who created workers compensation and factory law remedies for injured employees and industrially abused minors simply would not purposely deprive an illegally employed thirteen-year-old, who claims injury by the negligence of his employer, insurance protection granted routinely to almost everyone else … If the insurers hesitate to cover illegal employments, perhaps their remedy is reimbursement from the employer and not deprivation of the employee. The exclusion may not be applied to an illegally employed minor without violating New Jersey law."

The New Jersey superior court again considered the issue and arrived at the same conclusion in *Variety Farms, Inc. v. New Jersey Manufacturers Insurance Co.*, 410 A.2d 696 (N.J. Super. Ct. App. Div. 1980). Here, a fifteen-year-old lost an arm when allowed to operate power-driven equipment in spite of the state's labor law restricting anyone under sixteen from such work. As in Grange, the minor exercised his option to bring suit at common law rather than accept the statutory benefits. The insurer denied coverage based on the employers liability exclusion pertaining to employees employed in violation of the law with the knowledge of the insured. However, the court held that the exclusion could not apply. The exclusion "would be so repugnant to the letter and spirit of the state workers compensation law and so contrary to public policy as to be unenforceable in a case such as the one here involved."

Principals and Contractors

The workers compensation laws of a majority of states impose liability on principals for compensation benefits to employees of contractors or subcontractors under a certain condition. The statutes vary from state to state but usually are qualified by a provision imposing liability on the owner or general contractor (principal) *only* in the absence of workers compensation insurance provided by the subcontractor. For example, the statute of Wisconsin reads: "An employer shall be liable for compensation to an employee of a contractor or subcontractor who is not subject to this chapter, or who has not complied with the conditions of the statute in any case where such employer would have been liable for compensation if such employee had been working directly for him."

Court decisions have also reinforced this point. In the case of *Wentworth v. Becker Custom Building, Ltd.*, 947 N.E.2d 571 (2011), the Supreme Judicial Court of Massachusetts declared that the objectives of the liability imposing statutes is to prevent a general contractor from escaping its obligations under the workers comp act by hiring uninsured subcontractors. The court noted further that its interpretation of the statutes gives a general contractor a strong incentive to retain subcontractors that have workers compensation insurance because it otherwise has to pay the workers comp benefits and, in addition, is liable for any common law damages.

The status of the injured worker as an independent contractor or an employee is imputed by the facts of the situation. The Internal Revenue Service (IRS) has a checklist to determine the status of a worker for income tax purposes. Some of the items included are:

- who delivers instructions and who complies with them;

- how is training done;

- where does direction and control come from;

- who does the hiring, supervising, and paying;

- who sets the hours of work;

- who has the right to discharge a worker and terminate the work;

- who furnishes the tools and materials; and

- who has supplied the investment or capital?

The main consideration noted in this IRS list is the idea of control. Who controls the situation, and what is the relationship between the one who exercises control and the one injured? That idea of control is also behind the decisions of some courts when it comes to the status of injured persons.

In *Claim of Griffin*, 466 N.W.2d 148 (N.D. 1991), the supreme court in North Dakota stated that "in determining whether a person is an employee or an independent contractor, the primary test is the right to control. Under that test, if the person for whom the work is being done has the right of control, whether he exercises it or not, and is concerned not only with the result of the work but also with the manner and method of its doing, he is held to be an employer and the person doing the work is his employee. On the other hand, if he is concerned merely with the result of the work and has no control over the details of its doing, the person doing the work is held to be an independent contractor."

The *Griffin* case was mentioned in a case from Connecticut. In *Hanson V. Transportation General*, 716 A.2d 857 (1998), the Supreme Court of Connecticut reviewed a claim of a surviving spouse of a murdered taxicab driver; the workers compensation claim was denied by the workers compensation commission, the review board, and the appellate court. The Supreme Court said that the right to control test to determine whether the taxicab driver was an employee or an independent contractor for workers comp purposes was the proper procedure. The court found that the taxicab driver, who drove a cab under an owner-operator agreement with the company, was an independent contractor since, in the daily use of his cab, the driver could set his own hours, work anywhere in the company's service area, refuse to accept dispatch calls, and had sole responsibility for all expenses related to the operation of his cab.

In a case from Louisiana, the Court of Appeal of Louisiana, Third Circuit, ruled that a newspaper deliverer was an independent contractor and not the employee of the newspaper. The case is *Whitlow v. The Shreveport Times*, 843 So.2d 665 (2003).

In discussing the employer-employee relationship, the court said that the essence of the relationship is the right to control. The four primary evidentiary factors in deciding this are: selection and engagement; payment of wages; the power of dismissal; and the power of control. None of these factors is controlling, according to the court, so the totality of the circumstances must be considered and the burden of proof is on the party seeking to establish an employer-employee relationship. The court noted that the newspaper deliverer contracted with the newspaper to purchase newspapers at a wholesale rate for resale and delivery and this contract specifically designated the deliverer as an independent contractor. Moreover, the deliverer was not paid wages and was responsible for his own equipment and means of delivery. Thus, the newspaper deliverer was an independent contractor and was not entitled to workers comp benefits.

In *Hojnacki v. Last Rebel Trucking*, 689 S.E.2d 601 (2010), the Court of Appeals of North Carolina ruled that a truck owner was responsible under the workers compensation law for injuries sustained by the truck driver while connecting the truck to a trailer. The owner leased her trucks to a company for shipping services and the driver was hired to drive one of the trucks. Although there was no written employment agreement between the driver and owner, the driver agreed to drive the owner's truck, the owner paid the driver in exchange for his services, the owner provided the driver with an occupational accident insurance policy, the driver was required to call and report to the owner daily, and the owner required the driver to bring the truck to her if there were any problems. Thus, there was enough of the right to control factor in this instance to establish an employer-employee relationship.

Another example is *Cecil Young v. City of Bridgeport*, 135 Conn. App. 699 (2012), wherein both the trial court and the appeals court noted that the common law right to control test using the facts of the situation establish the status of the individual.

In general, a principal or contractor is not held responsible for the workers compensation claims of employees of contractors or subcontractors unless the subordinate employer has failed to provide coverage. This can happen, for example, through the expiration of a subcontractor's workers compensation insurance, the failure of a subcontractor to provide proper coverage, or because a subcontractor has too few employees to fall under the workers compensation statutes. There are, however, exceptions to this. By statute in several jurisdictions the principal may be liable: 1) if the work contracted is his usual business or occupation; or 2) if he retains control of the premises and supervises the work. In states where a minimum number of employees governs coverage under the act, liability may be passed upward to a contractor or principal who qualifies either because of the number of his own direct employees or because of the combined number involved with several nonqualifying subcontractors. A principal or contractor may also be held liable if the subcontractor's insurance is canceled or the subcontractor's insurer becomes insolvent.

When the principal or contractor is responsible for the compensation due an injured worker, the standard workers compensation and employers liability policy covers the benefits that are due. If the principal or contractor does not carry workers compensation insurance because he has no employees or not enough to require him to comply with the act, this obligation to the employees of subcontractors still applies.

What if the principal is a homeowner who has hired someone to do maintenance work? What if, further, the contractors and subcontractors hired for the job have no workers compensation policies and one of their employees is injured on the job? Typically, the homeowner will not have a workers compensation policy to cover the payment of any required benefits. What does the homeowner do for such coverage?

In general, it is unsafe in any of the states that impose liability on a principal or contractor to permit a contractor or subcontractor to work without workers compensation insurance. A person who fails to check the insurance protection of contractors or subcontractors is gambling for high stakes. This is especially true for homeowners, since homeowners forms do not apply to bodily injury to any person eligible to receive any benefits required to be provided by the insured under any workers compensation law. Therefore, the homeowner cannot rely on the homeowners policy to pay any required benefits.

This leaves few options for the homeowner. He can either self-insure or purchase a workers compensation policy, if possible. The self-insurance option could be expensive especially if the injury is serious or permanent. The purchasing of a workers compensation policy makes more sense financially but could run afoul of state regulations or, more likely, be nearly impossible to purchase in the standard marketplace. The best path for the homeowner would be, as intimated above, to make sure the contractor he hires for repair work carries proper and adequate workers compensation insurance.

In most cases, a principal or contractor that is compelled to pay compensation to an employee of another has an action against the person who is primarily liable. Homeowners should be aware of the fact that they or their insurer can seek recovery from another party if that other party is responsible for the employee's injury.

Wrap-Up Insurance Programs

Wrap-ups are consolidated insurance programs (CIP) whereby a sponsor secures and pays one or more insurance policies that insure multiple parties (e.g., sponsor, general contractor and subcontractors of all tiers). These programs can be utilized for a single project or multiple ongoing projects. For purposes of this chapter, we will refer to all such programs as CIPs.

As mentioned throughout this book, workers compensation is a "no-fault" type of system. Employees are guaranteed coverage if their injuries result from an accident occurring arose from and was within their scope of their employment. In return for this guarantee, employees receive tort immunity for injuries sustained by their employees. Both parties receive significant benefits from this arrangement. If an employee's injuries are caused by a third party, the employee may choose to accept workers compensation payments and bring a legal action against the negligent party.

CIPs create a new dynamic in this relationship between employer and employee. Since a CIP sponsor secures and pays for coverage for multiple parties, some courts have concluded that the sponsor is a statutory employer for purposes of workers compensation. As a statutory employer, the sponsor is immune from litigation from an employee of a CIP insured entity. For instance, Joe Smith is a welder for Smithback Welding. Smithback is a subcontractor to ACME General Contracting, who sponsors a CIP for the project. Joe Smith is badly injured when a piece he is working on collapses. Without a CIP, Joe would collect workers compensation benefits, and could sue the general contractor or another subcontractor if either or both contributed to his injuries. With a CIP, Joe may not be able to bring an action against the CIP sponsor.

The possibility of sponsors (and potentially others) being treated as statutory employers has created controversy between CIP sponsors, insured parties and injured workers. A variety of states have dealt with lawsuits testing these relationships and the applicability of state laws. Those states that find for the CIP sponsors generally do so for one or more of the following reasons:

- The sponsor paid for the CIP coverages.

- The sponsor provided the CIP coverages.

- One of the main objectives of the CIP is to reduce litigation.

Many of the cases that favorer the sponsors that paid CIP premiums were decided in Texas. The case of *Hector Garza v. Zachary Industrial, Inc. et al.*, No. 04-11-00101-CV (Tx. Ct. of App. 2012), is a recent example. The facts of this case are straight forward. Garza worked for DuPont at a plant in Texas. DuPont sponsored a CIP that insured Zachary, a subcontractor providing various services at the DuPont plant. Two of Zachary's employees assisted Garza with moving railcars and Garza was injured. He received workers compensation benefits from DuPont and sued Zachary and two of Zachary's employees. The defendants argued that subparts (a) and (e) of §406.123 of the Texas Labor Code specified that (a) a general contractor and a subcontractor may enter into a written agreement under which the general contractor provides workers compensation insurance coverage to the subcontractor and the employees of the subcontractor, and (e) an agreement under this section makes the general contractor the employer of the subcontractor and the subcontractor's employees only for purposes of the workers compensation laws. The court relied on this provision and several other cases in finding for the defendants.

Some states look favorably on sponsors that provide the CIP coverages. A Connecticut case is illustrative of this approach. In *Lisa Bishel v. Connecticut Yankee Atomic Power Company, Inc.*, 62 Conn. App. 537, (2001) the court concluded that the CIP sponsor was immune from civil liability because it paid the workers compensation benefits pursuant to Connecticut General Statutes §31-291. Bishel was employed by Burns International Security at defendant's power plant in East Hampton, CT. She slipped on ice on the power plant site and sustained injuries to her knee. She collected workers compensation and then sued Connecticut Yankee. Connecticut Yankee maintained a CIP which paid Bishel indemnity payments and her medical expenses. Connecticut Yankee argued that Connecticut General Statutes §31-291 specified that it enjoyed immunity from Bishel's claim because it paid Bishel's compensation expenses (… The provisions of this section shall not extend immunity to any principal employer from a civil action brought by an injured employee … unless such principal employer has paid compensation benefits under this chapter…). The court agreed.

Still other states look to the purpose of CIPs as a factor in their decision. *Stevenson v. HH&N/Turner*, 2003 WL 22480156 is a good example. The United States District Court for the Eastern District of Michigan considered that the Michigan Legislature determined that, as per the conditions of §418.621(3) of the Michigan Worker's Disability Compensation Act, a separate workers compensation policy may be issued to cover employers (and their employees) while performing work at a specified construction site. The court also considered the rationale behind CIPs and reasoned that allowing the plaintiff to recover in a court action would not be in congruence with the purposes of a CIP.

(Note that the alternative employer endorsement (WC 00 03 01 A) issued by NCCI would be ideal for a project owner of an OCIP to avoid having the owner defend itself and argue, where appropriate, that it is a statutory employer to contractors involved in the project.)

Leased Employees

A leased or borrowed employee is defined as one who is dispatched by his employer to another for some service. The leased employee must be loaned with his consent, and he must come under the exclusive control and direction of the employer to whom he is leased. Examples include temporary office workers or workers leased from an employment agency by a contractor to construct a building or drive trucks.

When the leased employee is injured on the job, does workers compensation or general liability insurance apply? If workers compensation applies, is it the exclusive remedy for the injured worker? Whose policy applies, the lessor's or the lessee's? (Or both? See for example the statement of the Court of Civil Appeals of Oklahoma in *Central Plains Construction v. Hickson*, 959 P.2d 998 (1998), that "the loaned servant [borrowed servant] doctrine allows the injured worker to bring workers compensation claims against either his actual employer or the secondary employer to whom he was loaned.)

In general, it can be said that the party that controls the work is the employer. When employer A lends an employee to employer B, the latter becomes liable for workers compensation coverage under certain circumstances. For example, a Florida appeals court, in *J.M. Foster, Inc. v. N.A. Logan, Inc.*, 483 So.2d 553 (Fla. Dist. Ct. App. 1986), decided that if the employee has an express or implied contract for hire with employer B, if the work being done is essentially that of employer B, and if the power to control details of the work being done resides in employer B, then employer B is liable for workers compensation benefits.

The three factors noted by the Florida court were also in evidence in a decision by a Louisiana court of appeals. In *Robbins v. Lee*, 505 So.2d 1161 (La. Ct. App. 1987), the court stated that Robbins was not a loaned employee because his act of helping to raise sheet metal was gratuitous and limited in scope and time. There was no contractual relationship and no control over Robbins exercised by Lee.

The United States Tax Court, in *Professional & Executive Leasing, Inc.* 89 TC 225 (1987), established a test consisting of seven factors to determine if an employment relationship exists. The court stated that the following areas had to be examined in order to accurately define the employment relationship: the degree of control over the work of the employees; any significant investment that the leasing company has made in the workplace; the realization of profit or loss by the leasing company; the integration of the work of the leased employees into the regular business operations of the leasing company; the right to hire and terminate; the type of work relationship (i.e., permanent job versus temporary job); how the parties treat the relationship and what the parties consider that relationship to be.

The United States Court of Appeals, Eleventh Circuit, added its views on the probative considerations of the borrowing principal's right to control in *Langfitt v. Federal Marine Terminals, Inc.*, 647 F.3d 1116 (2011). The court listed the following considerations: direct evidence that the general employer expressly transferred control to the borrowing principal or that the borrowing principal exercised control; evidence that the borrowing principal was responsible for paying the employee; evidence that the borrowing principal furnished equipment necessary for performance of the work; and evidence that the borrowing principal had the right to terminate its relationship with the employee.

A case from the United States District Court for the Northern District of Georgia offers a rather interesting analysis of the borrowed employee doctrine. This case is *U.S. Vinyl Manufacturing Corporation v. Colour & Design*, 32 F.Supp.3d 1253 (2013).

In this case, the manufacturer and distributor of vinyl wallcovering products brought claims of breach of contract, tortious breach of fiduciary duty, and constructive fraud against a vinyl wallcovering design firm. As part of the discussion of this case, the court was faced with an issue of fact as to whether the manufacturer loaned an employee to the design firm, holding that while the existence of a borrowed servant relationship is a question of law, the determination of the question is heavily fact based.

As part of its analysis, the court leaned on a determination of whether an individual was an employee by the Supreme Court where that court stated this should be based "on principles of the general common law of agency". Another court quoted by the District Court was the Eleventh Circuit which declared "... the focus is on the relationship between the two principals, that is, which of them had the right of control. Probative considerations of the borrowing principal's right to control might include: direct evidence that the general employer expressly transferred control to the borrowing principal or that the borrowing principal exercised control; evidence that the borrowing principal was responsible for paying the employee; evidence that the borrowing principal furnished equipment necessary for performance of the work; and evidence that the borrowing principal had the right to terminate its relationship with the employee".

The District Court said that no one of these factors is determinative, although control is first and foremost.

Now, there are contractual and statutory points that need to be considered in addition to legal doctrine.

A firm that leases its employees to another firm may have spelled out in the lease agreement which party must provide the workers compensation coverage. Presuming the existence of such a valid contract, the leased worker has the benefit of knowing coverage exists and all concerned parties are aware of their respective responsibilities.

Obviously, such a contractual agreement would have one of two alternatives. First, one or the other employer will provide workers compensation insurance and employers liability insurance. Second, both employers will provide the necessary coverage.

Under the first scenario, employer A (the lessor) may be required by employer B (the lessee) to provide workers compensation and employers liability insurance. Employer A may add the alternative employer endorsement, WC 00 03 01, to its existing workers compensation policy. This endorsement applies to bodily injury to employees in the course of special or temporary employment by the alternative employer named in the schedule. The insurer agrees, under the terms of WC 00 03 01, to reimburse the alternative employer for the benefits required if the insurer is not permitted to pay the benefits directly to the injured persons.

If both employers agree to provide workers compensation coverage and be liable for the benefits, each should have its own workers compensation policy. The agreement between the two employers may spell out the amounts of benefits and premiums to be paid by the respective parties. It should be noted that the other insurance clause in the workers compensation policy states that benefits and costs covered by the insurance are on a pro rata basis, subject to any limits of liability that may apply.

What if, however, one of the parties reneges on the contract or refuses to sign it? In this case, state laws vary, but, generally, if the lessee employer can't or won't provide workers compensation benefits, that burden will flow back to the lessor employer. One instance of litigation of such statutory employment status is found in *Dockery v. McMillan*, 355 S.E.2d 153 (N.C. Ct. App. 1987). In this case, a North Carolina appeals court held that a general employer is responsible for the payment of compensation benefits because that employer had failed to ascertain whether or not the borrowing employer had workers compensation insurance. The latter employer did not, and the general employer had to pay the benefits.

Any response from the general liability policy to an injured leased employee has to be considered in light of exclusions d. and e. in the commercial general liability coverage form; these are the exclusions dealing with obligations of the insured under workers compensation laws and due to employee injury. The CGL policy of the party deemed to be the employer would exclude coverage for injury to a leased employee. But, what is the result if a leased employee files a claim or a lawsuit against that employer not considered to be the employer of record? For example, the employee is leased from employer A to employer B, who becomes legally responsible for workers compensation benefits. The employee is injured while working for employer B; he receives workers compensation benefits from B and then files suit against employer A claiming negligence in the manner of his leasing. The CGL form of employer A should respond to such a claim. CGL Exclusion d. should not apply because the claim would not deal with any obligation arising from a workers compensation law. CGL Exclusion e. also should not apply because the claim is based on the alleged negligence of the insured (employer A) and not his employment of the injured worker. The worker is the employee of employer B.

If employer A then files a third-party-over suit against employer B seeking to share the damages, exclusion e. of B's CGL form would apply. CGL coverage is denied to B. However, if employer B carries employers liability insurance, the third-party-over suit can be handled by that coverage.

There are other facets of the commercial general liability form that should be mentioned at this time.

The ISO CGL exclusion e. does not apply to liability assumed by the insured under an insured contract. Using the example noted above, if the injured leased employee sues employer A for negligence in the manner of the leasing of the employee, and the lease agreement calls upon employer B to assume the tort liability of A, then the contractual coverage in the general liability policy of B would respond. B may respond depending (1) on the degree of hold harmless agreement (i.e., intermediate or broad); (2) whether any anti-indemnity statute otherwise permits it; and (3) the scope of contractual liability coverage (i.e., not subject, for example, to Contractual Liability Limitation endorsement CG 21 39). It is therefore possible for employer B to provide workers compensation benefits plus general liability damages to the same employee for the same incident.

The current ISO CGL form defines "employee" as including a "leased worker". This means that the CGL insurer does not want to provide general liability coverage for bodily injury to a leased worker. That leased worker is considered an employee of the named insured and, as such, is affected by the same exclusions d. and e. that preclude bodily injury coverage for a regular employee of the named insured. Bodily injury to a leased worker is meant to be covered under a workers compensation policy.

Note that the term "leased worker" in the ISO CGL form does not include a "temporary worker." A temporary worker means a person who is furnished as a substitute for a permanent employee on leave or to meet seasonal or short term work conditions. So why does exclusion e. apply to leased workers and not temporary workers? The answer lies in state workers compensation statutes. States tend to treat temporary workers as employees of the temporary service provider. For instance, the State of Kentucky has determined that the temporary help service provider is the employer of temporary workers [see Ky. Rev. Stat. Ann. §342.615(5)].

(Just as an aside, the October 2015 edition of Inside Counsel—a sister publication—noted that the National Labor Relations Board has broadened the standards for assessing joint-employer status under the National Labor Relations Act. The Board now finds joint employer status where one entity either actually directly controls another employer's employees' terms and conditions of employment, where that entity has indirect control of terms and conditions of employment or has simply reserved the right to exert such control.)

Alternate Employer Coverage

To the extent insurers are willing, an alternate employer endorsement (WC 00 03 01 A, for example) is a good way to protect entities that are involved in special employer situations; that is, where one entity borrows the employee of another entity and desires protection in the event the borrowed employee is injured while under the direction and control of the entity that has borrowed that employee.

An alternate employer endorsement (AEE) becomes significant when it is unclear which of the two employers (in a general-special or dual relationship) had control of the employee at the time of an accident. The endorsement also can be viewed as if there were two named insureds on a workers compensation policy enjoying immunity from suit. So, the AEE is the saving grace, so-to-speak, for an alternate employer. This is because the alternate employer is still protected when employees do not accept workers compensation benefits as the final settlement, but instead file suit despite those benefits—to the extent permitted by statute.

While there are differences by jurisdiction, it is generally accepted (according to Arthur Larson and Lex K. Larson, *Larson's Workers Compensation*, Vol. 2.ww.8, section 48) that when an employer (special employer) borrows an employee from another employer (general employer), or a general employer lends its employee to the recipient special employer, the special employer becomes liable for workers compensation only when the following three conditions are met: (a) the employee has made a contract of hire, express or implied, with the special employer; (b) the work being done is essentially that of the special employer; and (c) the special employer has the right to control the details of the work.

It is not always a simple matter to determine these criteria.

In the case of *Robert J. Ray and Amelia Ray v. Marcus Thomas*, 2009 WL 2600521, for example, the status of a special employer was held not to apply because there was no evidence of a contract of hire, implied or expressed. Briefly, Ray, who was employed by a contracting firm, was injured while working on the premises of another company. The injury came about when Thomas, an employee of this latter company, while transporting a pipe by a crane, dropped the pipe. After receiving statutory workers compensation benefits, Ray filed a complaint against Thomas alleging negligence and loss of consortium for his spouse. Thomas maintained that Ray's exclusive remedy was the statutory workers compensation benefits, because Ray was a special employee of the company for whom Thomas was employed and on whose premises Ray was injured.

In determining whether a special employer relationship existed, the court noted that the second and third of the above conditions had been met, but not the first one requiring that the employee had agreed to a contract of hire with the special employer. This was the court's decision even though Ray had reported to the premises every day for work and had received assignments from his supervisor, Thomas. The reason there was no contract of hire, even though Ray believed there was a contract, was that there was no evidence that Ray was aware of the contract's details.

Who had control at the time of injury also is often difficult to determine until after the fact, particularly with borrowed and lent employee arrangements, where employment is temporary, such as with staffing agencies. Much depends, for instance, on the three conditions previously mentioned, the first two of which can be determined prior to an injury and claim, but not the third one dealing with control. Thus, it is only after a claim is made and an investigation is conducted that one may be able to conclude who had control and should have had statutory workers compensation in place, the general or special employer. Sometimes, litigation is necessary to make the correct determination.

In that vein, there are a number of disputes over the alternate employer endorsement that have been litigated.

In *Regina Miller v. The Unity Group Inc.*, 2007 WL 8327961, a hotel housekeeping company that serviced hotels (Unity) had an agreement with a firm that supplied temporary employees (MBA). Since the contract between MBA and Unity required MBA to maintain workers compensation insurance, a certificate of insurance was issued by MBA's insurance representative listing Unity Group as a Certificate Holder Additional Insured.

A dispute arose after the claimant, who was injured on two separate occasions while performing services for Unity, made claims against Unity for these two work-related injuries. One of the questions before the court was whether Unity was a named insured on the workers compensation and employers liability policy issued to MBA. This particular policy contained an alternate employer endorsement which stated that workers compensation insurance would apply if an employee of MBA were injured "in the course of special or temporary employment by the alternate employer."

Since neither the policy nor the endorsement defined the term "alternate employer", the court decided that the endorsement created an ambiguity and, therefore, held that Unity qualified as an alternate employer. This decision was supported by the certificate of insurance, which not only referenced the workers compensation policy of MBA, but also stated that "coverage is provided for only those employees leased to but not subcontractors of the Unity Group". Thus, from the court's perspective, both the insurance certificate and the ambiguity created by the alternate employer endorsement supported the conclusion that Unity was an insured. (Note that this decision was reversed by the South Carolina Supreme Court in *Miller v. The Unity Group*, 2009 WL 9541389.)

(When a certificate of insurance is completed for these kinds of employment relationships, those who complete certificates should not assume or state anything on the certificate that is not also stated in the policy. In other words, the alternate employer should not be shown as a named insured or insured [which seems to be tossed around as being the equivalent of a named insured]. When an alternative employer endorsement is issued, it needs to be identified on the insurance certificate and nothing more. Once there is an attempt to clarify this endorsement's impact with such a description as named insured, insured, or additional insured, it can cause problems to the person who completes the insurance certificate.)

Although an alternate employer endorsement was sufficient for co-employers of a leasing arrangement to obtain immunity for an employee injury, additional steps were taken to seek that objective in *Brown v. Aztec Equipment, Inc.*, 921 S.W.2d 835 (1996).

Through client service agreements with small businesses, a staff leasing firm employed the existing work force of its clients and then leased them back to carry out the client's business. This relationship situation existed when the staff leasing company contracted with a business involved in the repair of oil and gas equipment (client). Under this arrangement, the staff leasing company agreed to carry workers compensation insurance covering all of its employees furnished to the client. The client service agreement also included a provision that the staff leasing company was the employer for some purposes and that the client would be considered the employer for certain other purposes. It also indicated that both the staff leasing company and the client were co-employers for still other purposes.

An employee who was furnished by the staff leasing company signed employment agreements on two separate occasions. He also agreed that for purposes of workers compensation insurance, he was an employee of both the staff leasing company and the client. These agreements stated that in the event of any injury, the employee agreed that his sole remedy was under the policy of the staff leasing company under the theory that both the staff leasing company and the client were co-employers. Following injury on two separate occasions, the employee sought workers compensation benefits, but after learning he was not entitled to benefits (for reasons not stated in this court case), he brought suit against both firms who claimed immunity. It turned out that the alternate employer endorsement and the agreement signed by the employee were both sufficient to hold that both firms had immunity to suit.

The alternate employer endorsement can be a spoiler for injured workers who are involved in situations involving special employments, such as temporary staffing companies. This is not a universal conclusion but certainly a situation that is intended by this endorsement. A case in point is *Antonio Perez Molina v. State Garden, Inc.*, 37 N.E.3d 39 (2013).

Molina, a general employee of American Resource Staffing Network (ARS), an entity in the business of providing temporary staffing, was assigned to provide on-site services to State Garden and was injured during the course of providing such services. ARS maintained a workers compensation and employers liability policy, which was amended with the alternate employer endorsement stating in part: "This endorsement applies only with respect to bodily injury to your employees while in the course of special or temporary employment by the alternate employer named [below]…Part One (Workers Compensation Insurance…will apply as through the alternate employer is insured."

The alternate employer endorsement on ARS's policy specifically identified State Garden as the alternate employer. Molina's employment with ARS was further subject to the terms of a signed waiver and release agreement, which provided in pertinent part as follows: "In recognition that any work related injuries which might be sustained by me are covered by state workers compensation statutes, and to avoid the circumvention of such state statutes which may result from suits against customers or clients of [ARS], based on the same injury or injuries, and to the extent permitted by law, I HEREBY WAIVE AND FOREVER RELEASE ANY RIGHTS I MIGHT HAVE to make claims or bring suit against any client or customer of [ARS], for damages based upon injuries which are covered under such workers compensation statutes."

It was undisputed that under the workers compensation act, ARS, the general employer was immune from any common law action arising out of Molina's injury. Molina, however, brought suit against State Garden, arguing that the statutory workers compensation bar did not apply to this entity (State Garden), because it was not his direct employer. State Garden, in turn, maintained that, while it was not Molina's direct employer, it nonetheless enjoyed immunity under the act by virtue of the alternate employer endorsement issued in conjunction with the ARS policy.

The court agreed with the argument of State Garden. In doing so, it stated that there was very limited Massachusetts case law that examined whether an entity named in an alternate employer endorsement to a workers compensation policy enjoyed the same immunity as the direct employer. What Massachusetts case law did exist, the court said, as well as authorities from other jurisdictions, led it to conclude that named alternate employers such as State Garden faced no common law liability through the exclusivity provisions of the act.

The case of *Allied Van Lines v. Fairfield Insurance Company*, 2010 WL 1254633 involved a dispute over which of two policies covered claims for injuries. An independent contractor (Jenkins) was the driver of a truck owned by (Allied) who, concerned for his health, hired another person (Storey) to assist in the loading and unloading of his van. While on a job, an accident occurred whereby Storey suffered serious injuries. The insurer (Fairfield) paid benefits under an occupational accident policy and not under the workers compensation policy.

Having received benefits under the occupational accident policy, Storey was not barred from recovery in tort and, therefore, filed suit against

Allied and others for damages. The defendants argued that since Storey was injured in the course and scope of his employment, he should have been paid under the workers compensation policy, which also would have barred Storey's suit. The trial court entered judgments against all defendants.

In the appeal, Allied and its insurer sued Fairfield for breach of contract in failing to pay under the workers compensation policy, which they claim exposed them to the payment of legal costs and a settlement of $200,000. The fallacy of this argument, according to the court, was that even if Allied were an insured under the alternate employer endorsement, and even if Storey had received workers compensation benefits, his effort to contest his employment status would have allowed him to pursue a tort remedy.

The appeals court also concluded that Allied was not an insured under the workers compensation policy issued by Fairfield to Jenkins by virtue of a certificate of insurance that referenced an alternate employer endorsement. While it was true that this endorsement listed Allied as an alternate employer, the endorsement also stated, "[t]his endorsement changes the policy to which it is attached and is effective on the date indicated on the Information page unless otherwise stated." The court noted, however, that the endorsement was not listed on the information page of the policy and, therefore, lacked an effective date. In light of the fact that the certificate did not amend, extend or alter the coverage afforded by the policies listed, Jenkins was the only insured. Since the alternate employer endorsement was not in effect, Allied's breach of contract allegation failed.

Note that it is necessary that the alternate employer endorsement is completed to reflect all of the states where it is to be applicable, particularly when an entity's workers compensation insurance is written by two or more insurers. This was the issue addressed in the case of *Metro Staffing, Inc. v. Workers' Compensation Appeal Board*, No. 2145 C.D. (Commonwealth Ct., PA. 2007) where, despite the fact that two insurers handled the workers compensation insurance, neither one had to pay benefits.

Metro Staffing, Inc. (employer) was a temporary employment agency with offices in Pennsylvania and Delaware. The claimant was hired by the employer at its Delaware location, which was covered by CNA through an independent producer, but assigned to work at Tasty Baking Company in Pennsylvania where he was injured. The employer's statutory coverage for Pennsylvania was purchased from the state workers compensation insurance fund (SWIF).

The policy issued by SWIF provided that it covered all of the employer's workplaces in items 1 and 4 of the information page; and it covered all other workplaces in item 3.A., unless the employer had other insurance or was self-insured for such workplaces. Item 3.A. stated that part one of the policy (workers compensation) applied under the law of Pennsylvania. The alternate employer endorsement issued in connection with the SWIF policy provided coverage for employees while in the course of special or temporary employment by the alternate employer in the state named in item 2 of the endorsement's schedule. The baking company was not named in this endorsement. (The SWIF knew there was an exposure in Pennsylvania but did not realize it was with the baking company.) Item 3.A. of this policy, on the other hand, applied to all workplaces in the state of Pennsylvania, unless other insurance was secured for such workplaces.

Thus, the SWIF policy covered only the employer's workplaces identified in items 1 and 4., those identified in the alternate employer endorsement, which was not issued for the baking company, and Pennsylvania workplaces not covered by other insurance. The Delaware office, where the claimant was employed, was not listed in items 1 or 4 of the SWIF policy. The CNA policy, on the other hand, was issued solely for the state of Delaware. With the alternate employer endorsement not being applicable to the baking company, the employer was left to retain the consequences of this injury and of the oversight in failing to properly designate the Delaware office on the SWIF policy.

The point to keep in mind here is that when policies have to split among different insurance producers or insurers, coverage gaps are more likely to occur than if all of the same coverages were consolidated with one insurer and producer. Unfortunately, it is not always possible to do so. This means that extra care must be taken to fill any gaps, since they can be costly, particularly with respect to workers compensation where the benefits payable for long periods can be enormous.

Another case that could have provided a special employer with protection had the endorsement listed that employer by name is *Salitsky Alloys Inc. v. Metz Personnel*, 29 Mass. L. Rptr. 558 (Mass. Super. Ct. 2012). Briefly, Metz leased employees to client much like a temporary staffing agency. The injured party was a direct employee of Metz whom Metz had leased to Salitsky and who was injured during the course of his leased employment. The employee sued Salitsky, claiming that the immunizing exclusivity provisions of the workers compensation act did not apply, because Salitsky was not his direct employer. The contract between Metz and Salitsky included an alternate employer endorsement, which could well have relieved Salitsky from common law liability. The parties, however, neglected to designate Salitsky as the alternate employer. The court accordingly held that, because the endorsement did not specify Salitsky by name as the alternate employer, the company was not entitled to immunity under the workers compensation act.

At times for a variety of reasons, the alternate employer endorsement may not be available as, for example, with workers compensation insurance written by a monopolistic state fund. (The single, most important advantage of this endorsement is that it views the alternate employer as if it were a policy named insured. As such, the alternate employer obtains defense on a primary and noncontributory basis, immunity from suit by the general employer's employee, and a built-in subrogation waiver.) If the endorsement is not available, the next best alternative would be for the alternate employer to obtain:

A contract of understanding between it and the general employer. This contract would also include the monetary arrangement. For example, the alternate employer may agree to reimburse the general employer for the workers compensation premium charge to the employees who will be working within the control of the alternate (special) employer;

A contract of understanding between it and each of the employee(s) of the general contractor who will be working within the control of the alternate (special) employer (this is an essential document in order to create the general-special employer relationship);

Proof of a workers compensation and employers liability policy and, when applicable, LHWCA and maritime general and excess liability policies;

A hold harmless and indemnity agreement between it and the general employer (the degree of such an assumption will depend on whether there is any applicable state anti-indemnity statute and exception;

A waiver of the general employer's rights of immunity specifically applicable to only the contractual relationship involved (the waiver is likely to be necessary because of the possibility of an action in tort and the fact that workers compensation commonly is the exclusive remedy; when effected, the general employer, in essence, waives its immunity granted by statute so as to become answerable to others (e.g., special employer), even after workers compensation benefits have been paid;

A waiver of subrogation to prevent the general employer's insurer from seeking payment of the benefits paid for an accident involving the general employer's employee while under the control of the alternate (special) employer;

Additional insured coverage under the general employer's CGL policy, including proof of contractual liability coverage encompassing the hold harmless agreement (a CGL policy may be especially helpful because a temporary employee is not an employee, which means that neither the workers compensation nor employers liability exclusions is applicable; some endorsements also may be necessary such as Coverage For Injury To Leased Workers, endorsement CG 04 24).

The general idea outlining the above steps is to ensure that the alternate employer is protected in the event of suit by an employee of the general employer after receipt of workers compensation benefits or before receipt if a state does not allow such actions after benefits are received. The more avenues taken, the better the chances of closing any gaps.

Illegal Immigrant Workers

When an illegal immigrant worker is injured on the job, is there going to be workers comp coverage for him or her?

In *HDV Construction Systems, Inc. v Aragon*, 66 So.3d 331 (2011), the District Court of Appeals of Florida, First District, ruled that the award of workers comp benefits was affirmed. The court said that in affirming this award, the decision emphasized that point that the purpose of workers compensation is to place on the industry, rather than the general taxpaying public, the expense incident to the hazards created by industry. Because the employer stands to benefit and profit from its employment of labor, and is in the best position to avoid the risk of loss, it would be improper to foist on society the costs of an injured worker. Moreover, in this instance, the court found that the state legislature clearly allowed and fully intended that illegal immigrants be covered under the state workers comp law.

The Supreme Court of Nebraska ruled in a similar fashion. In *Moyera v. Quality Pork International*, 825 N.W.2d 409, an employer sought a review of an award of permanent total disability workers comp benefits to a claimant who was an illegal alien for loss of earning power arising out of an accident in which the claimant's right foot was run over by a forklift. The court said that the state workers compensation act applies to undocumented employees under a contract of hire with a covered employer in the state. Moreover, said the court, a claimant's illegal residence or work status does not bar an award of indemnity for permanent total loss of earning capacity under the workers compensation act.

Of course, the fact is that hiring illegal immigrants may be deemed in violation of state law in some states. If so, will the workers comp policy have to pay the benefits? The workers comp policy states that the insured is responsible for any payments in excess of the benefits regularly provided by the workers compensation law because of the insured's knowingly employing an employee in violation of law. This means that the policy will pay the benefits due as required by the workers comp law, but any amount in excess of those benefits are the responsibility of the insured.

And, the insured should not look to the employers liability insurance coverage in the WC policy in such an instance since there is an exclusion in that section of the policy for bodily injury to an employee while employed in violation of law with the insured's actual knowledge.

Stop Gap Coverage

Employers liability insurance is normally part of the standard workers compensation policy. A problem arises when a standard workers compensation policy is not provided. This occurs when the workers compensation program is operated by a monopolistic state fund. In such cases, employers liability coverage is not offered by the state and a gap in coverage exists. Stop gap coverage plugs that gap.

Note first of all that stop gap coverage is not a substitute for workers compensation coverage. Stop gap coverage is designed only to provide liability insurance for an employer who is sued by an employee injured in the course of employment.

In monopolistic state fund jurisdictions, employers may be able to purchase stop gap coverage from private insurers (or they can self-insure the exposure). Stop gap coverage can mirror the employers liability coverage provided on the workers compensation policy. However, the terms are not automatically the same. Stop gap coverage is not a standardized policy and the insured needs to review the policy to be sure the needed coverage is being provided.

Guidelines provide for basic limits of liability of $100,000 each accident for bodily injury by accident; $100,000 each employee for bodily injury by disease; and $500,000 policy limit for bodily injury by disease. Higher limits are permitted. The premium is based on the workers compensation classifications and rates in the applicable rating organization's workers compensation manual.

Defense costs can also be provided by stop gap insurance. If an employee can sue an employer over work-related injuries, that lawsuit brings with it attorneys' fees and court costs—and stop gap can help defray those costs. Lawsuits brought by spouses or other family members of the injured employees for loss of consortium or services could be another item handled by stop gap coverage. And, dual capacity and third-party-over claims can likewise be subject matters for stop gap.

Stop gap coverage can be added as an endorsement to either a general liability or a workers compensation policy, depending on the underwriting guidelines of the insurer.

Workers Compensation and Volunteers

Workers compensation was created to apply to injuries of employees suffered in the course of employment. A question often arises when a volunteer is injured. Are volunteers employees? If the volunteers are considered employees, then the workers compensation system will respond if they are injured while performing their services. Unfortunately, there is no absolute standard on the status of volunteers under the workers compensation system. An entity that uses volunteers needs to know whether courts or statutes in its particular state have addressed the question of compensability of injuries to volunteers.

The following cases offer just a few examples of judicial thinking on this issue.

In Colorado, the state supreme court faced the issue of whether a claimant was an employee when he was injured on voluntary ski patrol in *Aspen Highlands Skiing Corp. v. Apostolou*, 866 P.2d 1384 (Colo. 1994). Apostolou was employed as a part-time ski instructor. He volunteered for ski patrol in exchange for ski passes for his girlfriend. During patrol, Apostolou fell and injured his knee. He sought workers compensation benefits, but the employer said he was a volunteer and not entitled to benefits. The state Supreme Court cited the definition of employee in the workers compensation statute; that is, "any person in the service of any private corporation under any contract of hire, express or implied." The court noted that Apostolou had negotiated with the employer for the ski passes. Apostolou had obligated himself to work and the employer had obligated itself to provide free passes. This established a contractual relationship, meaning that Apostolou was an employee within the terms of the statute.

Morales v. Workers' Compensation Appeals Board, 186 Cal App.3d 283 (1986) was a case where a county prisoner doing community work was found to be an employee entitled to workers compensation benefits. Morales was sentenced to sixty days in jail and put in a voluntary community work program. There was no monetary compensation offered and no contractual negotiations. The only consideration Morales received was freedom from the physical confinement of a jail cell while doing community work. Morales hurt his back during the work and sought workers compensation benefits. The California appeals court decided that consideration other than wages may support a contract of hire within the meaning of the state workers compensation law. Therefore, since Morales had received consideration in the form of semi-freedom in exchange for his work, a work contract could be said to exist. This meant Morales could be considered as an employee and entitled to workers compensation benefits.

In *McCreery v. Covenant Presbyterian Church*, 400 S.E.2d 130 (S.C. 1990), McCreery volunteered to help build a church and was injured during this work. He sought workers compensation benefits; coverage was disputed. A court of appeals found that McCreery was a volunteer and not an employee because he was not paid any money and received no other consideration for his services. Even though the Supreme Court reversed the lower court's decision on other grounds, the finding that McCreery was not an employee subject to the workers compensation statute was not denied by the Supreme Court.

In *Simmons v. SC Strong*, 739 S.E.2d 631 (2014), the Court of Appeals of South Carolina held that the claimant was a volunteer worker and thus was not entitled to receive WC benefits. The court said that to be considered an employee under a contract of hire, as required for eligibility for workers compensation benefits, a person must have a right to payment for his services. The claimant in this instance participated in a non-profit organization's program to rehabilitate former substance abusers, ex-convicts, and homeless adults but he neither received nor expected to receive any kind of pay for his services.

The Court of Appeals of Arizona, Division 1, in *Henderson-Jones v. Industrial Commission of Arizona*, 310 P.3d 976 (2013) ruled that the claimant who was teaching English in Africa at the time of injuries sustained in a motor vehicle accident, was a volunteer, as opposed to an employee of the non-profit organization from which she sought benefits. The court explained that a contract of hire is necessary to establish an employer-employee relationship under workers compensation statutes, and such a contract does not exist when someone labors for another on a gratuitous basis. The court added that the distinction between an employee and a volunteer in the workers comp context lies not so much in the employer's exercise of control over the individual, but in whether the individual expected to receive, and did receive, payment for services rendered; a volunteer does not expect to be paid a salary or wages.

In this case, the volunteer did receive a monthly stipend of $850, but the court said that stipends and reimbursements designed to offset the cost of volunteering are not payments for purposes of determining whether a workers compensation claimant is an employee.

So to a great degree then, the question of volunteer as employee rests upon whether consideration is granted for services. This consideration can be monetary or otherwise, but it can be seen as the basis of a contract between the worker and the other party. This can establish an employer-employee relationship.

Incidentally, most commercial general liability (CGL) coverage forms clearly distinguish a volunteer from an employee. So, if the volunteer is injured while performing services for the named insured, the volunteer may not be able to collect workers comp benefits, but he can file a lawsuit against the insured and seek benefits in that manner. Also, the medical payments coverage in the CGL form allows payments to volunteers for bodily injury to them caused by an accident on the premises of the insured or because of the operations of the insured.

Various Workers Compensation Doctrines

There are several legal theories relating to workers compensation that have been promulgated by courts throughout the country. These theories may affect coverage under the workers compensation system even though they are not all accepted in every state.

The Positional Risk Doctrine

The positional risk doctrine is a legal theory that proposes an employee injury may be said to arise out of his employment if the injury would not have occurred but for the fact that the conditions or obligations of the employment placed the employee in a position where he was injured by a neutral force. This neutral force must be one that is neither personal to the employee nor associated distinctly with the employment. The Supreme Court of Arkansas in *Jivan v. Economy Inn & Suites*, 260 S.W.3d 281 (2007) described the positional risk doctrine in just these terms.

In that case, the Court said that an injury is deemed to arise out of the employment under the positional risk doctrine if it is one that would not have occurred but for the fact that the conditions and obligations of the employment placed the claimant in the position where the injury occurred. The positional risk doctrine, the Court continued, is implicated in circumstances where a workers compensation claimant is injured by neutral risk to which he or she is exposed due to conditions and obligations of employment. And, a neutral risk means the risk that caused injury was neither personal to the claimant nor distinctly associated with the employment.

A common example of the positional risk doctrine is where a vehicle crashes through the building where the employee is working, injuring the employee. Some would argue that there is no causal connection between the employment and the injury. In jurisdictions that have adopted the positional risk doctrine, it is held that the employee was injured only because he was at work, in a position where he had to be because of his employment. Thus, workers compensation benefits should be paid. The doctrine declares that mere presence is enough if the injured employee would not have been injured otherwise. Jurisdictions that do not accept the positional risk doctrine emphasize the point that mere presence at the work place is not by itself enough to certify that an injury arose out of and in the course of employment.

The positional risk doctrine is a minority opinion in this country. An overwhelming majority of states require a causal connection. If a causal connection between the injury and the employment is disputed, such disputes are decided on a case-by-case basis, with the court taking several factors into consideration.

Foremost among these factors is the claimant's medical evidence. When an injured worker makes a workers compensation claim, it must be shown that the connection between the injury and the employment is based on reasonable medical probability. In other words, the employee must have a doctor report that the injury did (or most probably did) occur as a result of the employment.

Another factor is whether the activity was undertaken at the employer's request or order. The employer-employee relationship is determined on the right to control. The employer tells the employee what to do and how to do it. If the employee is injured in the process of complying with the employer's instructions, the employer cannot effectively deny that the injury was connected to work.

Additional factors considered are whether the employer either directly or indirectly compelled the employee's attendance at the place of injury and whether the employer benefited in some way by the employee's activity. If a workers compensation board or a court were to find that an employer did compel attendance or did benefit from the activity, the injury suffered by the employee will be declared work-related and the causal connection established.

Another example can be seen in *Zemis v. SCI Contractors, Inc./E.E. Black, Inc.*, 911 P.2d 77 (Haw. 1996). The supreme court of Hawaii discussed the positional risk doctrine in relation to an assault by one worker upon another. Zemis was involved in a car accident with the wife of a coworker. The coworker blamed Zemis for the accident and, two days later, confronted Zemis at the work site and hit him. Zemis sought workers compensation benefits; the employer denied the injury was in the course of employment. One of the theories put forth by Zemis was the positional risk doctrine. The state Supreme Court found in favor of the employer and pointed out that the positional risk doctrine applies only when the risk to the employee is neutral—that is neither personal to the claimant nor distinctly associated with the employment. In this case, the court decided that there was no reasonable inference that the nature of the employment created the risk.

Odd Lot Doctrine

The odd lot doctrine allows the finding of permanent total disability when a relatively small percentage of impairment caused by a work-related accident is combined with other factors to render a claimant unable to obtain employment. The employee does not have to be completely physically disabled under this doctrine. Some of the other factors to be considered are the age, education, and mental capacity of the claimant, as well as the claimant's ability to be trained. If a workers compensation board, after hearing the facts of the case, decides that the employee cannot obtain work because those factors preclude it, then permanent total disability can be granted.

Usual Exertion Doctrine

A majority of jurisdictions throughout the country apply the usual *exertion doctrine*. It states that an injury to an employee is compensable if the ordinary stress and strain of employment is shown to be a substantial cause of the injury. The unusual exertion rule requires a claimant to show that he was engaged in some form of unusual exertion or activity at the time of a job-related injury in order to collect workers compensation benefits.

These two principles usually come into play when disputes over workers compensation benefits arise because of preexisting conditions. For example, some would deny compensation to an employee who suffers a heart attack while on the job because that employee had a preexisting heart condition, unless it can be shown that the employee engaged in extraordinary or unusual exertion while working. Others support the idea that if an employee suffers a heart attack while engaged in the usual exertion of the job, compensation should be paid if a causal connection existed between the work related activity and the injury; the presence of a preexisting problem or disorder is not the main point.

Neither the usual exertion principle nor the unusual exertion rule have any direct effect on the workers compensation policy. The policy agreement states that the insurer will pay promptly when due the benefits required by the workers compensation law. Therefore, if a particular state workers compensation law (or court) declares that compensation is due, the workers compensation policy will respond.

Last Injurious Exposure Rule

Disputes may arise between employers or insurers over whether an injury is new or an aggravation of a prior injury. Under the last *injurious exposure rule*, it is the legal burden of the previous employer to show that the injury is a new one. If a new injury is proven, the current employer is responsible for compensation payments. If it is not proven, the previous employer may end up paying the compensation or splitting the payments, depending on how and to whom the workers compensation board apportions the injury.

Under this rule, if the current employer is ordered to make all the compensation payments, neither the employer nor its insurer is allowed to pursue the previous employer or its insurer for any contribution, unless state law permits such a course of action.

Peculiar Risk Doctrine

The peculiar risk doctrine, which is also known as the special risk doctrine, holds that a person who hires an independent contractor to perform work that is inherently dangerous (a peculiar risk) can be held liable for tort damages when the contractor's negligent performance causes injuries to others; the existence of a peculiar risk is determined by the facts of the particular incident. The reasoning behind the doctrine is that an innocent third party injured by the negligence of an independent contractor should not have to depend just on the contractor's ability to pay in order to receive compensation. Another source of compensation is the person who was to benefit from the contractor's work.

For a discussion of the peculiar risk doctrine see the Court of Appeal, Second District, Division 3, California in *Vargas v. FMI*, 233 Cal.App.4th 638 (2015), stated that under the doctrine of peculiar risk, a person that hires an independent contractor to perform work that is inherently dangerous can be held liable for tort damages when the contractor's negligent performance of the work causes injuries to others. The court also said that a hirer's liability under the doctrine is vicarious and this means that, irrespective of the hirer's lack of negligence, the hirer incurs liability for the hired contractor's act or omission in failing to use reasonable care in the performing the hired work.

(Such reasoning is not altogether unacceptable. Indeed, the owners and contractors protective liability coverage form is meant to apply to bodily injury and property damage arising out of operations performed for the named insured by a specified contractor.)

A problem arose, though, when some courts expanded the peculiar risk doctrine to allow a contractor's employees who were injured on the job through the negligence of the contractor to seek recovery from the person who hired the contractor, in addition to receiving workers compensation benefits.

A majority of courts around the country do not support this viewpoint— *Wagner v. Continental Casualty Co.*, 421 N.W.2d 835 (Wisc. 1988); *Peone v. Regulus Stud Mills*, 744 P.2d 102 (Idaho 1987); *Jones v. Chevron USA, Inc.*, 718 P.2d 890 (Wyo. 1986); and *Vertentes v. Barletta Co.*, 466 N.E.2d 500 (Mass. 1984). Also, in *Privette v. Superior Court of Santa Clara County*, 21 Cal.Rptr.2d 72 (1993), the California Supreme Court ruled that the peculiar risk doctrine provides no tort remedy against the person who hired the contractor for employees of that independent contractor who have been injured on the job through the negligence of the contractor.

However, see *McMillan v. The United States of America*, 112 F.3d 1040 (1997). In that case, the United States Court of Appeals, Ninth Circuit, noted that the general contractor or project owner is generally not liable for injuries sustained by employees of the subcontractor, but where the subcontractor is performing inherently dangerous work and the general contractor should have reasonable known of inherent danger, the general contractor has a nondelegable duty to ensure that the subcontractor employs safety precautions.

In this case, a logging contractor's employee sued the U.S. under the Federal Tort Claims Act, seeking to recover for injuries he sustained while felling trees in a national forest for which the U.S. had hired the contractor. The Circuit Court held that felling of trees was inherently dangerous, and so the U.S. had a nondelegable duty to ensure that the contractor employed proper safety precautions.

Personal Comfort Doctrine

As has been discussed, questions often arise about whether the employee is actually in the course of employment at the time of injury. For example, is an employee in the course of employment while visiting a coworker and talking about vacation plans? What about when the employee is on the phone talking to a relative? Are trips to the restroom just for personal grooming considered in the course of employment? Would workers compensation apply to injuries suffered under such circumstances?

These circumstances fit within the scope of the personal comfort doctrine. Virginia offers an example. *Kraf Construction Services, Inc. v. Ingram*, 437 S.E.2d 424 (Va. Ct. App. 1993) was a case in which a construction worker was injured while crossing a street to get a soft drink at a convenience store. The worker filed for workers compensation benefits, and the employer fought against it, saying the employee was not in the course of employment or even on the work premises. A Virginia appeals court said that an employee who seeks to satisfy his personal comfort is within the employment. However, there are restrictions on this notion: the employee has to use the facilities furnished to him by the employer, and is not supposed to go someplace else. In the Kraf case, the employee was not on the employer's premises; however, going for a soft drink was held to be incidental to employment.

The Oregon Supreme Court and the Wisconsin Supreme Court have both considered the issue. In *Fred Meyer, Inc. v. Hayes*, 943 P.2d 197 (Ore. 1997), the Oregon Supreme Court asked the question: was the conduct of the employee expressly or impliedly allowed by the employer? If so, activities personal in nature are reasonably incidental to employment and injuries suffered by the employee are compensable. In *Sauerwein v. Department of Industry and Human Relations*, 262 N.W.2d 126 (Wisc. 1978), the Wisconsin Supreme Court stated that "employees who engage in acts which minister to personal comfort do not thereby leave the course of employment, unless the departure is so great that an intent to abandon the job temporarily may be inferred, or unless the method chosen is so unusual and unreasonable that the conduct cannot be considered as incident of the employment". The court went on to list some activities that it considered permissible within the personal comfort doctrine: getting a drink; eating lunch on the premises; warming oneself; sleeping in a place provided by the employer; going to the bathroom; and going to get paid.

The bottom line is that such activities have to be reasonable and not expressly forbidden by the employer.

Successive Injury Cases

Many states, territories, and Canadian provinces provide for second or subsequent injury funds as a means to encourage employers to hire disabled workers. The reason for this is that an individual who already is partially disabled may become totally disabled if injured on the job. Without a second injury fund, an employer—or its workers compensation carrier—could be responsible for the cost of a total disability when, in fact, the second occupational accident alone would not result in disability.

The second or subsequent injury fund pays the difference in benefits between the combined disability and the required benefits if only the occupational injury had occurred. For example, an individual who was born with one hand may be hired. If the employee loses that hand in an occupational accident, the employer would be responsible for benefits based on the combined loss of both hands. This is much higher than for just the loss of one hand.

Even when second injury funds are not involved, issues often arise over which employer or workers compensation carrier is responsible when an employee who was previously injured in an occupational accident is injured in a second accident. This often results in disagreement over whether the second injury is an aggravation of a pre-existing condition or the recurrence of an old injury. Such disagreements are common when there are different employers or different insurance carriers during the two incidents, as well as when second injury payments are being considered.

There may be variations among states but, in general, an aggravation of a pre-existing condition usually is considered a new injury. The employer of record at the time of the injury usually is held responsible for workers compensation coverage. A recurrence of an old injury usually reverts to the employer of record when the original injury happened.

In *Kidder v. Coastal Construction Co., Inc.*, 342 A.2d 729 (Me. 1975), the Maine Supreme Court considered an employee who was temporarily disabled by two successive injuries that occurred in two separate employment situations. The two injuries combined to produce a single indivisible disabling case. The court listed three possible methods to decide who was responsible:

1.   Apply the Massachusetts-Michigan rule and place full liability on the carrier at the time of the most recent injury that contributed to the disability.

2.   Tap the second injury fund to pay the difference between permanent, total, and temporary partial disability.

3.   Apportion the loss between the two insurers of record at the time of each injury.

According to the Massachusetts-Michigan rule, liability is placed on the insurer that covers the risk at the time of the most recent injury that causally relates to the disability. In *Kidder*, the court ruled that each employer and respective carrier should pay equal portions of the disability benefits since each accident had contributed to the disabling condition.

In a follow-up case, the Supreme Judicial Court of Maine also declared that where it is found that two compensable injuries occurring in the course of and arising out of two successive employments combined to produce a single disabling injury, the workers compensation commissioner must determine as fact whether the causative contribution of each employer to the resultant medical disability can be ascertained, but if a solid basis for allocation of responsibility is not shown, the commissioner is justified in entering a decree of equal apportionment. This case is *Swan v. Andrew Crowe and Sons*, 434 A.2d 1008 (1981).

Chapter 14

Fraud

This chapter deals with fraud and workers compensation. The lead article comes from *Claims Magazine*, a sister publication, and is written by Stacey Golden, Director of Claims for Keenan. The article is followed by several workers compensation fraud related cases from various jurisdictions.

Three Keys to a Successful Workers Compensation Fraud Investigation

Unfortunately, workers compensation fraud has been on the rise. The poor state of the U.S. economy is certainly a factor in addition to the mortgage meltdown and government cutbacks. Even rising student debt in this environment is placing pressure on young people. Equally unfortunate are those who see fraud as a solution to their challenges. Many consider it easy money and are simply clueless to the potential consequences. There are also plenty of examples of sophisticated cases that require careful and persistent digging.

Insurers write more than $1 trillion in insurance premiums annually according to the Federal Bureau of Investigation (FBI), providing significant opportunities for fraud to be perpetrated. The FBI estimates the total cost of non-health insurance-related fraud to be more than $40 billion per year, costing the average U.S. family an estimated $400 to $700 per year in increased premiums.

The National Insurance Crime bureau says that Workers Compensation fraud accounts for approximately 25 percent of the fraud perpetrated, or approximately $7.2 billion annually and is one of the fastest growing areas of fraud. One insurance executive has said that "If Workers Compensation fraud were a legitimate business, it would rank among Fortune 500 companies."

Sadly, the cost of this fraud is not limited to any one entity; policyholders, employers, insurers, consumers and shareholders all bear the expense.

With cases of Workers Compensation fraud, there are three primary points of contact—the worker, the employer and the medical provider. Fraud may be committed for a variety of reasons including the following.

Claimants

- Financial problems

- Lack of medical insurance

- Sense of entitlement

- Layoffs looming

- Adverse employment action

Employers

- Reduce premiums

- Underbid competitors

- Reduce costs

- Bonus tied to safety programs

Providers

- Organized crime

- Exploitation of loopholes

- The competition is doing it

- Greed

In California, insurers are required to maintain a Special Investigations Unit (SIU). As a broker, Keenan does not fall under this mandate, but it does operate its own SIU as part of its service for providers.

Many compensability issues can be resolved by an informal inquiry by an examiner. In other cases, with high cost potential or complex subrogation issues, a referral to a licensed investigator may be appropriate.

What Is Insurance Fraud?

At its most basic, Workers Compensation fraud occurs when an individual purposely lies to obtain some benefit or advantage, or to cause some benefit that is due to be denied. It is a felony and can result in prison time and/or payment of restitution.

Employee fraud can involve a claim for an injury that did not occur or did not occur in relation to the job, or receipt of total temporary disability benefits as a result of lying about outside employment, re-employment or ability to work. In billing fraud, a provider submits a bill for services never provided, for a patient who was never examined, or for more services or time than was actually provided. Abuse, as opposed to outright fraud, can include sending claimants to specific attorneys, doctors or facilities, kickbacks for insurance reps of employees, and rewards or gifts for quick or favorable settlement of claims.

Here are some specific examples:

- Knowingly presenting, or causing to be presented, any false claim for the payment of a loss, including a loss under a contract of insurance.

- Knowingly presenting multiple claims for the same incident.

- Knowingly causing or participating in a vehicular collision for the purpose of presenting a false or fraudulent claim.

- Knowingly preparing, making or subscribing any writing with the intent to present or use it in support of a false or fraudulent claim.

A few caveats are in order here. Each case must be considered on its own merits. Do not designate people for special attention simply based on their origins, ethnicity, profession or area of practice or because they do a large volume of business. Avoid generalized and accusatory statements. Beware of withholding payments or making accusatory statements based on the serving of search warrants or the filing of criminal charges.

Evaluating the Potential Case

Although the process of pursuing Workers Compensation cases is fairly straightforward, attention to detail and the proper resources are essential for success. Solid experience and training on the part of the examiner is essential in identifying things that simply do not feel right in the early stages. The first step is to look for red flags. In training examiners, Keenan has identified forty-two indicators. They include things like the following.

- Claimant is exceedingly eager for a quick or discounted settlement

- Claimant lists P.O. box or hotel as their residence

- Claimant threatens to see a doctor or attorney if the claim is not settled quickly

- Claimed injuries are disproportionate to the impact of the accident

- Claimant has financial or marital problems

- Claimant wants a relative or friend to pick up settlement check

- Claimant will not provide a sworn statement or documentation to confirm loss or value

- Claimant has multiple prior claims or lawsuits

- Claimant "over documents" losses

- No independent witnesses or versions differ significantly

- Claimant recently purchased private disability insurance policy(ies)

- Accident is not the type in which the claimant should be involved

- First Report of Claim differs significantly from description of accident in medical report(s)

- Claimant reports an alleged injury immediately following disciplinary action, notice of probation, demotion or being passed over for a promotion

- Alleged injury relates to a pre-existing injury or health problem

Investigating Suspected Fraud

If there appear to be grounds for a case, an investigator is engaged. The first criterion, of course, is a valid and current license. Others include proven expertise in investigation of Workers Comp claims; a track record of well-managed, efficient and cost-effective investigations; use of state-of-the-art technology for surveillance; current knowledge on applicable legislation; availability for courtroom testimony; online case management system; and a process of internal audits.

The investigator will monitor the individual's activities, talk to neighbors, review medical conflicts and the like. Observation, including video surveillance and recorded statements, usually takes place over a period of two to three days to identify consistent behavior patterns.

Other resources include medical records, employment records, business/asset records, and the ISO Index of criminal records and previous injuries. Confirm all information with authenticated documentary evidence, which will be admissible in court. And when documenting claim notes, do not use the term "fraud," but instead use "potential fraud" or "alleged fraud."

Professionals who can assist in this process include defense counsel, regency investigations, accident reconstructionists, source/origin experts, Agreed Medical Evaluator/Qualified Medical Evaluator (AME/QME), technical experts and laboratories, and independent appraisers and analysts.

The following are some guidelines on when to utilize telephone, on-site and sub-rosa investigation methods.

Telephone (least expensive)

- Employer disputes the injury

- Injury was not reported to employee's supervisor, who can be interviewed by telephone

- There is another witness to the alleged injury

- Circumstances suggest that an on-site inspection is not required

- Apportionment or preexisting injury

- Short-term employee with Monday morning injury

- Alleged injury reported after termination

- Preliminary subrogation investigation

On-Site (moderately expensive)

- Multiple witnesses, unable to or uncomfortable with being interviewed by telephone

- Content of investigation is too extensive to be conducted by telephone

- Circumstances of alleged injury suggest employee was not performing regular job duties at time of injury, not supposed to be in the area, or not making full use of available safety equipment

- Review of personnel records required

- Extensive history of personal problems, medical problems, drug/alcohol abuse

- Employer disputes validity of claim

Activity Check/Sub Rosa *(most expensive)*

- Interview of witnesses discloses employee boasted about claiming to be injured in order to collect Workers' Compensation benefits

- Medical reports in the file do not appear to support the severity of alleged injury. Claimant is never available to take telephone calls at claimant's residence

- No Employment Development Department (EDD), unemployment or temporary disability is being paid

- Information is received that the employee is working

- Information is received that the applicant participates in sports or other activities that could have caused the alleged injury

Adhering to some overall best practices will significantly improve the validity of a case. Make sure to obtain authorizations for release of medical and employment records, request all records from the medical provider, do not include date of loss in records requested, closely review all documents and obtain records referred to in current records, and obtain complete written statements. If the claimant will not provide or counsel will not allow a written statement, request that the defense attorney perform a deposition if it has not already been done.

Once the investigation is complete, the next step is an evaluation, typically by a district attorney and the department of insurance to determine the viability of a case and the chances for success. A case may then take three to six months to build, part of which is to determine whether the situation involved abuse or fraud. The case is then presented to a judge, and in California the department of insurance makes the actual arrest.

Post-filing Investigation and Discovery

Finally, once the decision is made to proceed, it is advisable to take an aggressive defense posture. If the case appears to be fraudulent, have counsel make clear at the beginning that the company will try the case. Insist upon accurate and complete discovery. Closely review all discovery responses, especially verifications. Discuss with defense counsel the strategies for taking the offensive in litigation.

Also, keep in mind that regardless of what happens in the criminal prosecution of a fraud case, the underlying Workers Compensation claim must still be administered. Benefits do not stop just because there is a suspicion of fraud. Administration of the compensation claim must continue according to Workers Compensation laws.

Some claims may appear minor at first and then subsequently escalate, resulting in very costly surgery and indemnity costs, for example. Now more than ever, the role of the special investigations unit is absolutely critical in gathering accurate information quickly and helping to make strategic decisions early on that will impact the overall outcome of a claim.

Stacey Golden, director of claims for Keenan, is responsible for leading the firm's SIU/Fraud Unit, training and development, and vendor management. Golden is also an advisor to the California-based Employers' Fraud Task Force and a guest lecturer for the Insurance Educational Association (IEA). She has more than twenty years' experience and is certified by the IEA, Workers Compensation Claims Professionals Association and California Office of Self Insurance Plans.

WC Fraud Case Law

1. *People v. Brown*, No. D056908, 2010 WL 5167696 (Cal. Ct. App. Dec. 20, 2010).

While employed at the Ramada Plaza Hotel, Thomas Brown filed a workers' compensation claim for injuries allegedly sustained from a slip and fall that occurred while Brown was working in the kitchen on September 21, 2001. Brown's claim was that he slipped on liquid on the floor and sustained multiple injuries to his forearm, ribs, and head. Soon after the claim was filed, Brown was fired for unrelated reasons.

Brown visited the doctor on November 7, 2001 and told the doctor that he sustained injuries to his knee in the workplace accident and had no prior knee injuries. Zenith Insurance Company paid for a surgery for Brown's knee, as well as workers' compensation disability and other fees. Two years later Zenith was informed that the injury to Brown's knee was pre-existing, and he had filed a workers' compensation claim with a different insurance company in 1998. Brown was charged with a violation of the False and Fraudulent Claims Act.

2.   *Channels v. Bur. of Workers' Comp.*, 2011-Ohio-1173, 2.

Channels received workers' compensation for a valid injury on the work-site in 2005. Due to the nature of his previous employment, he was unable to return to his previous position and as a result he was enrolled in the Bureau of Workers' Compensation Vocational Rehabilitation Program. The Vocational Rehabilitation Program required Channels to make contact with prospective employers while benefiting from the program. While on his way into his home to retrieve the name and address of a prospective employer, Channels fell and broke his ankle. He filed a claim seeking workers' compensation for the ankle injury. The claim was rejected when the court found that the injury did not occur in the "course of employment" or "arise out of participation" in the rehabilitation program.

3.   *United States v. Catone,* 769 F.3d 866, 869 (4th Cir. 2014).

Joseph Catone Jr. worked at the USPS for twenty-nine years before filing a workers' compensation claim for injuries arising from extended periods of driving. Catone received benefits for his injuries. While Catone was receiving workers' compensation benefits he also worked for a custodial company, and failed to disclose his subsequent employment to the Office of Workers' Compensation Programs (OWCP). While receiving benefits, Catone was required to fill out forms that required him to disclose if he had, during the past fifteen months, (1) "work[ed] for any employer;" (2) was "self-employed or involved in any business enterprise;" (3) earned "monetary or in-kind compensation" for "volunteer work;" or (4) was "unemployed for all periods." Catone failed to mention his employment on the forms. During interviews with the OWCP Catone alleged that his wife was the one in the family that was employed with the custodial company. Testimony during trial revealed that Catone was indeed employed with the custodial company. Catone was convicted and forced to pay restitution and serve sixteen months in prison.

4.   *ARCTEC Servs. v. Cummings*, 295 P.3d 916 (Alaska 2013).

Cummings received workers' compensation for a 2006 work-site injury. In 2007 Cummings was videoed by private investigators while helping out at her boyfriend's herb shop. In 2008, ARCTEC, her former employer, filed a petition for a finding of fraud, alleging that she had misrepresented her physical capabilities and work status. In 2013, on appeal, the Supreme Court of Alaska ruled in favor of Cummings, thus affirming the Commission's earlier decision. The court's decision in this case hinged on whether Cummings knowingly committed fraud. "Knowingly" requires a subjective intent to defraud. Cummings testified that she considered her activities at the store to be a hobby and not employment, thus she did not knowingly misstate her employment status. In addition, she had not misrepresented her physical capabilities to doctors.

5.   *Bellino v. Verizon Wireless*, 435 N.J. Super. 85, 99, 86 A.3d 751, 759 (App. Div. 2014).

In 2006 Bellino tripped over some boxes and fell while working as a sales representative for Verizon Wireless. Bellino received extensive medical treatment over the course of the next few months. Verizon claimed that Bellino had violated the Workers' Compensation Act's anti-fraud provision on the basis of the fact that Bellino had not disclosed all prior medical conditions to those doctors. Bellino testified that she had attempted to answer doctors truthfully but could not remember everything because she had been to many doctors in the past. The Superior Court of New Jersey ruled in favor of Bellino, finding that there was not sufficient evidence of fraud, and that her disability was supported by substantial evidence. The court reasoned that "It is not enough that the moving party show the worker made an inaccurate or false statement or omitted material facts. Rather, the moving party must show (1) the injured worker acted purposefully or knowingly in giving or withholding information with the intent that he or she receive benefits; (2) the worker knew that the statement or omission was material to obtaining the benefit; and (3) the statement or omission was made for the purpose of falsely obtaining benefits to which the worker was not entitled." Bellino had not made any false statements or omissions purposefully or knowingly.

6.   *Regency Oaks Corp. v. Norman-Spencer McKernan, Inc.*, 129 A.D.3d 1454, 12 N.Y.S.3d 398 (N.Y. App. Div.) *appeal dismissed sub nom. Regency Oaks Corp. v. Norman-Spencer-McKernan, Inc.*, 26 N.Y.3d 980, 40 N.E.3d 570 (2015).

Regency Oaks Corporation sued an insurance agency for fraud after an agency employee provided the company with a falsified workers compensation policy that was not actually from the agency. The defendant argued that justifiable reliance was not met because it could not be liable for the acts of its employee and the plaintiff's reliance on "apparent authority" was not reasonable. The Supreme Court of New York ruled in favor of the plaintiff for three reasons. First, the plaintiff reasonably relied upon apparent authority of the employee to act for the defendant; second, the plaintiff fulfilled its duty to inquire about the authority of the employee to act for the agency; and third, the plaintiff reasonably relied on the agency employee's explanation that the company that prepared a proposal for the organization was a division of the agency. Importantly, statements from the agent are not enough. The insurance agency must have given the plaintiff reason to believe that the agent possessed the authority to do what he was doing. The defendant assigned the employee to work with the plaintiff. Under these circumstances it was reasonable for the company to rely on this employee's word.

7.   *Desadier v. W. Frasier, Inc.*, 48,303 (La. App. 2 Cir. 8/7/13), 122 So. 3d 584.

Desadier suffered a shoulder injury in 2010 while working as a lumber grader. He sought medical treatment and informed his employer that he could now only do light duty. In 2011 he informed his supervisor that he could no longer work at all. He was then fired. He then filed a workers' compensation claim based on the shoulder injury and an alleged knee injury. It was later revealed that Desadier had a long history of injury to his shoulder previous to the 2010 incident and that this history was so extensive that any statements he made otherwise could only have been made with the intent to deceive. Desadier's wife also testified that he made money mowing lawns during the time that he claimed to be unable to work. The Court of Appeal of Louisiana held that sufficient evidence that claimant committed workers' compensation fraud supported determination that the claimant was ineligible for benefits.

8.   *Kraeuter v. W.C.A.B. (Ajax Enterprises, Inc.)*, 82 A.3d 513 (Pa. Commw. Ct. 2013).

Kraeuter suffered a work related shoulder injury and began to receive workers' compensation. Her benefits were later suspended and she filed a petition alleging fraud. An incorrect piece of paperwork stated that Kraeuter had begun working again and the claims adjuster never verified this as he should have. The company obtained her signature on the final receipt, acknowledging an end to her benefits, by calling her in to sign where she normally signed for compensation checks. She never received notice of the suspension because her name and address were misspelled on the mailed notice. She believed that she was signing another compensation check. The Commonwealth Court of Pennsylvania ruled in Kraeuter's favor, ruling that conduct of the claims adjuster constituted fraud. The court further ruled that evidence supported the Workers' Compensation Judge's decision to impose a 50 percent penalty against the employer for unreasonably delaying payment.

9.   *Daniel v. Point To Point Directional Drilling, Inc.*, 2013-1407 (La. App. 3 Cir. 5/7/14), 139 So. 3d 613, 615 *writ denied*, 2014-1165 (La. 9/19/14), 149 So. 3d 245.

While travelling for work Mr. Daniel was involved in a horrific car accident. For about a half hour before emergency help arrived he worked helping to free and assist others who had been hurt. He witnessed badly injured and screaming people and mangled and severed corpses. He subsequently developed post-traumatic stress disorder (PTSD), and as a result, an addiction. He sought medical help through his parents' health insurance rather than through his work, but this was not successful. He was later fired for failing a drug test. After repeated failed attempts at treatment, Mr. Daniel filed for workers' compensation. Point to Point argued that it should not have to pay due to the fact that Mr. Daniel had been dishonest about his drug use prior to developing PTSD. The court ruled that his misstatements were inadvertent and inconsequential. The court also ruled that the health insurer was not entitled to reimbursement from the workers' compensation, that the employer was not entitled to enforce a health-care cap for payment of unauthorized expenses, and that Mr. Daniels was entitled to an award of penalties for Point to Point's failure to reasonably convert a claim for medical expenses.

10. *Urbano v. Bletsas Plumbing & Heating Corp.*, 124 A.D.3d 1025, 2 N.Y.S.3d 636 (N.Y. App. Div. 2015).

Urbano was injured on the job and filed for workers' compensation. As a result of this, the insurer became aware that the employer had committed fraud by paying employees off the books and under-reporting the number of employees to the insurer. An argument arose as to whether an insurer is liable for workers' compensation payments when the employer purchasing the insurance has committed fraud but the injured employee is totally innocent in the matter. The Supreme Court of New York ruled in favor of the employee, citing previous case law (*Matter of Cruz v. New Millennium Constr. & Restoration Corp.*, 17 A.D.3d 19, 22–24, 793 N.Y.S.2d 548 [2005]). The insurer argued that an amendment to workers' compensation law (*McKinney's Workers' Compensation Law* § 52) made after the previous case law superseded it. The Court disagreed with this interpretation of the new statute, reasoning that the amendment was intended to punish fraud perpetrated by the employer, not rescind coverage.

11. *In re Arellano*, 2015 WY 21, 344 P.3d 249 (Wyo. 2015).

Mr. Arellano was an alien working in the United States without authorization. Mr. Arellano obtained work by falsely filling out documents under penalty of perjury, using a fake driver's license. About four months later he injured his back at work and filed for workers' compensation. His claim was denied by the Office of Administrative hearings due to the fact that he had fraudulently filled out documents. Arellano petitioned, arguing that the decision was "arbitrary, capricious, an abuse of discretion or otherwise not in accordance with law." On appeal, the Wyoming

Supreme Court held that (1) Arellano was an employee within the meaning of the Workers' Compensation Act, and (2) provisions in the Act regarding making misrepresentations to obtain benefits did not apply in this situation. According to Wyo. Stat. Ann. § 27–14–102(a)(vii), the term employee includes "aliens whom the employer reasonably believes, at the date of hire and the date of injury based upon documentation in the employer's possession, to be authorized to work by the United States Department of Justice, Office of Citizenship and Immigration Services." This included Mr. Arellano. In addition, the court reasoned that the fraud provisions of the Workers Compensation Act dealt specifically with misstatements concerning medical conditions, not authorization to work in the United States.

12. *Roberts v. Montgomery Cty.*, 436 Md. 591, 84 A.3d 87 (2014).

Roberts was injured while driving his motorcycle from physical training at a school for his work as a firefighter to the fire station. The County contested his workers' compensation claim because it did not consider his injury to be in the course of employment. It considered his time of injury to be under the definition of "going and coming to work" instead, because he was not technically travelling between two different sections of the employer's premises. The going and coming rule bars people from collecting workers' compensation due to injury from normal commuting. The Court of Appeals of Maryland disagreed with the County's argument. Even though the school was not owned by the employer, Roberts was conducting activity related to his employment there, so he was travelling from one work related activity to another. Travel incidental to employment cannot be excluded from coverage.

13. *Omian v. Chrysler Grp. LLC*, 309 Mich. App. 297, 869 N.W.2d 625 *appeal denied sub nom. Omian v. Chrysler Grp., L.L.C.*, 498 Mich. 886, 869 N.W.2d 605 (2015).

Omian incurred a back injury while working for Chrysler in 2000. He later pled guilty to conspiracy and aiding and abetting structuring financial transactions to evade reporting requirements, in a completely unrelated case. Chrysler filed a petition to stop benefits, contending that he had been incarcerated for activities that demonstrated his physical and mental abilities to earn money, contrary to his claim of disability. Omian countered that his activities did not prove that he was capable of his previous work at Chrysler. The court chose not to allow testimony as to whether activities such as repackaging controlled substances, altering stamps, and laundering profits demonstrated work skills. The court found that Omian was disabled, based on doctor testimony, and did not consider his proof of illegal activity to be proof of job skills. Chrysler further argued that Omian should be barred from receiving benefits by the wrongful-conduct rule. The court rejected this argument because Chrysler had waited for appeal to raise it for the first time, but noted that they would have rejected it even if it had been raised on time. In order to bar Omian from collecting under the wrongful-conduct rule there would have had to have been a proximate cause between the injury and the illegal act. This decision was based off of previous case law from Michigan (*Manning v. Bishop of Marquette,* 345 Mich. 130, 136, 76 N.W.2d 75 (1956)) and Mississippi (*Meador v. Hotel Grover,* 193 Miss. 392, 9 So.2d 782 (1942)).

14. *SCF Gen. Ins. Co. v. Indus. Comm'n of Arizona,* 236 Ariz. 545, 342 P.3d 1285 (Ct. App. 2015).

SCF General Insurance accused an insured employer of fraud after the employer filed a false statement claiming that no injuries had occurred since the cancellation date, when requesting reinstatement of the policy. After reinstatement, the employer then attempted to collect for an injury that occurred during the gap between coverage. This injury specifically occurred after the request for reinstatement but before the reinstatement. An administrative law judge initially awarded the claim to the injured worker. The insurer appealed. The Court of Appeals of Arizona held that SCF was entitled to rescind the contract. "Misrepresentations, omissions, concealment of facts and incorrect statements shall not prevent a recovery under the policy unless: 1. Fraudulent. 2. Material either to the acceptance of the risk, or to the hazard assumed by the insurer. 3. The insurer in good faith would either not have issued the policy, or would not have issued a policy in as large an amount, or would not have provided coverage with respect to the hazard resulting in the loss, if the true facts had been made known to the insurer as required either by the application for the policy or otherwise." (*SCF Gen. Ins. Co. v. Indus. Comm'n of Arizona*). Given that the failure of the employer to give the insurer the full information met all three of these standards, SCF was entitled to rescind the contract. The award of benefits was also set aside.

15. *People v. Fuentes,* No. A138058, 2014 WL 2921808 (Cal. Ct. App. June 27, 2014).

Oscar Josef Fuentes was an employee of the state, and was injured on the job in 2003 and filed a workers' compensation claim that was resolved in 2006. It was determined that Fuentes was 45 percent disabled. Due to his injuries he was awarded disability benefits and medical benefits related to injuries on his back, neck, and upper extremities. In 2004 Fuentes stopped working for the state and began doing part-time work as a machinist helper from 2005-2007. In 2007 Fuentes participated in rehabilitation and told his counselor that he wanted to become a contractor and start working on building projects on several properties he owned. He told his counselor that he could drive for up to two hours, lift up to 150 pounds, and sit or stand for up to 30 minutes at a time. Despite these claims, Fuentes filed a petition to reopen his workers' compensation claim and increase his disability to 100percent. In the petition Fuentes claimed that he could not lift more than 20 pounds, sit or stand for extended periods of time, lift his arm above his shoulder, or engage in recreational activities. During investigations, Fuentes was recorded working on cars, participating in his son's sports team practices (for up to six hours a day), and unloading vehicles, among other activities. Fuentes' second claim was found to be fraudulent, and he was ordered to serve six months in jail and was not allowed to submit any subsequent workers' compensation claims.

16. *Carroso v. State*, 129 So. 3d 374, 375 (Fla. Dist. Ct. App. 2013).

Kenneth Carroso was involved in a truck accident within the scope of employment. He filed a workers compensation claim based on a spiral fracture in his left arm and complications from that injury sustained from the truck accident. Carroso received temporary total disability benefits for more than one year. During the deposition Carroso misrepresented and omitted some chiropractic and minor medical treatment he had received earlier, possibly related to off-the-job automobile accidents. The possible fraud was reported to the state, and Mr. Carroso was charged with insurance fraud in the second degree.

17. *Pipkin v. Buchanan Pump & Supply Co.*, 2015 WL 9097448 (W. Va.).

This is an unpublished opinion. Steven Pipkin appeals his decision by the West Virginia Workers' Compensation Board of Review. His workers' compensation claim was denied and he wants it reopened for further consideration of temporary disability benefits. Pipkin injured his left shoulder while maintaining a pump shaft. Because of the injury Pipkin went to a doctor to begin treatment and had two shoulder arthroscopies performed. After the arthroscopies he still complained of shoulder pain and was referred to a pain management specialist by his doctor. An independent medical evaluation was done and that doctor said that Pipkin would reach maximum improvement in eight weeks after completing physical therapy.

His employer, Buchanan Pump & Supply Company, alleged that Pipkin was committing workers' compensation fraud because Pipkin has since been arrested for three felony counts relating to the sale of prescription narcotics. His employer also provided a copy of the criminal complaint. This case affirmed the Board of Review denying workers' compensation.

Chapter 15

Canadian Workers Compensation

Similarities and Differences between the United States and Canadian Workers Compensation Systems

Similarly to the way that workers compensation claims are handled in the United States (U.S.), on a state-wide basis, Canada has several worker compensation boards (WCB) that are responsible for workers compensation in federal, provincial, and territorial jurisdictions throughout the country. The WCB's provide insurance for workplace injuries and illnesses. The driving difference between the Canadian system and the United States system is the stark contrast between the dominance of the competitive market in the U.S., and the public administration model that has held fast and kept costs down in Canada. The Canadian system is remote from the government, and is sheltered from political influence, allowing even the Minister responsible only minimal powers. Unlike the United States system, the Canadian system does not allow for self-insurance.

Convention

In the U.S., workers compensation coverage is mandatory for most employers in almost every state, with a few exceptions. Most states allow mutual and stock insurance companies to compete to write workers compensation coverage, ending up with a largely competitive private insurance market. In Canada, industries that require workers compensation coverage can only receive that coverage through a WCB. The monopolistic WC states in the U.S. have similar composition to the Canadian system.

Funding

The Canadian insurance programs are funded by the employers that require the coverage, and not the provincial governments with which they are associated, while the various U.S. monopolistic systems may fall back upon federal funds and taxpayer money if funds run low. Each employer pays into the system at a rate based upon payroll, industry sector, and history of injuries in the workplace.

The first responsibility of the WCB after they receive a claim is to review the incident and determine benefits entitlement. This process is analogous to the compensability decision in U.S. workers compensation decisions.

Cost Drivers

Unlike the U.S., where cost is driven mainly by medical benefits, in Canada the loss of earnings benefits and wage loss benefits are the primary cost drivers. This is likely because of the publically funded nature of the Canadian healthcare system. Features of the Canadian system are that it has fewer administrative costs and minimal over-utilization of the system, two things that the U.S. system is lacking.

Workplace Safety and Insurance Board (WSIB)

The Canadian Workplace Safety and Insurance Board (WSIB) is an independent trust agency that handles compensation and no-fault insurance. The WSIB takes care of claims and ensures a swift claim process for the employee, and help and support to help employees return to work after an injury or illness. The WSIB is entirely funded by employers. Although the WSIB is based out of Ontario, all of the WCB's mentioned in the Departments Contacts section below are partners in the Association of Workers' Compensation Boards of America.

Employer Schedules

Canadian employers fit into two schedules which are governed by the Workplace Safety and Insurance Board.

Schedule 1 employers are not individually liable to pay benefits directly to workers or their survivors under the insurance plan. (*Workplace Safety and Insurance Act* s.88(2)) Employers included in Schedule 1 must contribute to the insurance fund. The insurance fund is comprised of annual premiums paid by the Schedule 1 employers. The amount each Schedule 1 employer is asked to contribute is determined based on business activity and total payroll.

Schedule 2 employers are compulsorily covered through a system of individual liability. If a workplace injury or illness occurs, Schedule 2 employers must individually pay the total costs of benefits for their injured employees. (*Workplace Safety and Insurance Act* s.90(1)) In order to cover costs incurred by a Schedule 2 employer, the WSIB may ask for a deposit from the employer.

Specifics for employer schedule designation can be found on the WSIB website at www.wsib.on.ca.

Second Injury Fund

The WSIB employs a Second Injury and Enhancement Fund that is paid for by Schedule 1 employers. Schedule 1 employers comprise most private sector employers and some public sector employers. Schedule 1 employers pay into the SIEF because it generally will help to reduce claims costs that qualify by about 50 percent.

Experience Rating

The purpose of experience rating in workers compensation is to ensure that employers are being charged a premium that accurately reflects the risks they represent. Industry groups are compared within themselves, and each individual employer's loss experience is compared as well. In Canada, employer's experience ratings are taken very seriously in an effort to keep healthcare costs down, and to equitably distribute the cost of work-related injury and illness across employers.

Most of the provinces have established experience rating programs, but the programs can vary from province to province.

Maximum Assessable/ Insurable Earnings for 2015

Maximum assessable/insurable earnings refer to the maximum annual earnings on which a premium is calculated for each worker of a covered employer. Benefits for a person who was injured at work are calculated based on the maximum assessable earnings of the province where the claim is brought.

Province	Maximum Assessable/ Insurable Earnings
Manitoba	$121,000
Alberta	$95,300
Northwest Territories and Nunavut	$86,000
Yukon	$84,837
British Columbia	$78,600
Saskatchewan	$65,130
Newfoundland and Labrador	$61,615
New Brunswick	$60,900
Prince Edward Island	$52,100
Ontario	$85,200
Quebec	$70,000
Nova Scotia	$56,800

Assessments and Premiums

Since the WCB's are funded by employers and not the government, in order to maintain sufficient funding the employers are charged a certain amount per $100 of their payroll. The amount paid is called the "assessment rate". Not all employers pay into workers compensation. For information regarding this please refer to the provinces workers' compensation legislation. The money collected from employers for workers' compensation goes into a fund known as the accident fund. The money in the accident fund generally goes toward providing wage loss benefits to the injured employee, providing medical aid and rehabilitation to the injured employee, and the administration of the WCB.

Generally each employer is asked to pay an average assessment rate, but not all employers pay that average rate. Sometimes, individual employers have different rates that are based on differences in industry or class, or the experience (or lack thereof) that an employer has dealing with workers' compensation cases.

Roles and Responsibilities

The workers compensation legislation (generally known as the Workers Compensation Act) outlines the roles and responsibilities of the worker, employer, and WCB when an injury or illness occurs in the workplace. Federal government employees are governed under the Federal Government Employees Compensation Act (GECA).

Although they may change from province to province, and between the two acts, the general responsibilities are as follows.

The **worker** must:

- Report the illness or injury to the employer

- Diminish further loss and

- Cooperate with the employer if modified duties are offered, so long as they are suitable alternatives.

The **employers** must:

- Immediately provide first aid and arrange (and pay for) transport for medical treatment if necessary.

- Pay full wages and benefits for the shift on which the injury or illness occurred.

- Investigate the incident, and document the steps taken to correct any issues discovered through the process of investigation.

- Report the injury or illness to the WCB.*

- Provide accurate information.

- Provide an offer of suitable, modified work to allow for early and safe return to work.

The **WCB** must:

- Review all reported incidents and determine benefit entitlements.

- Issue medical benefits and/or loss earnings/wages benefits wherever applicable.

- Arrange specialist appointments and independent medical examinations.

- Interpret and enforce workers compensation legislation.

- Review evidence and make decisions on any appeals that are initiated by an appropriate party.

When to report:

Employers are generally required to report a work-related accident or illness within seventy-two hours of:

- Learning that the worker requires professional medical treatment; or

- Is absent from the next shift of regular work; or

- Earns less than regular pay for regular work (has hours reduced); or

- Requires modified work at less than regular pay.

- Employers Beware

Cost Drivers

Unlike the U.S., where cost is driven mainly by medical benefits, in Canada the loss of earnings benefits and wage loss benefits are the primary cost drivers. This is likely because of the publically funded nature of the Canadian healthcare system. Features of the Canadian system are that it has fewer administrative costs and minimal over-utilization of the system, two things that the U.S. system is lacking. Because of these stipulations, the main cost in Canadian workers compensation claims is the lost work time.

An employer working under the WCB system should make sure to offer modified duties to a worker at the onset of a workers compensation claim. It is important to have a regular and proactive program in place to help employees return to work immediately. Such programs, immediately offering modified duties to recovering employees, will help immensely in cost-control efforts by employers.

Workers Compensation Fraud

Despite the employee friendly, helpful nature of Canadian workers compensation there are still employees that attempt to defraud the insurance system. Numbers for the amount of workers compensation fraud that occurs in Canada are scarce, but experts estimate that the statistics track with those projected in the United States, costing employers millions of dollars each year. In order to report suspected fraud, visit the provinces' website for reporting details.

Department Contacts

As previously mentioned, although these are generally the provisions that are provided for in Canadian WCB's, there are differences between each of the individual provinces. If any uncertainties come to light, please contact the department or visit their website.

Federal Workers Compensation Service (FWCS)

Employment and Social Development Canada (ESDC) [previously HRDCC]
Ottowa, ON, K1A 0J2
http://www.labour.gc.ca/eng/health_safety/compensation/index.shtml

Alberta

Workers Compensation Board of Alberta
9912 – 107 Street
PO Box 2415
Edmonton AB T5J 2S5
http://www.wcb.ab.ca

British Columbia

WorkSafeBC (Workers Compensation Board of British Columbia)
6951 Westminster Highway
Richmond BC V7C 1C6
http://www.worksafebc.com

Manitoba

Workers Compensation Board of Manitoba
1 Portland Street
PO Box 160
Saint John NB E2L 3X9
http://www.wcb.mb.ca

New Brunswick

WorkSafe NB (Workers Compensation Board of British Columbia)
1 Portland Street
PO Box 160
Saint John NB E2L 3X9
http://www.worksafenb.ca/

Newfoundland and Labrador

Workplace Health, Safety & Compensation Commission of Newfoundland and Labrador
146-148 Forest Road
PO Box 9000
St. John's NL A1A 3B8
http://www.whscc.nf.ca/

Northwest Territories and Nunavut

Workers Compensation Board of the Northwest Territories and Nunavut
5022 49th Street 5th Floor
Centre Square Tower PO Box 8888
Yellowknife NT X1A 2R3
http://www.wscc.nt.ca/

Nova Scotia

Workers Compensation Board of Nova Scotia
5668 South Street
PO Box 1150

Halifax NS B3J 2Y2
http://www.wcb.ns.ca

Ontario

Workplace Safety and Insurance Board
200 Front Street West
Toronto ON M5V 3J1
http://www.wsib.on.ca

Prince Edward Island

Workers Compensation Board of Prince Edward Island
14 Weymouth Street
PO Box 757
Charlottetown PE C1A 7L7
http://www.wcb.pe.ca

Quebec

**Commission de la sante et de la securite du travail du Quebec (CSST)
(Occupational Health and Safety Commission)**
1199, rue de Bleury
CP 6056, Succursale <<centre-ville>>
Montreal QC H3C 4E1
http://www.csst.qc.ca/portail/fr/

Saskatchewan

**Saskatchewan Workers Compensation Board
Head Office**
200-1881 Scarth Street
Regina SK S4P 4L1

Saskatoon Office

115-24th Street East
Saskatoon SK S7K 1L5
http://www.wcbsask.com

Yukon

Yukon Workers Compensation, Health and Safety Board
401 Strickland Street
Whitehorse YK Y1A 5N8
http://wcb.yk.ca/

Association of WCB's of Canada

AWCBC
40 University Avenue, Suite 1007
Toronto ON M5J 1T1
http://awcbc.org/
email: contact@awcbc.org

Citations

Amaxx Risk Solutions Inc. *Prior Workplace Injury Records Useful to Obtain Second Injury Funds in Canada.* (Accessed October 15, 2015) Web Search for: blog.reduceyourworkerscomp.com/2009/04/prior-workplace-injury-records-useful-to-obtain-second-injury-funds-in-canada/.

Association of Workers Compensation Boards of Canada. *Comparative Tables*, (Accessed October 13, 2015).

Association of Workers Compensation Boards of Canada. Facts Sheets, (Accessed October 13, 2015) Web search for: awcbc.org/?page_id=63.

Brief Summary of Canadian Workers Compensation System, (Accessed October 13, 2015).

www.actuaries.org/CTTEES_SOCSEC/Documents/Canada_Workers_Comp.pdf.

Canadian Workers Compensation Law, (Accessed October 12, 2015) www.workerscompensationinsurance.com/workers_compensation/canada.htm.

Kristen Moskal, Understanding the Canadian Workers Compensation System, (Accessed October 12, 2015).

web-files.crawco.com/extranet/CA/UnderstandingCanadianWorkers Comp.pdf.

Provincial Workers Compensation Boards in Canada, (Accessed October 12, 2015) www.ccohs.ca/oshanswers/information/wcb_canada.html.

What Is a State Compensation Insurance Fund, (Accessed October 12, 2015) www.insureon.com/blog/post/2014/05/29/state-workers-compensation-fund.aspc.

Workers Compensation Act, R.S.O., 1990, as amended. Sections 1(3), 5, 6 103, 107, 109(2). Reg. 1102, R.R.O. 1990.

Workers Compensation Board of Nova Scotia. *Summary of Workplace Injury Insurance*, (Accessed October 13, 2015) www.wcb.ns.ca/Workplace-Injury-Insurance/Summary-of-Workplace-Injury-Insurance.aspx.

Workers Compensation Insurance, (Accessed October 12, 2015) www.naic.org/cipr_topics/topic_workers_comp.html.

Workplace Safety and Insurance Act, 1997, as amended. Sections 67, 68, 74, 88(2), 90(1), 91, 92, 183(2) *O. Reg. 175/98*, Schedule 1, Schedule 2, s.12.

Canadian Workers Compensation Summary

The government provides benefits to employees under the *Government Employees Compensation Act*. The government uses services already available through provincial workers' compensation boards. There is no cost to the employees for the services, the government of Canada reimburses the provincial boards for the cost of compensation to the employees.

Types of Payments

1. Temporary payments for lost income

2. Permanent payments paid out following a final settlement

3. Payments to cover medical expenses

4. Payments to cover medical treatments

5. Payments to cover rehabilitation expenses

6. Payments to cover a physical disability

How it Works

When workers are victims of a work related injury, they receive compensation from the Workers Compensation Board (WCB) in their providence. If you are entitled to receive the WCB payments you have to provide the WCB with: (1) the start and end date of the payment, (2) daily or weekly amount paid by the WCB, (3) amount of payment in the first week, (4) amount of payments in the last week – if known, and (5) types of payments. WCB temporary payment rates are calculated on a basis of five days a week – Monday through Friday.

If the WCB decides that the injury prevents the worker from returning to work or any other occupation, the WCB may issue permanent payments after a final settlement of a claim. A final settlement can also be made if the worker is able to work at any job, but not at the previous salary level.

There are payments no considered earning and therefore are not allocated. Those are (1) lump sum amounts or pensions paid following a final settlement, (2) payments used to cover injury or illness-related expenses, and (3) payments used for permanent impairment.

What to do

Upon an injury immediately tell a supervisor. The employer will then complete and process a report for compensation. You may also be asked to give the report directly to the WCB.

Can Claims Be Disallowed?

A claim could be disallowed if there is (1) insufficient information supplied, (2) accident was not related to work, (3) injury is not considered to be due to the accident, or (4) accident was caused solely by the serious and willful misconduct of the employee.

http://www.servicecanada.gc.ca/eng/ei/information/work_accident.shtml

http://www.labour.gc.ca/eng/health_safety/compensation/pubs_wc/accident.shtml.

Appendix A

WORKERS COMPENSATION AND
EMPLOYERS LIABILITY INSURANCE POLICY

WC 00 00 01 A

Original Printing   Issued May 1, 1988   Standard

INFORMATION PAGE

Insurer

POLICY NO.

1. The Insured: _____Individual   _____Partnership

   Mailing address: _____Corporation or_____

2. The policy period is from _____ to _____ at the insured's mailing address.

3. A.   Workers Compensation Insurance: Part One of the policy applies to the Workers Compensation Law of the states listed here.:

   B.   Employers Liability Insurance: Part Two of the policy applies to work in each state listed in Item 3.A. The limits of our liability under Part Two are:

   Bodily Injury by Accident $_____ each accident

   Bodily Injury by Disease $_____ policy limit

   Bodily Injury by Disease $_____ each employee

   C.   Other States Insurance: Part Three of the policy applies to the states, if any, listed here:

   D.   This policy includes these endorsements and schedules:

4. The premium for this policy will be determined by our Manuals of Rules, Classifications, Rates and Rating Plans. All information required below is subject to verification and change by audit.

Classifications	Code	Premium Basis	Rate Per	Estimated
	No	Total Estimated	$100 of	Annual
	Annual	Remuneration	Remuneration	Premium

Total Estimated Annual Premium $

Minimum Premium $ Expense Constant $

Countersigned by _____

1987 National Council on Compensation Insurance

WORKERS COMPENSATION AND EMPLOYERS LIABILITY INSURANCE POLICY   WC 00 00 00 C

1st Reprint   *Effective January 1, 2015*   **Standard**

WORKERS COMPENSATION AND EMPLOYERS LIABILITY INSURANCE POLICY

In return for the payment of the premium and subject to all terms of this policy, we agree with you as follows:

GENERAL SECTION

A. The Policy

This policy includes at its effective date the Information Page and all endorsements and schedules listed there. It is a contract of insurance between you (the employer named in Item 1 of the Information Page) and us (the insurer named on the Information Page). The only agreements relating to this insurance are stated in this policy. The terms of this policy may not be changed or waived except by endorsement issued by us to be part of this policy.

B. Who is Insured

You are insured if you are an employer named in Item 1 of the Information Page. If that employer is a partnership, and if you are one of its partners, you are insured, but only in your capacity as an employer of the partnership's employees.

C. Workers Compensation Law

Workers Compensation Law means the workers or workmen's compensation law and occupational disease law of each state or territory named in Item 3.A. of the Information Page. It includes any amendments to that law which are in effect during the policy period. It does not include any federal workers or workmen's compensation law, any federal occupational disease law or the provisions of any law that provide nonoccupational disability benefits.

D. State

State means any state of the United States of America, and the District of Columbia.

E. Locations

This policy covers all of your workplaces listed in Items 1 or 4 of the Information Page; and it covers all other workplaces in Item 3.A. states unless you have other insurance or are self-insured for such workplaces.

PART ONE
WORKERS COMPENSATION INSURANCE

A. How This Insurance Applies

This workers compensation insurance applies to bodily injury by accident or bodily injury by disease. Bodily injury includes resulting death.

1. Bodily injury by accident must occur during the policy period.
2. Bodily injury by disease must be caused or aggravated by the conditions of your employment. The employee's last day of last exposure to the conditions causing or aggravating such bodily injury by disease must occur during the policy period.

B. We Will Pay

We will pay promptly when due the benefits required of you by the workers compensation law.

C. We Will Defend

We have the right and duty to defend at our expense any claim, proceeding or suit against you for benefits payable by this insurance. We have the right to investigate and settle these claims, proceedings or suits.

We have no duty to defend a claim, proceeding or suit that is not covered by this insurance.

D. We Will Also Pay

We will also pay these costs, in addition to other amounts payable under this insurance, as part of any claim, proceeding or suit we defend:

1. reasonable expenses incurred at our request, but not loss of earnings;
2. premiums for bonds to release attachments and for appeal bonds in bond amounts up to the amount payable under this insurance;
3. litigation costs taxed against you;
4. interest on a judgment as required by law until we offer the amount due under this insurance; and
5. expenses we incur.

E. Other Insurance

We will not pay more than our share of benefits and costs covered by this insurance and other insurance or self-insurance. Subject to any limits of liability that may apply, all shares will be equal until the loss is paid. If any insurance or self-insurance is exhausted, the shares of all remaining insurance will be equal until the loss is paid.

F.   Payments You Must Make

You are responsible for any payments in excess of the benefits regularly provided by the workers compensation law including those required because:

1. of your serious and willful misconduct;

2. you knowingly employ an employee in violation of law;

3. you fail to comply with a health or safety law or regulation; or

4. you discharge, coerce or otherwise discriminate against any employee in violation of the workers compensation law.

If we make any payments in excess of the benefits regularly provided by the workers compensation law on your behalf, you will reimburse us promptly.

G.   Recovery From Others

We have your rights, and the rights of persons entitled to the benefits of this insurance, to recover our payments from anyone liable for the injury. You will do everything necessary to protect those rights for us and to help us enforce them.

H.   Statutory Provisions

These statements apply where they are required by law.

1. As between an injured worker and us, we have notice of the injury when you have notice.

2. Your default or the bankruptcy or insolvency of you or your estate will not relieve us of our duties under this insurance after an injury occurs.

3. We are directly and primarily liable to any person entitled to the benefits payable by this insurance. Those persons may enforce our duties; so may an agency authorized by law. Enforcement may be against us or against you and us.

4. Jurisdiction over you is jurisdiction over us for purposes of the workers compensation law. We are bound by decisions against you under that law, subject to the provisions of this policy that are not in conflict with that law.

5. This insurance conforms to the parts of the

workers compensation law that apply to:

a. benefits payable by this insurance;

b. special taxes, payments into security or other special funds, and assessments payable by us under that law.

6. Terms of this insurance that conflict with the workers compensation law are changed by this statement to conform to that law.

Nothing in these paragraphs relieves you of your duties under this policy.

PART TWO
EMPLOYERS LIABILITY INSURANCE

A.   How This Insurance Applies

This employers liability insurance applies to bodily injury by accident or bodily injury by disease. Bodily injury includes resulting death.

1. The bodily injury must arise out of and in the course of the injured employee's employment by you.

2. The employment must be necessary or incidental to your work in a state or territory listed in Item 3.A. of the Information Page.

3. Bodily injury by accident must occur during the policy period.

4. Bodily injury by disease must be caused or aggravated by the conditions of your employment. The employee's last day of last exposure to the conditions causing or aggravating such bodily injury by disease must occur during the policy period.

5. If you are sued, the original suit and any related legal actions for damages for bodily injury by accident or by disease must be brought in the United States of America, its territories or possessions, or Canada.

B.   We Will Pay

We will pay all sums that you legally must pay as damages because of bodily injury to your employees, provided the bodily injury is covered by this Employers Liability Insurance.

The damages we will pay, where recovery is permitted by law, include damages:

1. For which you are liable to a third party by reason of a claim or suit against you by that third party to recover the damages claimed

WORKERS COMPENSATION AND EMPLOYERS LIABILITY INSURANCE POLICY   **WC 00 00 00 C**

1st Reprint   *Effective January 1, 2015*   **Standard**

against such third party as a result of injury to your employee;

2. For care and loss of services; and

3. For consequential bodily injury to a spouse, child, parent, brother or sister of the injured employee; provided that these damages are the direct consequence of bodily injury that arises out of and in the course of the injured employee's employment by you; and

4. Because of bodily injury to your employee that arises out of and in the course of employment, claimed against you in a capacity other than as employer.

C. **Exclusions**

This insurance does not cover:

1. Liability assumed under a contract. This exclusion does not apply to a warranty that your work will be done in a workmanlike manner;

2. Punitive or exemplary damages because of bodily injury to an employee employed in violation of law;

3. Bodily injury to an employee while employed in violation of law with your actual knowledge or the actual knowledge of any of your executive officers;

4. Any obligation imposed by a workers compensation, occupational disease, unemployment compensation, or disability benefits law, or any similar law;

5. Bodily injury intentionally caused or aggravated by you;

6. Bodily injury occurring outside the United States of America, its territories or possessions, and Canada. This exclusion does not apply to bodily injury to a citizen or resident of the United States of America or Canada who is temporarily outside these countries;

7. Damages arising out of coercion, criticism, demotion, evaluation, reassignment, discipline, defamation, harassment, humiliation, discrimination against or termination of any employee, or any personnel practices, policies, acts or omissions;

8 Bodily injury to any person in work subject to the Longshore and Harbor Workers' Compensation Act (33 U.S.C. Sections 901 et seq.), the Non-appropriated Fund Instrumentalities Act (5 U.S.C. Sections 8171 et seq.), the Outer Continental Shelf Lands Act (43 U.S.C. Sections 1331 et seq.), the Defense Base Act (42 U.S.C. Sections 1651–1654), the Federal Mine Safety and Health

Act (30 U.S.C. Sections 801et seq. and 901-944), any other federal workers or workmen's compensation law or other federal occupational disease law, or any amendments to these laws;

9. Bodily injury to any person subject to the Federal Employers' Liability Act (45 U.S.C. Sections 51 et seq.), any other federal laws obligating an employer to pay damages to an employee due to bodily injury arising out of or in the course of employment, or any amendments to those laws;

10. Bodily injury to a master or member of the crew of any vessel, and does not cover punitive damages related to your duty or obligation to provide transportation, wages, maintenance, and cure under any applicable maritime law;

11. Fines or penalties imposed for violation of federal or state law; and

12. Damages payable under the Migrant and Seasonal Agricultural Worker Protection Act (29 U.S.C. Sections 1801 et seq.) and under any other federal law awarding damages for violation of those laws or regulations issued thereunder, and any amendments to those laws.

D. **We Will Defend**

We have the right and duty to defend, at our expense, any claim, proceeding or suit against you for damages payable by this insurance. We have the right to investigate and settle these claims, proceedings and suits.

We have no duty to defend a claim, proceeding or suit that is not covered by this insurance. We have no duty to defend or continue defending after we have paid our applicable limit of liability under this insurance.

E. **We Will Also Pay**

We will also pay these costs, in addition to other amounts payable under this insurance, as part of any claim, proceeding, or suit we defend:

1. Reasonable expenses incurred at our request, but not loss of earnings;

2. Premiums for bonds to release attachments and for appeal bonds in bond amounts up to the limit of our liability under this insurance;

3. Litigation costs taxed against you;

4. Interest on a judgment as required by law until we offer the amount due under this insurance; and

5. Expenses we incur.

F. **Other Insurance**

We will not pay more than our share of damages and costs covered by this insurance and other insurance or self-insurance. Subject to any limits of liability that apply, all shares will be equal until the loss is paid. If any insurance or self-insurance is exhausted, the shares of all remaining insurance and self-insurance will be equal until the loss is paid.

G. **Limits of Liability**

Our liability to pay for damages is limited. Our limits of liability are shown in Item 3.B. of the Information Page. They apply as explained below.

1. Bodily Injury by Accident. The limit shown for "bodily injury by accident—each accident" is the most we will pay for all damages covered by this insurance because of bodily injury to one or more employees in any one accident.

    A disease is not bodily injury by accident unless it results directly from bodily injury by accident.

2. Bodily Injury by Disease. The limit shown for "bodily injury by disease—policy limit" is the most we will pay for all damages covered by this insurance and arising out of bodily injury by disease, regardless of the number of employees who sustain bodily injury by disease. The limit shown for "bodily injury by disease—each employee" is the most we will pay for all damages because of bodily injury by disease to any one employee.

    Bodily injury by disease does not include disease that results directly from a bodily injury by accident.

3. We will not pay any claims for damages after we have paid the applicable limit of our liability under this insurance.

H. **Recovery From Others**

We have your rights to recover our payment from anyone liable for an injury covered by this insurance. You will do everything necessary to protect those rights for us and to help us enforce them.

I. **Actions Against Us**

There will be no right of action against us under this insurance unless:

1. You have complied with all the terms of this policy; and

2. The amount you owe has been determined with our consent or by actual trial and final judgment.

This insurance does not give anyone the right to add us as a defendant in an action against you to determine your liability. The bankruptcy or insolvency of you or your estate will not relieve us of our obligations under this Part.

PART THREE
OTHER STATES INSURANCE

A. **How This Insurance Applies**

1. This other states insurance applies only if one or more states are shown in Item 3.C. of the Information Page.

2. If you begin work in any one of those states after the effective date of this policy and are not insured or are not self-insured for such work, all provisions of the policy will apply as though that state were listed in Item 3.A. of the Information Page.

3. We will reimburse you for the benefits required by the workers compensation law of that state if we are not permitted to pay the benefits directly to persons entitled to them.

4. If you have work on the effective date of this policy in any state not listed in Item 3.A. of the Information Page, coverage will not be afforded for that state unless we are notified within thirty days.

B. **Notice**

Tell us at once if you begin work in any state listed in Item 3.C. of the Information Page.

PART FOUR
YOUR DUTIES IF INJURY OCCURS

Tell us at once if injury occurs that may be covered by this policy. Your other duties are listed here.

1. Provide for immediate medical and other services required by the workers compensation law.

2. Give us or our agent the names and addresses of the injured persons and of witnesses, and other information we may need.

3. Promptly give us all notices, demands and legal

papers related to the injury, claim, proceeding or suit.

4. Cooperate with us and assist us, as we may request, in the investigation, settlement or defense of any claim, proceeding or suit.

5. Do nothing after an injury occurs that would interfere with our right to recover from others.

6. Do not voluntarily make payments, assume obligations or incur expenses, except at your own cost.

PART FIVE—PREMIUM

A. **Our Manuals**

All premium for this policy will be determined by our manuals of rules, rates, rating plans and classifications. We may change our manuals and apply the changes to this policy if authorized by law or a governmental agency regulating this insurance.

B. **Classifications**

Item 4 of the Information Page shows the rate and premium basis for certain business or work classifications. These classifications were assigned based on an estimate of the exposures you would have during the policy period. If your actual exposures are not properly described by those classifications, we will assign proper classifications, rates and premium basis by endorsement to this policy.

C. **Remuneration**

Premium for each work classification is determined by multiplying a rate times a premium basis. Remuneration is the most common premium basis. This premium basis includes payroll and all other remuneration paid or payable during the policy period for the services of:

1. all your officers and employees engaged in work covered by this policy; and

2. all other persons engaged in work that could make us liable under Part One (Workers Compensation Insurance) of this policy. If you do not have payroll records for these persons, the contract price for their services and materials may be used as the premium basis. This paragraph 2 will not apply if you give us proof that the employers of these persons lawfully secured their workers compensation obligations.

D. **Premium Payments**

You will pay all premium when due. You will pay the premium even if part or all of a workers compensation law is not valid.

E. **Final Premium**

The premium shown on the Information Page, schedules, and endorsements is an estimate. The final premium will be determined after this policy ends by using the actual, not the estimated, premium basis and the proper classifications and rates that lawfully apply to the business and work covered by this policy. If the final premium is more than the premium you paid to us, you must pay us the balance. If it is less, we will refund the balance to you. The final premium will not be less than the highest minimum premium for the classifications covered by this policy.

If this policy is canceled, final premium will be determined in the following way unless our manuals provide otherwise:

1. If we cancel, final premium will be calculated pro rata based on the time this policy was in force. Final premium will not be less than the pro rata share of the minimum premium.

2. If you cancel, final premium will be more than pro rata; it will be based on the time this policy was in force, and increased by our short-rate cancelation table and procedure. Final premium will not be less than the minimum premium.

F. **Records**

You will keep records of information needed to compute premium. You will provide us with copies of those records when we ask for them.

G. **Audit**

You will let us examine and audit all your records that relate to this policy. These records include ledgers, journals, registers, vouchers, contracts, tax reports, payroll and disbursement records, and programs for storing and retrieving data. We may conduct the audits during regular business hours during the policy period and within three years after the policy period ends. Information developed by audit will be used to determine final premium. Insurance rate service organizations have the same rights we have under this provision.

WC 00 00 00 C   **WORKERS COMPENSATION AND EMPLOYERS LIABILITY INSURANCE POLICY**

Standard   *Effective January 1, 2015*   **1st Reprint**

PART SIX—CONDITIONS

A. **Inspection**

We have the right, but are not obliged to inspect your workplaces at any time. Our inspections are not safety inspections. They relate only to the insurability of the workplaces and the premiums to be charged. We may give you reports on the conditions we find. We may also recommend changes. While they may help reduce losses, we do not undertake to perform the duty of any person to provide for the health or safety of your employees or the public. We do not warrant that your workplaces are safe or healthful or that they comply with laws, regulations, codes or standards. Insurance rate service organizations have the same rights we have under this provision.

B. **Long Term Policy**

If the policy period is longer than one year and sixteen days, all provisions of this policy will apply as though a new policy were issued on each annual anniversary that this policy is in force.

C. **Transfer of Your Rights and Duties**

Your rights or duties under this policy may not be transferred without our written consent.

If you die and we receive notice within thirty days after your death, we will cover your legal representative as insured.

D. **Cancelation**

1. You may cancel this policy. You must mail or deliver advance written notice to us stating when the cancelation is to take effect.

2. We may cancel this policy. We must mail or deliver to you not less than ten days advance written notice stating when the cancelation is to take effect. Mailing that notice to you at your mailing address shown in Item 1 of the Information Page will be sufficient to prove notice.

3. The policy period will end on the day and hour stated in the cancelation notice.

4. Any of these provisions that conflict with a law that controls the cancelation of the insurance in this policy is changed by this statement to comply with the law.

E. **Sole Representative**

The insured first named in Item 1 of the Information Page will act on behalf of all insureds to change this policy, receive return premium, and give or receive notice of cancelation.

Appendix B

Workers Compensation Experience Rating

WORKER'S COMPENSATION EXPERIENCE RATING

Risk Name: Happy Hotel Co.[1] **Risk ID:** 123456789[4]

Rating Effective Date: 07/15/2015[2] **Production Date:** 09/04/2015[3] **State:** Florida[5]

Carrier: Any **Policy No. WC 2011** **Effective Date:** 7/15/2011 **Expiration Date:** 7/15/2012

Code[6]	ELR[7]	D-Ratio[8]	Payroll[9]	Expected Losses[10]	Exp Prim Losses[11]	Claim Data[16]	LJ[15]	OF[14]	Act Inc Losses[13]	Act Prim Losses[12]
8810	.10	.43	983,795	984	423	281937585[17]	05	F	1,834	1,834
9052	1.57	.45	3,172,676	49,811	22,415	171953685	06	F	421	421
9058	1.11	.49	1,375,693	15,270	7,482	784942730	06	F	2,075	2,075
9807	ADDITIONAL PREMIUM		0	0	0	181672485	06	F	2,878	2,878
						NO. 10[18]	06	*	6,410	6,410
						041807485	09	F	34,024	15,500
						415021730	09	F	51,140	15,500

Subject Premium: 127,892 **Total Act Inc. Losses:** 98,782

Policy Total: 5,532,164

Carrier: Any — Policy No. WC 2012 — Effective Date: 7/15/2012 — Expiration Date: 7/15/2013

Code	ELR	D-Ratio	Payroll	Expected Losses	Exp Prim Losses	Claim Data	IJ	OF	Act Inc Losses	Act Prim Losses
8810	.10	.43	1,050,397	1,050	452	NO. 2	05	*	2,834	2,834
9052	1.57	.45	3,244,353	50,936	22,921	13201781	05	F	3,632	3,632
9058	1.11	.49	1,476,697	16,391	8,032	13201088	06	F	3,946	3,946
98C7	ADDITIONAL PREMIUM			0	0	NO. 9	06	*	6,375	6,375
9841	DRUG FREE CREDIT			-3,419	-1,570					

Policy Total: 5,771,447 — Subject Premium: 147,599 — Total Act Inc. Losses: 16,787

Carrier: Any — Policy No. WC 2013 — Effective 7/15/2013 — Date: — Expiration Date: 7/15/2014

Code	ELR	D-Ratio	Payroll	Expected Losses	Exp Prim Losses	Claim Data	IJ	OF	Act Inc Losses	Act Prim Losses
8810	.10	.43	1,050,397	1,050	452	NO. 2	05	*	2,834	2,834
9052	1.57	.45	3,244,353	50,936	22,921	13201781	05	F	3,632	3,632
9058	1.11	.49	1,476,697	16,391	8,032	13201088	06	F	3,946	3,946
9765	WORKPLACE SAFETY C			-1,281	-589					
9807	ADDITIONAL PREMIUM			0	0					
9841	DRUG FREE CREDIT									

Policy Total: 5,411,877 — Subject Premium: 152,847 — Total Act Inc. Losses: 90,862

Basic Manual—2001 Edition—ILLINOIS

MISCELLANEOUS RULES

Effective 31 Dec 2015 12:00:01

ILLINOIS WORKERS COMPENSATION PREMIUM ALGORITHM

The following algorithm provides the framework for premium charges and credits. Where not specified, the premium base would be the result from the prior line.[*]

	PREMIUM ELEMENTS	EXPLANATORY NOTES
	MANUAL PREMIUM	[(PAYROLL/100)* RATE]
+	Supplementary Disease (foundry, abrasive, sandblasting)	[(SUBJECT PAYROLL/100)* DISEASE RATE]
+	USL&H Exposure for non-F classification codes	[(SUBJECT PAYROLL/100)* (RATE* USL&H FACTOR)]
	TOTAL MANUAL PREMIUM	
+	Waiver of Subrogation factor[**]	[% applied to the portion of Total Manual Premium where waiver is applicable]
+	Employers Liability (E/L) increased limits factor	[% applied to Total Manual Premium]
+	Employers Liability increased limits charge	[Balance to E/L increased limits minimum premium]
+	Employers Liability increased limits factor (Admiralty, FELA)	[Factor applied to the portion of Manual Premium where Admiralty/FELA coverage is applicable]
+	Employers Liability/Voluntary Compensation flat charge	[Coverage in Monopolistic State Funds]
−	Small Deductible credit	[% applied to Total Manual Premium]
	TOTAL SUBJECT PREMIUM	
×	Experience Modification (Exp Mod)	

PREMIUM ELEMENTS	EXPLANATORY NOTES
TOTAL MODIFIED PREMIUM	
× Contracting Class Prem Adj Program factor (1 – CCPAP credit %)	
+ Employee Leasing Rating Adjustment	
+ Supplemental Disease Exposure (Asbestos,[NOC])[†]	
+ Atomic Energy Radiation Exposure[NOC][†]	
+ Charge for nonratable catastrophe loading[†]	
+ Aircraft Seat Surcharge	
+ Balance to Minimum Premium (State Act)	[Balance to minimum premium at Standard Limits]
+ Balance to Minimum Premium (Admiralty, FELA)	
TOTAL STANDARD PREMIUM	
– Premium Discount[§]	[% applied to Standard Premium]
+ Coal Mine Disease Charge	[Underground, surface, surface auger]
+ Expense Constant	
+ Terrorism	[(PAYROLL/100)* TERRORISM VALUE]
+ Catastrophe (other than Certified Acts of Terrorism)	[(PAYROLL/100)* CATASTROPHE (OTHER THAN CERTIFIED ACTS OF TERRORISM) VALUE]
ESTIMATED ANNUAL PREMIUM	

[**]Premium charges established for Waiver of Subrogation are not filed by NCCI for the voluntary market.

[NOC] = Not Otherwise Classified.

[†]Nonratable Element Premiums generated by nonratable portion of manual rate are subject to all applicable premium elements applied to the policy, however, not subject to experience rating or retrospective rating.

[§]For policies subject to premium adjustments under a retrospective rating plan, premium discount does not apply.

Note: For short rate cancellations, short rate percentage/short rate penalty premium factor is subject to experience rating, included in Total Subject Premium, and applied prior to Experience Modification.

[*] The above rating method would be used in absence of independent carrier filings.

Appendix C

Application of Workers Compensation Laws

State	Who is Covered						Statutory Reference
	Exclusive Remedy[1]	Executive Officers[2]	Partners[3]	Sole Proprietors[4]	Agricultural Workers[5]	Domestic Employees[6]	
Alabama	X	X					§25-5-50, 25-5-53
Alaska	X	X	X	X			§23.30.230, 23.30.239, 23.30.240, 23.30.055
Arizona		X			X		§23-901, 23-1022, 23-1024
Arkansas	X	X		X			§11-9-102, 11-9-105
California	X				X	X	Labor Code §3351, 3602
Colorado	X	X			X	X	§8-41-104, 8-41-202, 8-40-302
Connecticut	X		X	X	X	X	§31-275, 31-284
Delaware	X	X			X	X	Tit. 19, §2304, 2307, 2308
District of Columbia	X	X			X	X	§32-1501, 32-1504, §
Florida	X	X			X		§440.02, 440.11
Georgia	X	X			X		§34-9-2.2, 34-9-11
Hawaii	X	X			X	X	§386-4, 386-5
Idaho	X	X			X		§72-209, 72-212, 72-213
Illinois	X	X			X	X	Tit. 820, §305/1, 305/5
Indiana	X	X			X	X	§22-3-2-6, 22-3-6-1
Iowa	X	X			X	X	§85.1, 85.1A, 85.20
Kansas	X	X			X	X	§44-501, 44-508
Kentucky	X	X			X	X	§342.012, 342.640, 342.690
Louisiana	X	X	X	X	X		§23:1032, 23:1035

State	Exclusive Remedy[1]	Executive Officers[2]	Partners[3]	Sole Proprietors[4]	Agricultural Workers[5]	Domestic Employees[6]	Statutory Reference
				Who is Covered			
Maine	×	×			×		§39-A-401
Maryland	×	×			×	×	Labor and Employment Code §9-206, 9-219, 9-227, 9-509
Mass.		×			×	×	Ch.152 §1, 24
Michigan	×	×	×		×	×	§418.118 418.131
Minnesota	×	×			×	×	§176.031, 176.041, 176.011
Mississippi	×	×					§71-3-5, 71-3-9
Missouri	×	×			×		§287.030, 287.035, 287.120
Montana	×	×			×		§39-71-118, 39-71-411
Nebraska	×	×					§48-110, 48-115
Nevada	×	×					§616A.020, 616A.105
New Hampshire	×				×	×	§281-A:2, 281-A:8, 281-A:18-a
New Jersey	×	×			×	×	§34:15-8, 34:15-36
New Mexico	×	×		×			§52-1-6
New York	×	×			×	×	Workers Compensation Law §2, 11
N. Carolina	×	×			×	×	§97-2, 97-10.1
N. Dakota	×						§65-01-02, 65-01-08
Ohio	×	×			×	×	§4123.01, 4123.74
Oklahoma	×	×			×	×	Tit. 85, §2, 12
Oregon	×	×		×	×		§656.018, 656.027, 656.128

State						Statutes
Pennsylvania	X			X		Tit. 77, §463, 481
Rhode Island	X					§28-29-2, 28-29-20
S. Carolina	X			X	X	§42-1-130, 42-1-360, 42-1-540
S. Dakota	X			X	X	§62-1-2, 62-1-7, 62-3-2
Tennessee	X					§50-6-102, 50-6-108
Texas	X		X	X	X	Labor Code §406.097, 408.001
Utah	X			X	X	§34A-2-103, 34A-2-104, 34A-2-105
Vermont	X			X	X	Tit. 21, §601, 622
Virginia	X			X	X	§65.2-101, 65.2-307
Washington	X	X		X	X	§51.12.020, 51.32.010
W.Virginia	X	X	X	X		§23-2-1, 23-2-6
Wisconsin	X	X	X	X		§102.03, 102.075, 102.076
Wyoming	X			X		§27-14-102, 27-14-104

1. Some states allow employees to opt out of the workers compensation system. Some jurisdictions also allow employees to sue their employers for injuries or death arising from willful conduct, physical assault, fraudulent concealment, sexual harassment, sexual assault, defective products made by employers, invasion of privacy, infliction of emotional distress, or gross negligence.
2. Although executive officers are subject to workers compensation in most states, some states allow officers to be exempt from workers compensation coverage.
3. Partners are not subject to workers compensation in most states, but many jurisdictions allow partners to elect coverage. A few states that subject partners to workers compensation allow them to choose exemption.
4. Sole proprietors are not generally subject to workers compensation, but most states allow them to elect coverage. A few states that require coverage allow sole proprietors to choose exemption.
5. Some jurisdictions cover agricultural workers the same as other employees; some carry specific limitations.
6. Many stipulations apply to coverage for domestic employees.

Residual Market Systems

The following states use Assigned Risk Plans (Pools):		
Alabama	Massachusetts	Tennessee
Alaska	Michigan	Vermont
Arizona	Minnesota	Virginia
Arkansas	Mississippi	Wisconsin
Connecticut	Missouri	
Delaware	Nebraska	
District of Columbia	Nevada	
Georgia	New Hampshire	
Hawaii	New Jersey	
Idaho	New Mexico	
Illinois	North Carolina	
Indiana	Oregon	
Iowa	South Carolina	
Kansas	South Dakota	

These states use the state fund:	
California	Ohio
Colorado	Oklahoma
Kentucky	Pennsylvania
Louisiana	Rhode Island
Maine	Texas
Maryland	Utah
Montana	Washington
New York	West Virginia
North Dakota	Wyoming
Florida uses a Joint Underwriting Association.	

These states use the monopolistic construct:	
Ohio	Washington
North Dakota	Wyoming

Successive Injury Funds

STATE	COVERED INJURIES	EMPLOYER OBLIGATION	FUND OBLIGATION	FUND SOURCES	OTHER PROVISONS
Alabama			Successive Injury Fund Eliminated		
Alaska Statutory ref: 23.30.040; 23.30.205	Second injury which, when combined with pre-existing permanent impairment results in greater disability than from second injury alone.	104 weeks of disability resultant from second impairment.	Excess of 104 weeks.	Compensation up to 6% paid to fund; no-dependents death cases - $10,000; civil penalties.	"Permanent impairment" as shown, or would support award of 200 weeks or more.
Arizona Stat. ref: 23-1065	Second injury, combined with pre-existing work-related disability or non-industrially related physical impairment, which results in disability of work.	Resultant disability from second injury.	Fund and employer are equally responsible for remaining difference between compensation for second injury and combined disability.	Cost of self- insurance and 1.5% of all premiums. Up to 0.5% of yearly premiums may be allocated to fund to keep it sound.	Employer must know of existing nonindustrial physical impairment.
Arkansas Stat. ref: 11-9-525 REPEALED JANUARY 1, 2008	Second injury which when combined with previous partial impairment or disability, results in greater disability/ impairment than from second injury alone.	Resultant disability from second injury.	Difference between compensation for second injury and previous permanent disability.	A portion of premium tax is allocated to the Second Injury Fund; the Permanent Total Disability and Death fund receives $500 from no-dependency death cases.	
California Labor Code 4751, 62.5	Second permanent partial injury, when combined with a pre- existing permanent partial disability, and results in 70% or more permanent disability. Unless prior injury involved a major member and second injury is to the opposite and corresponding member for at least 5%, second injury must account for 35% of disability.	Resultant disability from second injury.	Difference between compensation for most recent injury and permanent total disability.	Legislative appropriations from non-administrative expenses of the workers compensation program.	

STATE	COVERED INJURIES	EMPLOYER OBLIGATION	FUND OBLIGATION	FUND SOURCES	OTHER PROVISONS
Colorado			Successive Injury Fund Eliminated		
Connecticut			Successive Injury Fund Eliminated		
Delaware Stat. ref: Title 19, §2327	Disease or second injury which, when added to any pre- existing permanent injury, results in permanent total disability.	Resultant disability from second injury.	Difference between compensation for second injury and permanent total disability.	Premium received by insurance carriers is taxed at 2%.	
District of Columbia			Successive Injury Fund Eliminated		
Florida			Successive Injury Fund Eliminated		
Georgia Stat. ref: 34-9-241, 34-9-360 CLOSED TO NEW INJURIES AFTER JUNE 2006	Disease or second injury which, when combined with pre- existing permanent impairment, results in greater disability than from second injury alone.	Resultant disability from second injury for first 102 weeks.	Income benefits over 104 weeks; for medical and rehabilitation expenses from $5000 to $10,000 are reimbursed to employer at 50%. Medical and rehabilitation expenses above $10,000 are reimbursed at 100%.	Carriers and self- insureds are proportionately assessed up to 175% of disbursements from fund to annual compensation benefits paid, less net assets in fund.	Employer must know of prior impairment before second injury occurs. When no funds are needed assessments may be suspended or reduced.
Hawaii Stat ref: HRS 386-33, 386-151	Second injury which when added to previous permanent partial disability results in permanent total disability or greater permanent partial disability.	Resultant disability for the first 104 weeks.	Benefits beyond the first 104 weeks.	Assessments on insurers and self- insurers, plus a percentage of maximum weekly benefit rate in no- dependency death cases and the unpaid balance in permanent total and permanent partial disability cases with no dependents.	
Idaho Stat. ref: 72-332	Second injury when added with prior permanent physical impairment causes permanent total disability.	Resultant disability from the second injury.	Difference between compensation for second injury and permanent disability.	Assessments based on semi-annual reporting of indemnity payments paid, not less than $200.	

State	Second Injury	Resultant disability	Difference	Fund Contribution	Payments
Illinois Stat. ref: 820 ILCS 305/7 and 305/8	Second injury involving loss of use of major members or loss of eye, when combined with pre-existing loss of member, causes permanent total disability.	Resultant disability from the second injury.	Difference between compensation for second injury and permanent disability.	Employers contribute a percentage of compensation payments.	Payments are not required when the funds reach $600,000; reduced by half when the fund is at $500,000. Payments increase or are reinstated when the fund reaches $300,000 or $400,000.
Indiana Stat. ref: 22-3-3-13	Second injury involving loss or loss of use of foot, leg, arm, hand or eye, when combined with a pre-existing loss or loss of use or member, results in a permanent total disability.	Resultant disability from second injury.	Difference between compensation for second injury and permanent total disability.	Throughout the calendar year 25% of all benefits to injured employees is paid into the fund. An assessment may be charged if the fund drops below $1,000,000 on or before October 1.	
Iowa Stat. ref: 85.64-65	Second injury involving loss of use of member or loss of eye, when combined with pre-existing loss of member, causes permanent disability.	Resultant disability from second injury.	Difference between compensation for second injury and permanent disability, less the value of the previously lost member or organ.	Dependent death cases–$12,000; no-dependent death cases– $45,000. Payments due but not paid to nonresident alien dependents.	
Kansas			Successive Injury Fund Eliminated		
Kentucky			Successive Injury Fund Eliminated		
Louisiana Stat. ref: 23-10:1378	Second injury, when combined with known prior permanent partial disability, results in substantially greater disability or death than from second injury alone. Or second injury would not have occurred if not for pre-existing permanent partial disability.	Complete disability for the first 104 weeks; 175 weeks for death.	Reimburses employer for weekly compensation after the first 104 weeks; or 175 for death.	Assessments on carriers and self-insurers.	If no assessment payment is made there is no reimbursement.

STATE	COVERED INJURIES	EMPLOYER OBLIGATION	FUND OBLIGATION	FUND SOURCES	OTHER PROVISONS
Maine			Successive Injury Fund Eliminated		
Maryland Stat. ref: 10-204	Second injury, when added with pre-existing permanent impairment due to disease, congenital condition or accident, causes a greater combined disability constituting an impediment to employment. Total disability must be 50% of body or equivalent as a whole.	Resultant disability from second injury.	Additional compensation to employee if permanent disability resulting from prior and subsequent impairment exceeds 50% of the body as a whole. Prior and second injuries must each be compensable for at least 125 weeks.	Percentage of compensation on all awards and settlement agreements.	
Massachusetts Stat. ref: Title 21 152 §65	Second injury, when added to pre-existing physical impairment which results in substantially greater disability of death.	Disability benefits for the first 104 weeks.	After the first 104 weeks the employer is reimbursed for up to 75% of benefits.	Employer assessment.	
Michigan Stat. ref: 418.521, 351-9	Second injury which involves loss of eye or member, when added to pre-existing loss of eye or member, results in permanent total disability.	Resultant disability from second injury.	Difference between payment for second injury and permanent total disability.	Carrier and self-insurer assessments.	Fund is credited with balance above $200,000.
Minnesota			Successive Injury Fund Eliminated		
Mississippi Stat. ref: 71-3-73	Second injury involving loss or loss of use of eye or member, when combined with pre-existing loss or loss or use, causes permanent total disability.	Resultant disability from second injury.	Difference between payment for second injury and permanent total disability.	Up to $200,000 may be transferred from the Administrative Expenses Fund . $300 in dependency death cases. $500 in no-dependence death cases.	When fund reaches $300,000 payments are suspended, and reinstated when fund reaches $150,000.
Missouri Stat. ref: 287.222, 287.715	Previous partial permanent industrial disability of at least 12 ½% body as a whole 15% of major extremity exists, and presents additional disability of at least 12 ½ % body as a whole or 15% of major extremity exists.	Resultant disability from second injury.	Difference between payment for second injury and combined disability.	Surcharge set annually as a percentage of premiums paid by all insured and self-insured premium equivalent.	

State					
Montana Stat. ref: 39-71-907	Second injury, when added to certified pre-existing physical impairment, which results in disability or death.	Medical benefits for 104 weeks following the injury and the first 104 weeks of indemnity benefits.	Re-imbursement of employer after first 104 weeks.	Surcharge of employers.	Workers must be certified as vocationally handicapped.
Nebraska			Successive Injury Fund Eliminated		
Nevada	Nevada administers four separate successive injury funds, each with different qualifications and requirements.				
New Hampshire Stat. ref: 281-A:54	Second injury, when added to pre-existing physical impairment, which results in greater disability.	Disability benefits for the first 104 weeks.	Reimbursement for employers after the first 104 weeks, plus 50% of anything over $10,000 during the first 104 weeks.	Assessment against insurers and self-insurers.	An employer is reimbursed 50% of cost of modification if it makes modification to retain an injured worker, not to exceed $5,000 yearly per employee.
New Jersey Stat. ref: 34: 15-94 and 95	Second injury, when added to pre-existing partial disability, which results in total disability.	Resultant disability from second injury.	Difference between payment for second injury and pre-existing disability.	Annual surcharge on policyholders and assessment of self-insurers.	Up to $12,500 per year may be transferred to the fund for administrative expenses.
New Mexico			Successive Injury Fund Eliminated		
New York Workers Comp code: 15 CLOSED TO NEW INJURY AFTER 6/30/2007	Second injury, when pre-existing permanent, physical impairment results in a permanent disability caused by materially and substantially greater conditions than that which have resulted from the second injury alone.	Benefits for death or disability for first 260 weeks.	Reimbursement of employer after first 260 weeks.	Assessment against carriers and self-insurers.	

STATE	COVERED INJURIES	EMPLOYER OBLIGATION	FUND OBLIGATION	FUND SOURCES	OTHER PROVISONS
North Carolina Stat. ref: 97-35	Second injury involving the loss of eye or other member, when combined with pre-existing injury results in permanent total disability, provided the prior and subsequent disability were each 20% of the entire member.	Resultant disability from second injury.	Difference between payment for second injury and permanent total disability.	Employer of insurer assessments.	
North Dakota			Monopolistic State Fund		
Ohio Stat. ref: 4123.343	Second injury aggravates pre-existing condition or disease and causes death, temporary or permanent total disability, and disability compensable under a particular schedule.	Resultant disability from occupational disease or injury sustained in employment.	Determined by Bureau.	Statutory Surplus funds.	
Oklahoma Stat. ref: title 85 §172-3 : Statute repealed.					
Oregon Stat. ref: 656.628	Any new compensable injury.	First $1000 of expenses.	Payment determined by Bureau; subsequent injuries throughout the claimant's working career as the result of the condition.	Percentage of hourly wages paid by the worker and employer.	Reimbursement from fund requires approval from department.
Pennsylvania Stat. ref: title 77, §516 and 517	Second injury involving loss or loss of use, when added to a pre-existing loss or loss of use of a hand, arm, foot, leg, or eye, causes total disability.	Resultant disability as a result of second injury according to schedule of benefits.	Any remaining compensation due to total disability.	Assessment against carriers and self-insurers.	

State / Stat. ref	Definition	Disability covered	Reimbursement / Benefits	Funding	Special provisions
Rhode Island			Successive Injury Fund Eliminated		
South Carolina Stat. ref: 42-9-400, 42-7-310 CLOSED TO DATES OF NEW INJURY AFTER 7/1/2008	Second injury, when combined with any prior permanent physical impairment, results in substantially greater disability or death.	The first 78 weeks of disability compensation and medical care caused by second injury.	Reimbursement of employer for all benefits after 78 weeks, plus 50% of medical payments over $3,000 during the first 78 weeks.	Assessment of carriers and self-insurers.	Employer must prove prior knowledge of impairment or that worker was unaware of impairment.
South Dakota			Successive Injury Fund Eliminated		
Tennessee Stat. ref: 50-6-208	Second injury, when added to pre-existing impairment or disability, results in permanent total disability.	Resultant disability from second injury.	Benefits exceeding 100% total disability to body as a whole.	Premium tax on insurers and self-insurers.	Employer must prove knowledge of pre-existing disability.
Texas Stat. ref: 403.006, 403.007	Subsequent compensable injury added to the effects of a previous injury.	Benefits that would have accrued if only the subsequent injury had occurred and not the previous injury.	Balance of lifetime income benefits.	Maintenance tax, and 364 weeks no dependency death case benefits.	
Utah			Successive Injury Fund Eliminated		
Vermont			Successive Injury Fund Eliminated		
Virginia Stat. ref: 65.2-1100-1105	Second injury involving 20% loss or loss of use of eye or member, when combined with pre-existing disability of 20% or more, and causes partial or total disability.	Resultant disability from second injury.	Pro-rata reimbursement to employer for compensation has expired, and up to $7,500 for vocational and medical rehabilitation expenses.	Premium tax on carriers and self-insurers.	Payments are suspended when the fund reaches $250,000 and reinstated when the fund drops to $125,000.

STATE	COVERED INJURIES	EMPLOYER OBLIGATION	FUND OBLIGATION	FUND SOURCES	OTHER PROVISONS
Washington Stat. ref: 51.16.-20 51.16.-40	Second injury or disease, which, when added to pre-existing injury or disease, causes permanent total disability or death.	Resultant disability from second injury.	Difference between charges assessed against employer at time of second injury and total cost of pension reserve.	Transfer from accident fund and self-insurers assessment.	
West Virginia Stat. ref: 23-3-1	Second injury, when combined with prior disabilities, results in permanent total disability.	Resultant disability from second injury.	Remainder of compensation due for permanent total disability.	Assessment of self-insurers.	Self-insurers required to subscribe to Second Injury Fund.
Wisconsin Stat. ref: 102.59	Second injury with permanent disability for 200 weeks or more, with a pre-existing disability of 200 weeks or more.	Resultant disability from second injury.	The disability caused by the lesser of two injuries. If the combined disabilities cause permanent total disability, the fund pays the difference between compensation for second injury and permanent total disability.	$20,000 for loss of hand, arm, foot, leg, or eye.	
Wyoming			No Successive Injury Fund.		

Type of Law by State

Jurisdiction of Law	Type Permitted	Waivers	State Fund	Pvt. Carrier	Additional Information
Alabama	Compulsory	No	No	Yes	Contact an employee of the compliance section for more information
Alaska	Compulsory	Yes	No	Yes	marie.marx@alaska.gov
Arizona	Compulsory	Yes	Competitive	Yes	A.R.S. 23-901 or www.azica.gov
Arkansas	Compulsory	Yes	No	Yes	info@awcc.state.ar.us
California	Compulsory	No	Competitive	Yes	DIRInfo@dir.ca.gov
Colorado	Compulsory	Yes	Competitive	Yes	Cdle_workers_compensation@state.co.us
Connecticut	Compulsory	Yes	No	Yes	
Delaware	Compulsory	No	No	Yes	
Dist. of Col.	Compulsory	No	No	Yes	
Florida	Compulsory	Yes	No	Yes	
Georgia	Compulsory	Yes	No	Yes	
Hawaii	Compulsory	No	Competitive	Yes	
Idaho	Compulsory	No	Competitive	Yes	
Illinois	Compulsory	No	No	Yes	
Indiana	Compulsory	No	No	Yes	
Iowa	Compulsory	Yes	No	Yes	
Kansas	Compulsory	Yes	No	Yes	
Kentucky	Compulsory	Yes	Competitive	Yes	

Jurisdiction of Law	Type Permitted	Waivers	State Fund	Pvt. Carrier	Additional Information
Louisiana	Compulsory	Yes	Competitive	Yes	
Maine	Compulsory	Yes	Competitive	Yes	
Maryland	Compulsory	Yes	Competitive	Yes	
Massachusetts	Compulsory	No	No	Yes	
Michigan	Compulsory	Yes	Competitive	Yes	
Minnesota	Compulsory	No	Competitive	Yes	
Mississippi	Compulsory	No	No	Yes	
Missouri	Compulsory	No	Competitive	Yes	
Montana	Compulsory	Yes	Competitive	Yes	
Nebraska	Compulsory	Yes	No	Yes	
Nevada	Compulsory	No	No	Yes	
New Hampshire	Compulsory	No	No	Yes	
New Jersey 1, 2	Compulsory	No	No	Yes	
New Mexico	Compulsory	Yes	Competitive	Yes	
New York	Compulsory	No	Competitive	Yes	
North Carolina	Compulsory	Yes	No	Yes	
North Dakota	Compulsory	No	Exclusive	No	
Ohio	Compulsory	Yes	Exclusive	No	
Oklahoma	Compulsory	No	Competitive	Yes	
Oregon	Compulsory	No	Competitive	Yes	
Pennsylvania	Compulsory	No	Competitive	Yes	
Puerto Rico	Compulsory	No	Exclusive	No	

Rhode Island	Compulsory	No	Competitive	Yes
South Carolina	Compulsory	Yes	No	Yes
South Dakota	Compulsory	Yes	No	Yes
Tennessee	Compulsory	Yes	No	Yes
Texas 3	Elective	No	Competitive	Yes
Utah	Compulsory	No	Competitive	Yes
Vermont	Compulsory	Yes	No	Yes
Virginia	Compulsory	Yes	No	Yes
Virgin Islands	Compulsory	No	Exclusive	No
Washington	Compulsory	No	Exclusive	No
West Virginia	Compulsory	No	Exclusive	Yes
Wisconsin	Compulsory	No	No	Yes
Wyoming 4	Compulsory	No	Exclusive	No
United States*				
FECA	Compulsory	No	Exclusive	No
LHWCA	Compulsory	No	No	Yes

* Federal Employee's Compensation Act.
Longshore and Harbor Workers' Compensation Act.

FOOTNOTES

1. New Jersey: Workers compensation coverage may be terminated by either party upon sixty days notice in writing prior to any accident.
2. New Jersey: Permits ten or more employers licensed by the State as hospitals to group self-insure.
3. Texas: Provides for mandatory workers' compensation coverage under Title 25 of State statutes regarding rules and regulations for "Carriers" (Article 911-A, Sec. II, Motor Bus Transportation and Regulations by the Railroad Commission).
4. Wyoming: The law is compulsory for all employers engaged in extra-hazardous occupations and elective for all other occupations.

Appendix D

Scopes Manual

Posted 01 March 2014 12:00:01

8810

States Not Applicable:	Replaced By:
Not Applicable	Not Applicable
States Exceptions to the National Code:	
AK, CA, MA, MT, NJ, NY, OR, TX	
Established:	**Retained:**
Date Unknown	Not Applicable
Discontinued:	**NCCI Schedule and Group:**
Not Applicable	Schedule 35, Group 350

PHRASEOLOGY CLERICAL OFFICE EMPLOYEES NOC

(N/A MA, TX)

Note: Subject to the Rule 1-B-2.

Description:

Code 8810 is applied to clerical office employees provided they are not otherwise classified in the *Basic Manual*. Clerical employees who perform telecommuting activities may qualify for Code 8871—Clerical Telecommuter Employees. Refer to Code 8871's scope for conditions under which a telecommuting employee's pay should be assigned to this code.

Code 8810 employees are common to so many businesses that they are considered to be Standard Exceptions unless they are specifically included within the phraseology of a basic classification. The duties of a clerical office employee include creation or maintenance of financial or other employer records, handling correspondence, computer composition, technical drafting, and telephone duties, including sales by phone. The clerical office classification continues to apply to a qualified clerical office employee who performs a duty outside of a qualified clerical office area when that duty does not involve direct supervision or physical labor and is directly related to that employee's duties in the office. These duties do not exclude depositing funds at the bank, purchasing office supplies, and pickup or delivery of mail, provided they are incidental and directly related to that employee's duties in the office. However, for purposes of this rule, the definition of clerical duties excludes outside sales or outside representatives; any work exposed to the operative hazards of the business; and any work, such as a stock or tally clerk, which is necessary, incidental or related to any operations of the business other than a clerical office.

A clerical office is a work area separated and distinguishable from all other work areas and hazards of the employer by floors, walls, partitions, counters, or other physical barriers.

A clerical office excludes work or service areas and areas where inventory is located, products are displayed for sale, or to which the purchaser customarily brings the product from another area for payment.

If the principal business of an insured is a clerical operation, the operations of all employees not included in the definition of clerical shall be assigned to the separate basic classification that most closely describes their work.

Certain Internet service providers may also have their principal business described by a clerical classification. Under these circumstances, these Internet service providers are classified in the same manner as described above. These risks usually offer electronic mail services and access to World Wide Web sites, Internet chat rooms, and Internet news groups.

Other employments or operations assigned by analogy to Code 8810 include telephone answering services; designers, proofreaders, and editors of newspaper publishers or magazine printers; employees performing computerized photographic composition or automated platemaking, which is used in the graphic arts industry as well as specialists engaged in such operations; clubs employing only clerical employees; horse and dog racetrack pari-mutuel clerks and cashiers; bus terminal ticket sellers; airline or helicopter ticket sellers and information clerks away from airport or heliport locations; and employees of highway toll roads confined to keeping books and records.

Code 8810 is applicable to traveling auditing, accounting, or other type clerical employees of business concerns such as manufacturers, chain stores, restaurants, hotels, gasoline stations, etc., who perform clerical duties at their temporary location. These traveling clerical employees, sometimes referred to as "internal auditors," may travel to various branches and remain at these branches for a period of several days or weeks, auditing or monitoring procedures at these locations. These employees are not included within the scope of Code 8803—Accountants—Traveling and are assigned to Code 8810. These employees are not classified to Code 8803 since their employers are not in the business of providing auditing or accounting services for others.

Special Conditions:

In instances where clerical or drafting employees perform any other duties, the total payroll of such employees would be assigned to the highest rated classification representing any part of their work. This is in accordance with Rule 2-G.

Related Operations Not Classified to Code 8810:

Certain Code 8810 operations are designated as "not otherwise classified" (NOC). These NOC operations will apply to an insured only when no other classification more specifically describes the insured's operations. The following is a representative list of classifications somewhat related in nature to Code 8810 operations that are not assigned to Code 8810:

8803—Auditors, Accountant or Factory Cost or Office Systematizer—Traveling
8820—Attorney
8855—Banks and Trust Companies—All Employees, Salespersons, Drivers & Clerical
8861—Charitable or Welfare Organization—Professional Employees and Clerica
8856—Check Cashing Establishments—All Employees, Salespersons, Drivers & Clerical
8871—Clerical Telecommuter Employees
8814—Federal Employer's Liability Act: Clerical Office Employees
8723—Insurance Companies—Including Clerical & Salespersons
8799—Mailing or Addressing Company or Letter Service Shop—Clerical Staff
8800—Mailing or Addressing Co
8901—Telephone or Telegraph Co.—Office or Exchange Employees & Clerical

In addition to this representative list, one should review sources such as the alphabetical index in this manual to determine whether a classification other than Code 8810 or a classification other than one on the above list is applicable to the operations being reviewed for classification purposes.

CROSS-REF. COMPUTER SYSTEM DESIGNERS OR PROGRAMMERS—EXCLUSIVELY OFFICE

(N/A TX)

CROSS-REF. PUBLIC LIBRARY OR MUSEUM—PROFESSIONAL EMPLOYEES & CLERICAL

(N/A TX)

Description:

As evidenced by this classification's cross-reference phraseology, professional employees of public libraries or museums operated by any municipality, i.e., village, town, county, city, or state, are assigned by analogy to Code 8810. In addition to clerical employees of public libraries, this classification includes library professionals such as administrators, librarians and their assistants, and page persons. In instances where employees of public libraries operate mobile library units, the drivers are assigned to Code 7380. Librarians who travel in their private automobiles from their homes to mobile library locations where they perform their normal duties are properly assigned to Code 8810 since these duties are the same as those performed at central or branch public libraries. In addition to clerical employees of public museums, this classification includes museum professionals such as administrators, curators and their assistants, librarians, tour directors, and lecturers, who may at times conduct classes for public education. Museum professionals who prepare various types of exhibits and restore art works are additionally assigned to Code 8810.

It should be noted that even though the above references refer to public libraries and museums, private libraries and museums are classified by analogy in a manner similar to public libraries and museums.

Refer to Code 9101 for the classification of all other than professional or clerical employees of libraries and museums.

CROSS-REF. RACETRACK OPERATION—HORSE OR DOG—PARI-MUTUEL CLERKS, CASHIERS, AND CLERICAL OFFICE EMPLOYEES

(N/A TX)

Appendix E

Interplay Among the FMLA, ADA, and Workers Comp Statutes

Comparison of the Statutes

The following pages contain a chart that displays the comparisons between the Family and Medical Leave Act, the Americans with Disabilities Act, and workers compensation statutes. This information is presented to the reader in a compact manner to make it easier to understand the differences among those laws that have such a great impact on the employer-employee relationship.

The chart first appeared in an article written by Mr. Walter E. Zink II and Ms. Jill Gradwohl Schroeder from the *Defense Counsel Journal*, Volume 66, January, 1999. The chart was reprinted with permission.

Comparisons between the Family and Medical Leave Act, the Americans with Disabilities Act, and General Workers' Compensation Statutes.

Issue	FMLA	ADA	WC
What number of employees must be employed?	50 or more employees.	15 or more employees.	One or more employees.
Does the act apply to applicants for employment?	No. The FMLA applies to employees after 12 months employment with a minimum 1250 hours in the previous 12 months.	Yes.	Generally, no, although individuals injured during tryouts may be covered.
To whom is the act applicable?	May include absences for the employee to care for family members.	Only the worker is included.	Only the worker is included, except that survivors may receive indemnity benefits if worker suffered a fatal work-related injury.
Who is covered by the act?	It covers employees with serious health conditions, those who need to care for a family member, those who have experienced the birth of a child, those who will be caring for an adopted or foster child, and family members taking care of covered service members.	The ADA applies to qualified employees and job applicants who suffer from, have a record of, or are regarded as having a disability.	The state statutes generally apply to individuals who suffer accidents or illnesses which arise out of and in the course of the employment.

Issue	FMLA	ADA	WC
How is the disability defined?	A "serious health condition" may encompass any illness, injury, impairment, physical or condition that involves inpatient care or continuing treatment by a health care provider.	A "physical or mental impairment" which "substantially limits one or more major life activities," including "major bodily functions." Disabilities include impairments that are episodic or in remission. An applicant or employee is "regarded as" disabled if he or she is subject to an action prohibited by the ADA based on an impairment that last longer than 6 months and is major.	State statutes generally include physical or mental injuries or illnesses which were caused by the employment.
What is the primary obligation of the employer under the act?	To grant unpaid leave to employee.	To provide reasonable accommodations the employee, and not discriminate because of disability.	To pay statutory indemnity benefits and medical expenses to or on behalf of the injured worker, and possibly to accommodate the worker or restore him or her to employment.
Can the employer assert undue hardship as a defense?	No.	Yes.	Generally, yes, although it is not expressed in those terms in statutes.

Issue	FMLA	ADA	WC
May the employer transfer the employee?	The employer may temporarily transfer the employee for intermittent or reduced leave so long as the pay and benefits are equivalent.	An employer may reassign an employee who is no longer able to perform the essential functions of his or her original position.	The employer is generally able to transfer the employee so long as it is reasonable. The ability of the employer to transfer may be governed by specific statutory vocational priorities.
Must the employee be returned to equivalent pay and benefits?	Yes.	Yes, unless no job with equivalent pay and benefits is available.	Not necessarily. If employee is returned to lower pay, loss of earning power benefits may be owed, depending on nature of injury.
Is the employer mandated to provide requested leave?	Employer must provide leave to eligible employee even if accommodations exist to keep employee at work.	Employer may deny request for leave and provide alternative reasonable accommodation that allows employee to remain on the job.	Employer may deny a request for leave and provide alternative or transitional duty for the employee.
If an employee wishes to return to work after medical leave, may he or she do so?	Yes, unless leave didn't qualify under FMLA, job was eliminated for other reasons, employee cannot perform an essential function of job because of physical or mental condition, or employee a "key" employee whose return would cause substantial and grievous economic injury to employer. Notice must be given if employee not permitted to return.	Yes, unless the employer demonstrates that holding the job open would impose an undue hardship.	Whether the employer may reject employee's request to return is dependent upon state statutes governing workers comp cases and whether the employment is "at will". Vocational priorities may mandate granting the employee's request to return.

Issue	FMLA	ADA	WC
Must benefits be continued while the employee is off work?	Group health coverage must be continued throughout the leave.	Employer must provide coverage for employee taking leave or working part-time only if employer also provides coverage for other employees in the same leave or part-time status.	Dependant on state statutes.
What type of medical inquiries may an employer make?	Employers may require that a request for leave be supported by a certification issued by a health care provider for the employee or family member.	Employers may inquire as to medical conditions so long as the inquiries are job related and consistent with business necessity.	Generally an employer has access to all medical records relating to the current condition and may have access to records of prior conditions if it can justify the need for them.
May the employer obtain its own opinion as to the nature and extent of the employee's condition?	Yes. The employer may obtain a second opinion. A binding third opinion may also be used. Exams are at the employer's expense.	The employer may perform a post-offer physical examination so long as it is related to the disability and is consistent with business necessity.	In most jurisdictions, the employer has a right to have a "defense examination" performed upon an injured worker.
Are there consequences if employee doesn't submit to an examination scheduled by the employer?	The employee may jeopardize any claim under the FMLA.	The employee may jeopardize any claim under the ADA.	The employee may suffer reduced or discontinued indemnity or medical benefits.

Issue	FMLA	ADA	WC
Can return to work physical examinations be performed?	Yes. Such examinations are limited to the serious medical condition for which the leave is sought. Employers may require "fitness-for-duty" tests if doing the job raises a significant risk of harm to themselves or others.	Yes. Such examinations must be job-related and consistent with business necessity.	Generally, an employer has a right to have a "defense examination" performed at occasional intervals.
Does the act mandate that medical records be kept confidentially?	Medical records created for FMLA are to be maintained as confidential medical records separate from usual personnel files. If ADA also applicable, records are to be maintained in conformance with ADA confidentiality requirements. To protect employee's privacy, direct supervisors are prohibited from getting an employee's medical information when FMLA certification is needed.	Confidentiality of medical records is required. Supervisors and managers may be informed regarding accommodations required by employees.	Confidentiality provisions vary from state to state.
May an action be brought against a co-employee for violating the act?	Liability under the FMLA is limited to the employer.	Although there is a split in decisions as to whether the ADA provides for individual liability, the majority position is that there is no individual liability under the Act.	The extent to which exclusive remedy provisions bar suits against co-employees varies from state to state.

Issue	FMLA	ADA	WC
May intermittent leave or a reduced schedule be taken by the employee?	Yes, if leave requested is due to serious health condition of employee or qualified family member of employee. Such leave may not be taken for birth or adoption of a child, unless employee and employer agree otherwise.	Yes, as a reasonable accommodation.	While intermittent leave or a reduced schedule may not be mandated, it may be used as a form of light duty designed to restore the employee to full duty.
What must the employee show in order to be granted intermittent or reduced leave?	That the employee or a qualified family member suffer from a serious health condition for which such leave is medically necessary.	That such leave will enable the employee to perform the essential functions of the job.	The employer may wish to offer such leave to the employee to reduce its exposure for temporary total disability or vocational rehabilitation benefits.
What is the duration of the leave?	12 weeks; 26 weeks unpaid caregiver leave for relatives of covered servicemembers.	Unlimited, but bound by the concept of "reasonable" accommodations.	State statutes may vary.
Must the employee take the initiative in reporting a qualifying event or condition?	Employee must inform the employer that there is a serious health condition or other reason for which leave is necessary. The employee does not need to elaborate as to details, however the employee may be required to provide certification.	Generally, the employee must inform the employer of the disability or must request a reasonable accommodation.	Employee must inform employer of work-related accidents. In limited situations, employer may be obligated to inquire as to whether condition is related to the employment.

Appendix F

ERM-14 FORM—CONFIDENTIAL REQUEST FOR OWNERSHIP INFORMATION
Effective 01 Dec 2003

All items must be answered completely or the form may be returned.

The following confidential ownership statements may be used only in establishing premiums for your insurance coverages. Your workers compensation policy requires that you report ownership changes, and other changes as detailed below, to your insurance carrier in writing within 90 days of the change. If you have questions, contact your agent, insurance company, or the appropriate rating organization. Once completed, this form must be submitted to the rating organization by you, your insurance carrier(s), or your agents. If this form does not provide the means to explain the transaction, enter as much information on the form as possible and supplement the form with a narrative on the employer's letterhead, signed by an owner, partner, or executive officer.

Section A—Transaction and Entity Information

Check all that apply	Type of Transaction Columns A, B, and C referenced below are found in Section B.	Effective Date Enter effective date of transaction	Reported Date Enter date reported in writing to your insurance provider
	Name and/or legal entity change—Complete column A for former entity and column B for newly named entity. Complete Type of Entity portion for each entity to reflect such change.		
	Sale, transfer or conveyance of all or a portion of an entity's ownership interest—Complete column A for ownership before the change and column B for ownership after the change.		
	Sale, transfer or conveyance of an entity's physical assets to another entity that takes over its operations—Complete column A for the former entity and column B for the acquiring entity.		
	Merger or consolidation (attach copy of agreement)—Complete columns A and B for the former entities and column C for the surviving entity.		
	Formation of a new entity that acts as, or in effect is, a successor to another entity that: (a) Has dissolved (b) Is non-operative (c) May continue to operate in a limited capacity.		
	An irrevocable trust or receiver, established either voluntarily or by court mandate—Complete column A before the change and column B after the change.		
	Determination of combinability of separate entities—Complete a separate column in Section B for each entity to be reviewed for common ownership (attach additional forms if necessary).		

ENTITY 1—Complete Column A on Page 3

Complete Name of Entity (including DBA or TA) _____

Risk ID _____ FEIN _____

Type of Entity (check all that apply)   Carrier _____   Policy # _____   Eff. Date _____

☐ Sole Proprietorship   ☐ Limited Partnership   ☐ Temporary Labor Service   ☐ School District   ☐ Irrevocable Trust
☐ Partnership   ☐ Limited Liability Corporation   ☐ Publicly Traded   ☐ For Profit   ☐ Religious Organization
☐ Domestic Corporation   ☐ Joint Venture   ☐ State Agency   ☐ Not for Profit   ☐ Charitable Organization
☐ Foreign Corporation   ☐ Association (including unincorporated)   ☐ County Agency   ☐ Non-Profit   ☐ Franchise
☐ Sub-Chapter S-Corp   ☐ Employee Leasing   ☐ Municipality   ☐ Revocable Trust   ☐ ESOP

Primary Address

Street _____   City, State, Zip _____

Telephone Number _____   Fax Number _____   E-mail Address _____

Contact Name _____   Web Site _____

Mailing Address (if different than Primary Address) _____

Additional Location(s) _____

ERM-14 (Rev. 12/03)   NC790

Page 1 of 4

© 2002 National Council on Compensation Insurance, Inc.   Oct 2003 (1)

277

ENTITY 2—Complete Column B on Page 3

Complete Name of Entity (including DBA or TA) _____

Risk ID _____   FEIN _____

Type of Entity (check all that apply)   Carrier _____   Policy # _____   Eff. Date _____

☐ Sole Proprietorship   ☐ Limited Partnership   ☐ Temporary Labor Service   ☐ School District   ☐ Irrevocable Trust
☐ Partnership   ☐ Limited Liability Corporation   ☐ Publicly Traded   ☐ For Profit   ☐ Religious Organization
☐ Domestic Corporation   ☐ Joint Venture   ☐ State Agency   ☐ Not for Profit   ☐ Charitable Organization
☐ Foreign Corporation   ☐ Association (including unincorporated)   ☐ County Agency   ☐ Non-Profit   ☐ Franchise
☐ Sub-Chapter S-Corp   ☐ Employee Leasing   ☐ Municipality   ☐ Revocable Trust   ☐ ESOP

Primary Address

Street _____   City, State, Zip _____

Telephone Number _____   Fax Number _____   E-mail Address _____

Contact Name _____   Web Site _____

Mailing Address (if different than Primary Address) _____

Additional Location(s) _____

ENTITY 3—Complete Column C on Page 3

Complete Name of Entity (including DBA or TA) _____

Risk ID _____   FEIN _____

Type of Entity (check all that apply)   Carrier _____   Policy # _____   Eff. Date _____

☐ Sole Proprietorship   ☐ Limited Partnership   ☐ Temporary Labor Service   ☐ School District   ☐ Irrevocable Trust
☐ Partnership   ☐ Limited Liability Corporation   ☐ Publicly Traded   ☐ For Profit   ☐ Religious Organization
☐ Domestic Corporation   ☐ Joint Venture   ☐ State Agency   ☐ Not for Profit   ☐ Charitable Organization
☐ Foreign Corporation   ☐ Association (including unincorporated)   ☐ County Agency   ☐ Non-Profit   ☐ Franchise
☐ Sub-Chapter S-Corp   ☐ Employee Leasing   ☐ Municipality   ☐ Revocable Trust   ☐ ESOP

Primary Address

Street _____   City, State, Zip _____

Telephone Number _____   Fax Number _____   E-mail Address _____

Contact Name _____   Web Site _____

Mailing Address (if different than Primary Address) _____

Additional Location(s) _____

Section B—Ownership

1. Have any of these entities operated under another name in the last four years? ☐ Yes ☐ No

2. Are any of the entities **currently** related through common majority ownership to any entity not listed on the front of the form? ☐ Yes ☐ No

3. Have any of these entities been **previously** related through common majority ownership to any other entities in the last four years?
   ☐ Yes ☐ No

4. If you answered Yes to questions 1, 2, or 3 above, provide additional information, indicating which question(s) your answer references:
   ☐ 1 ☐ 2 ☐ 3

Name of Business	Principal Location	Carrier and Policy Number	Effective Date

5. Were the assets and/or ownership interest (all or a portion) of this entity acquired from a previously existing business? ☐ Yes ☐ No
   If yes, you must provide complete ownership information for the prior owner in column A and ownership information for the new owner in column B.

6. If this is a partial sale, transfer, or conveyance of an existing business (i.e., sale of one or more plants or locations):
   a. Explain what portion or location of the entire operation was sold, transferred, or conveyed.
   _____

   b. Was this entity insured under a separate policy from the remaining portion? ☐ Yes ☐ No
      If not, specify the entities with which it was combined:
   _____

ERM-14 (Rev. 12/03)   NC790

7. Did the legal status of this entity change? ☐ Yes ☐ No
    If yes, you must complete the Type of Entity portion for each entity to reflect such change.

8. Is this transaction a result of bankruptcy? ☐ Yes ☐ No
    If yes, please indicate under which Chapter the bankruptcy was filed. _____

Corporations—List all names of owners of 5% or more of voting stock and number of shares owned. Submit shareholder proposal if transaction involved exchange of stock.

Partnerships—List each partner and appropriate share in the profits. If the entity is a limited partnership, list name(s) of each general partner(s).

Other—If no voting stock, list members of board of directors or comparable governing body.

Information	Column A	Column B	Column C
	Enter name used in Section A for Entity 1 **Entity 1**	Enter name used in Section A for Entity 2 **Entity 2**	Enter name used in Section A for Entity 3 **Entity 3** If applicable, use this column for multiple combinations or entities resulting from mergers and consolidations
Name of Entity			
Ownership See reference above to ownership information required for corporations, partnerships, and other entities.			
Total Ownership Interest or Number of Shares			

NOTE: If your business has changed significantly to result in a change to the primary (governing) classification and the process and hazard of the operation have also changed, contact your agent, insurance company or rating organization for additional information.

Section C—Additional Information

Please include any additional information you believe pertinent to the transaction detailed above that cannot be expressed due to the format of this form. If there is not enough space below, attach the information on the entity's letterhead, signed by an owner, partner, or executive officer.

_____

_____

_____

_____

_____

Section D—Did You Remember to . . .

- Indicate the type of transaction, check all that apply, and include transaction and notification dates?
- Complete all necessary entity information? **Note:** You can use more forms if the number of entities exceeds three.
  - Entity name
  - Risk identification number (if you know it)
  - Federal Employer Identification Number (FEIN)
  - Type of entity
  - Primary address, telephone, and other contact information
  - Mailing address and additional locations if applicable
- Fill out the ownership table completely?
  - Include the names of the entities as listed in Section A?
  - Include all owners, partners, board of director members, members and/or manager of LLCs, general partners of LPs, or any other comparable governing body?
  - Include percentage of ownership for each owner, partner, board of director member, member and/or manager of LLCs, general partner of LPs, or any other comparable governing body?
- Answer questions 1 though 8?

Section E—Certification

This is to certify that the information contained on this form is complete and correct.

All forms will be returned if this Certification Section is incomplete.

Name of person completing form:_____

Check which entity or entities the signer represents: ☐Entity 1 ☐Entity 2 ☐Entity 3 ☐Other_____

Signature of Owner, Partner, Member, or Executive Officer	Title	Carrier
Print name of above signature	Date	Carrier Address

Section F—For Rating Organization Use Only

Associate/automated _____

Date received _____

Date complete _____

Assessment—form complete? What is missing? _____

Ruling _____

Revisions necessary—Yes/No _____

Revisions complete and mailed—Yes/No/NA _____

Rating Effective Date impacted—Yes/No—if Yes, which ones? _____

Risk ID impacted—list all impacted, any deactivated? Indicate deactivated #s _____

All carriers/rating organizations notified? _____

ERM-14 (Rev. 12/03)   NC790

Appendix G

Workers Compensation Requirements for Employers

Workers Compensation varies from state to state. This table shows the workers compensation requirements of employers depending on the state.

State	Administrator	Requirements	Website
Alaska	Marie Marx, Director	Requires each employer having one or more employees to obtain workers' compensation insurance, unless the employer has been approved as a self-insurer.	http://www.labor.state.ak.us/wc/home.htm
Alabama	Charles Delamar, Director	The manner or method by which you choose to insure your workers' compensation liability is your decision.	https://labor.alabama.gov/wc/
Arizona	Kathleen McLeod, Claims Manager	Requires all public and private employers with at least one employee to carry workers' compensation insurance. The law makes coverage optional for domestic servants, working partners and sole proprietors.	http://www.ica.state.az.us/Claims/Claims_main.aspx
Arkansas	Omar Abdullah, Support Services	Most employers with three or more employees are required to have workers' compensation insurance coverage for their employees. There are exceptions to the three-or-more requirement, so employers with fewer than three should check with authorities before assuming they do not fall under the workers' compensation laws	http://www.awcc.state.ar.us/employerbasicfacts.html
California	Christine Baker, Director of DIR	Required in every work situation, normally covered under your owners insurance, if not you can obtain a policy through the CA State Fund. The annual premium is based on the annual salary the employee makes, and then they monitor ALL the tax filings each quarter and then at the end of the year they will do an audit to make sure the client paid the correct premium.	http://www.dir.ca.gov/DWC/

State	Administrator	Requirements	Website
Colorado		All public and private employers with limited exceptions, must provide workers' compensation coverage for their employees if one or more full or part-time persons are employed. A person hired to perform services for pay is presumed by law to be an employee. This includes all persons elected or appointed to public sector service and all persons appointed or hired by private employers for remuneration.	https://www.colorado.gov/cdle/dwc
Connecticut	John Mastropietro, Chairman	All businesses with one or more employees are required to have workers compensation insurance except those able to self-insure. There are exemptions for household employees who work 26 hours or less per week, Sole proprietors, multiple member LLC's, corporate officers and partnerships, who may elect not to carry workers compensation insurance for themselves. However, they must always provide coverage for their employees.	http://wcc.state.ct.us/
Delaware		Employers with one or more employees are required to carry workers' compensation insurance. Employers may not charge an employee any portion of the premium or expense of carrying workers' compensation insurance. Workers' Compensation benefits have certain entitlement requirements which must be met in order to receive benefits.	http://dol.delaware.gov/about.php
Florida	Tanner Holloman, Director	If you are in an industry, other than construction, and have four or more employees, you are required to carry workers' compensation coverage.	http://www.myfloridacfo.com/division/wc/

State	Administrator	Requirements	Website
Georgia	Delece Brooks, Director/Chief Operating Officer	Every employer, individual, firm, association, or corporation, regularly employing three or more persons, shall provide workers' compensation insurance coverage.	http://sbwc.georgia.gov/
Hawaii		Any employer, other than those excluded having one or more employees, full-time or part-time, permanent or temporary, is required to provide WC coverage for its employees.	http://labor.hawaii.gov/
Idaho	Kenneth Edmunds, Director	Employers with one or more full-time, part-time, seasonal, or occasional employees are required to maintain a workers' compensation policy unless specifically exempt from the law. Workers' Compensation is required to be in place when the first employee is hired. Employment that may be exempt from required coverage includes: Household domestic service, Employment of family members living in the employer's household	http://www.iic.idaho.gov/
Illinois	Michael Arnold, Deputy Counsel	Required in every work situation.	http://www.iwcc.illinois.gov/
Indiana	Linda Hamilton, Chairman	All public and private employer-employee relationships are covered by the Worker's Compensation and Occupational Diseases Acts. It does not matter how many workers are employed in a business; all employees must be covered.	http://www.in.gov/wcb/

State	Administrator	Requirements	Website
Iowa	Joseph Cortese II, Worker's Compensation Commissioner	Most employers are required to purchase workers' compensation liability insurance. Insurance is mandatory if you have eligible employees, unless you are self-insured.	https://www.iowaworkforcedevelopment.gov/
Kansas		All employers carry occupational injury compensation insurance, but there are certain exceptions also. The obligation applies only to those employers whose annual payroll gross exceeds $20000. Agricultural employers are also exempted.	http://www.dol.ks.gov/workcomp/
Kentucky		All employers whether private or a government organization are legally obligated to have an occupational injury compensation insurance. The number of employees does not matter.	http://www.labor.ky.gov/workersclaims/Pages/Department-of-Workers'-Claims.aspx
Louisiana		All employers must provide workers compensation insurance for their employees, and must show proof that they have the financial means to carry Louisiana workers compensation insurance. There are some exemptions such as the crews of any airplane working in dusting or spraying operations, real estate brokers, musicians and performers, and others.	http://www.laworks.net/WorkersComp/OWC_MainMenu.asp
Maine	Paul Fortier, Deputy Director	Any business with one or more employees must provide workers compensation insurance coverage.	http://www.state.me.us/wcb/

State	Administrator	Requirements	Website
Maryland	R. Karl Aumann, Chairman	With few exceptions, every employer with one or more employees is required by law to provide workers' compensation insurance. Agricultural employers with less than three employees or an annual payroll for full-time employees which does not exceed $15,000, are not required to carry worker's compensation insurance.	http://www.wcc.state.md.us/
Massachusetts		All businesses must carry workers compensation insurance coverage regardless of the amount of hours worked. This also includes owners that are considered employees. Employees in domestic service who work at least 16 hours a week also require coverage.	http://www.mass.gov/lwd/workers-compensation/
Michigan		All employers are required to carry a workers compensation insurance policy. There are NO exemptions provided for workers compensation insurance.	http://www.michigan.gov/wca
Minnesota	Ken Peterson, Commissioner	Does not provide any waiver to any of the employers working in this state. All employers are legally obligated to provide insurance coverage to all their employees, including the ones that are not even US citizens or are still minor.	http://www.doli.state.mn.us/workcomp.asp
Mississippi	Joyce Wells, Commission Secretary	Most employees qualify to use the workers compensation system. However, there can be exceptions. For example, if you are working for an employer who has less than five employees in their organization, you may not be covered under such insurance plan. Employers with less than 5 employees are not obligated to carry workers compensation insurance coverage. Other workers that may not be covered include farm workers and independent contractors.	http://www.mwcc.state.ms.us/

State	Administrator	Requirements	Website
Missouri	John Hickey, Director	It is required for all employers that have five or more employees. However, if a business is in the construction industry then coverage must be provided if there are one or more employees. The statutory definition of "employee" includes both full and part-time employees, seasonal, and even temporary employees.	http://labor.mo.gov/dwc
Montana	Fam Bucy, Commissioner	Legally mandatory for the employers to carry workers compensation insurance coverage for all their employees.	http://wcc.dli.mt.gov/
Nebraska		Require all employers to carry occupational injury insurance policies in order to ensure timely payments to injured workers as and when needed.	http://www.wcc.ne.gov/
Nevada	Steve George, Administrator	All employers who have at least one worker must carry proper occupational injury insurance coverage. However, they have the option either to be self-insured or to buy the coverage from a Nevada based private insurance carrier. Some employers may qualify for certain exemptions as well. For example, if the employee is already covered under a private disability plan that ensures equal or higher benefits may not qualify for occupational injury compensation.	http://dirweb.state.nv.us/wcs/employee.htm
New Hampshire	Kathryn Barger, Deputy Commissioner	Any business who employs one full or part-time employee is required to provide workers compensation insurance, regardless of that employee's family relation.	http://www.nh.gov/labor/workers-comp/

State	Administrator	Requirements	Website
New Jersey		Requires all employers, not covered by Federal programs, have workers compensation coverage or be approved for self-insurance. Even out-of-state employers may need workers compensation coverage if a contract of employment is entered into in New Jersey or if work is performed in New Jersey.	http://lwd.dol.state.nj.us/labor/wc/employer/employer_index.html
New Mexico		Employers with three or more employees are required to carry workers compensation insurance through a New Mexico workers compensation policy or a New Mexico certified self-insurance program. Employers in the construction industry, however, must carry coverage regardless of the number of employees.	http://www.workerscomp.state.nm.us/
New York	Robert Beloten, Chair	Covers all types of employees regardless of whether they are working as a part-time, fulltime or a leased worker. The laws specifically mention that teachers for public schools, County workers working under hazardous conditions, and even volunteers working for a profitable business can also qualify for occupation injury compensation benefits	http://www.wcb.ny.gov/
North Carolina		All employers who have more than three employees or workers working for them are legally required to carry proper occupational injury insurance. However, if there are less than three employees in an organization, the employer can be exempted from this insurance requirement.	http://www.ic.nc.gov/

State	Administrator	Requirements	Website
North Dakota		It is legally mandatory for all employers to carry workers compensation insurance coverage. There are no numeral exceptions under North Dakota workers compensation laws. Waivers are also not permitted.	http://www.nd.gov/risk/workers-compensation
Ohio		All employers with one or more employees must carry workers compensation insurance coverage	https://www.bwc.ohio.gov/
Oklahoma	Mark Costello, Commissioner	It is legally mandatory for all employers to carry occupational injury coverage to all employees. No waivers are allowed. Even those who have just one part-time worker must meet these insurance requirements.	http://ok.gov/wcc/
Oregon	Lori Graham, Director	It is compulsory for all employers to carry occupational insurance. Waivers are not permitted. Even if there is just one part-time worker in the organization, there must be adequate workers comp insurance policy in place. There are no numeral exceptions applicable.	http://www.cbs.state.or.us/wcd/index.html
Pennsylvania	Kathy Manderino, Secretary	It is mandatory for all employers provide occupational insurance. However, the employers have the option to provide the insurance through self-insuring, competitive state fund, or a private insurance carrier. Even domestic servants and agricultural employees are entitled to compensation benefits.	http://www.portal.state.pa.us/portal/server.pt/community/workers'_compensation/10386
Rhode Island	Scott Jensen, Director	It's mandatory for all employers to carry occupational insurance coverage, but there are certain exemptions, such as for independent contractors, sole proprietors, and partners. Besides that, some agricultural and real employers and those having domestic servants may also be exempted.	http://www.dlt.ri.gov/wc/

State	Administrator	Requirements	Website
South Carolina	Gary Cannon, Executive Director	Employer who regularly employs four or more workers full-time or part-time is required to have workers compensation insurance. Agricultural employees, railroads, and railway express companies and their employees, and employers who had a total annual payroll during the previous year of less than $3,000, regardless of the number of workers employed during that period are exempt.	http://www.wcc.sc.gov/Pages/default.aspx
South Dakota	Marcia Hultman, Secretary	All employers must carry adequate amount of insurance coverage. Employers have the option either to buy this coverage from a private insurance carrier or to get self-insured.	http://dlr.sd.gov/workerscomp/default.aspx
Tennessee	Burns Phillips, Commissioner	It's legally mandatory for every employer with more than five employees to carry insurance coverage for work-related accidents. However, this rule does not apply to those engaged in construction business (including subcontractors); even if they have five or less than five employees in their organizations, they must carry workers compensation insurance coverage. Certain waivers are also permitted in specific cases.	http://www.tn.gov/
Texas		Does not make it mandatory for all employers to carry occupational insurance. But there are still some exceptions, such as construction contracts for governmental entities; in such cases, the insurance requirements are mandatory. But, workers have the legal right to file compensation claims if they think they have a genuine case and the employer is still refusing to pay monetary benefits.	http://www.tdi.texas.gov/wc/index.html

State	Administrator	Requirements	Website
Utah	Sherri Hayashi, Commissioner	All employers are legally required to carry appropriate workers compensation insurance coverage. However, the organizations with agricultural workers that have a payroll of up to $50000 are exempted from this legal requirement.	http://laborcommission.utah.gov/divisions/IndustrialAccidents/WCClaimsProcess.html
Vermont	Anne Noonan, Commissioner	It is mandatory for all employers to carry adequate amount of insurance coverage. There are no numerical exceptions to this legal requirement but waivers are permitted in specific cases.	http://labor.vermont.gov/workers-compensation/
Virginia	Wesley Marshall, Chairman	Requires every employer who regularly employs three or more full-time or part-time employees to purchase and maintain workers' compensation insurance. Employers with fewer than three employees may voluntarily come under the Act.	http://www.vwc.state.va.us/
Washington		It is compulsory for all employers to carry appropriate insurance coverage to ensure timely payments of compensation benefits as and when needed. There are no numerical exceptions. Waivers are not permitted.	http://www.lni.wa.gov/claimsins/claims/
West Virginia	Michael Riley, Commissioner	It's legally mandatory for all employers to carry adequate insurance coverage, but there are a few employers who are exempt from this requirement, such as an agricultural employer with less than five workers and a casual employer with less than three workers.	http://www.wvinsurance.gov/WorkersCompensation.aspx

State	Administrator	Requirements	Website
Wisconsin		Those who have less than three employees in their organizations are exempt from this requirement. No waivers are permitted under the laws though. Even domestic servants must also be provided with voluntary worker's compensation coverage.	https://dwd.wisconsin.gov/wc/
Wyoming	John Cox, Director	Not all employers can choose to be self-insured, as there are certain eligibility criteria set by the laws to qualify for the same. There are no numerical exceptions to this legal requirement and even waivers are also not permitted.	http://www.wyomingworkforce.org/businesses/workerscomp/

Appendix H

Canadian Experience Rating Program

Province	Name of Supervising System	Website	Maximum Assessable Earnings	Experience Rating Program
Alberta	Workers' Compensation Board of Alberta	http://www.wcb.ab.ca	$95,300	Premium rate will increase or decrease based on experience up to 200% increase or 40% decrease.
British Columbia	WorkSafeBC	http://www.worksafebc.com	$78,600	Premium rate will increase or decrease based on experience up to 500% or 40% decrease.
Manitoba	Workers' Compensation Board of Manitoba	http://www.wcb.mb.ca	$121,000	Premium rate will increase or decrease based on experience up to 200% increase or 40% decrease
New Brunswick	WorkSafeNB	http://www.worksafenb.ca/	$60,900	Premium Rate will increase or decrease based on experience up to 80% increase or 40% decrease
Newfoundland and Labrador	Workplace Safety and Compensation Commission	http://www.whscc.nf.ca/	$61,615	Premium Rate will increase or decrease based on experience up to 100% increase or 20-40% decrease
Northwest Territories and Nunavut	Northwest Territory/Nunavut Workers' Safety and Compensation Commission	http://www.wscc.nt.ca/	$86,00	Merit/Demerit program in place
Iqaluit	Workers Safety and Compensation Commission	http://www.wcb.nt.ca	$84,200	None
Nova Scotia	WorkSafe Nova Scotia	http://www.wcb.ns.ca	$56,800	Premium Rate will increase or decrease based on experience up to 60% increase or 40% decrease

Province	Name of Supervising System	Website	Maximum Assessable Earnings	Experience Rating Program
Ontario	Workplace Safety and Insurance Board (WSIB)	http://www.wsib.on.ca	$85,200	Yearly penalty or refund based on experience. An invoice is issued for up to 200% of the premium at year end.
Prince Edward Island	Compensation Board of Prince Edward Island	http://www.wcb.pe.ca	$52,100	Premium rate will increase or decrease based on experience up to 100% increase or 25-50% decrease
Quebec	Commission de la Sante et de la Sescurite du Travail (CSST)	http://www.csst.qc.ca/portail/fr/	$70,000	Three-tiered program. 1. Yearly Penalty or refund based on experience. An invoice issued for up to 100% of the premium at year end. 2. Premium rate will increase or decrease based on experience p to 100% increase or 40% decrease 3. Large employers can select "insurance level" to increase or decrease premium based on projected experience.
Saskatchewan	Saskatchewan Workers' Compensation Board	http://www.wcbsask.com	$65,130	Premium rate will increase or decrease based on experience up to 100% increase or 25-40% decrease
Yukon	Yukon Workers' Compensation Health and Safety Board	http://wcb.yk.ca/	$84,837	None

Index